MAJORITY RULE VERSUS

CONSENSUS

AMERICAN POLITICAL THOUGHT
Wilson Carey McWilliams and Lance Banning, Founding Editors

DATE DUE

BRODART, CO.

Cat. No. 23-221

Majority Rule

VERSUS

Consensus

THE POLITICAL THOUGHT

OF JOHN C. CALHOUN

James H. Read

University Press of Kansas

Published by the University Press of Kansas (Lawrence, Kansas
66045), which was organized by the Kansas Board of Regents and is
operated and funded by Emporia State University, Fort Hays State
University, Kansas State University, Pittsburg State University,
the University of Kansas, and Wichita State University

Library of Congress Cataloging-in-Publication Data

Read, James H., 1958–
Majority rule versus consensus : the political thought of John C.
Calhoun / James H. Read.
p. cm. — (American political thought)
Includes bibliographical references and index.
ISBN 978-0-7006-1635-0 (cloth : alk. paper)
1. Calhoun, John C. (John Caldwell), 1782–1850. 2. Political
science—Philosophy. 3. Consensus (Social sciences)—United States.
4. Majorities. 5. Slave trade—United States. 6. South Carolina—
Politics and government—1775–1865. 7. United States—Politics
and government—1815–1861. I. Title.
JC212.C3R43 2009
320.01—dc22
2008033340

British Library Cataloguing-in-Publication Data is available.

Printed in the United States of America

10 9 8 7 6 5 4 3 2 1

To my parents, Herbert and Charlotte Read

Contents

Acknowledgments

This project started as a spinoff from my first book, which examined the political thought of James Madison, Alexander Hamilton, James Wilson, and Thomas Jefferson. Madison and Jefferson paved my peculiar route to John C. Calhoun. A couple of conference papers expanded to a full-length book as Calhoun became my key to understanding the crisis over sovereignty and slavery that led to the Civil War; and as I began to discover surprising echoes of Calhoun's political theory in Northern Ireland, Yugoslavia, and South Africa.

Work on the project began in earnest in fall 2002 with a residential fellowship at the International Center for Jefferson Studies in Charlottesville, Virginia. The grounds of Kenwood Farm were perfect for reading and reflection. My 2002–2003 sabbatical from the College of St. Benedict and St. John's University gave me the time to read Calhoun's *Papers*, volume by volume.

I am indebted beyond words to Michael Zuckert and Peter Onuf for inspiring and encouraging this project, and for their indispensable feedback over seven years. Michael remarked to me years ago that there were few good studies of Calhoun's political theory and challenged me to enter the competition. My conversations with Peter in Charlottesville about antebellum political economy and the meaning of nationalism sent the project in new directions I could not have glimpsed on my own.

Parts of the work were presented in draft form to the International Center for Jefferson Studies; the British Association for American Studies in Swansea, Wales; the Rhetoric Society of Southern Africa in Cape Town, South Africa; the Society for Historians of the Early American Republic; the Bay Area Seminar for Early American History; the Association for Political Theory; and (several times) to the Midwest Political Science Association. A faculty exchange program enabled me to present a synopsis of the book to the Political Science Department of Morehouse College in Atlanta; I want to thank Morehouse students for their interest and probing questions, and Sharon Vaughan and Gregg Hall for generously hosting my visit. My examination of Madison's response to nullification was presented at the symposium "James Madison: Life, Times, and Legacy" sponsored by the International Lincoln Center at Louisiana State University, Shreveport, an opportunity for which I thank Bill Pederson. I gave an on-campus presentation on Calhoun's constitutional thought for the Collegial Conversations series at the College of St. Benedict and St. John's University.

My discussion of the former Yugoslavia in chapter 7 profited from a summer 2003 faculty study trip to that region, led by my colleague Nick Hayes and sponsored by Dan Whalen and the Whalen Foundation. My understanding of the tragic failure of the consensus model of politics in Yugoslavia also owes a large debt to the work of Robert Hayden, who generously read and commented on a draft of chapter 7.

In working for many years on a theorist (John C. Calhoun) about whom I was deeply ambivalent, I was helped along at key times by a number of people who responded to my writing and kept the project moving forward. Brian Schoen took an early interest in the project and has offered valuable comments at every stage. This book continues my longtime exchange of ideas with Alan Gibson, who also gave the work a boost at a crucial time.

Others who have read drafts and in one way or another kept it moving forward include David Siemers, Dee Andrews, Eugene Genovese, Dick Holway, Herbert Sloan, Andrew Shankman, John Vile, Jon Schaff, Craig Grau, Tony Iaccarino, James Lewis, Nina Gladziuk, Zoltan Vajda, Dan Sabia, David Schultz, and Les Benedict.

My Political Science colleague Gary Prevost gave me timely feedback on chapter 7. I am indebted to Gene Garver for an ongoing intellectual exchange and for setting up the Cape Town panel. My understanding of antebellum economic history profited from conversations with John Olson, Chuck Rambeck, and Louis Johnston of the Economics Department.

Suzanne Reinert has been unfailingly helpful with the logistics of a project I've worked on at a baffling variety of locations over the years.

Fred Woodward at the University Press of Kansas took an immediate interest in the project and told me he'd been looking for a good Calhoun manuscript for years.

Pia Lopez has been from beginning to end my most exacting and loving critic. She has patiently read everything I've written, good or bad. Now that the book is finished we'll have time for the serious business of hiking, biking, and mountain climbing.

Parts of chapter 2 will be published as "James Madison's Response to Nullification" in William Pederson, John Vile, and Frank Williams, editors, *James Madison: Philosopher, Founder, and Statesman,* forthcoming from Ohio University Press; an abbreviated version of chapter 7 will appear as "John C. Calhoun's Federalism and Its Contemporary Echoes" in Lee Ward and Ann Ward, editors, *The Ashgate Research Companion to Federalism.*

My parents, Herbert and Charlotte Read, have set a lifelong example of political commitment, intellectual independence, and democratic participation with all its highs and lows. To them in gratitude I dedicate this book.

ONE

■

Introduction

Ancient political theorists identified three basic types of political rule: rule by one, rule by a few, rule by the majority. To these, one could add anarchy, rule by no one. Early modern political thinkers, whatever their other differences with the ancients, adopted this basic tripartite classification.[1] Good and bad variants of each numerical category were recognized, and constitutions were possible that combined elements of the one/few/many principle. But the tripartite classification remained fundamental.

And under any constitution, however mixed and blended, someone ruled and someone else was ruled. Rulers might alternate over time (especially in a democracy as a result of elections), but at any given moment in time, someone decided matters over the opposition of someone else. Consensus—rule by unanimous agreement—was not considered a practicable form of government by most ancient or modern political theorists.

But for every rule there is an exception, and this work explores the exception. In the history of political thought John C. Calhoun of South Carolina (1782–1850) stands out as the most thoroughgoing advocate of the consensus model of government as an alternative to majority rule. His political theory invites us to consider whether a regime is possible that is neither rule by one, few, or many, nor yet anarchy—but rule by all. The idea is certainly an attractive one, for clearly decisions to which all genuinely consent are preferable to decisions made by some (no matter how many) at the expense of others. Calhoun did not aim merely to reform majority rule but to replace it with something fundamentally different.

There has always been a tension between democracy's goal and its principal mechanism. The goal is rule by and for the community as a whole, "the people," which suggests collective pursuit of a common good. The mechanism is majority vote, rule by the greater part of the community over the rest. Nothing guarantees that the mechanism will accomplish the goal, because the majority might or might not consider the views and interests of the rest of the community. Democratic theory and practice has attempted in various ways to resolve this tension. No remedy permanently solves the problem.

One remedy is to subject majority rule to constitutional limits designed to make it deliberate rather than hasty and thus more likely to consider broader perspectives and longer-term interests. These limits include separating legislative, executive, and judicial branches of government; requiring that laws apply equally and impartially to all—to those in the majority as well as those in the minority; and guaranteeing freedom of speech and press, which provide outvoted minorities the opportunity to change the majority's mind and sometimes to replace the existing majority with a new one.

Another, complementary remedy is federalism, which constitutionally distinguishes between matters affecting the whole community, to be decided by the majority of the whole, and matters principally affecting particular states or districts, to be decided by majorities within those states or districts. Federalism might prevent a national majority from deciding local or regional matters about which it cares little and knows nothing.

All these constitutional checks reduce but do not eliminate the danger that majority rule will become oppressive. Freedom of speech and press do not guarantee that the majority will actually listen and respond to the minority's arguments and interests. Formally neutral laws and procedures can be used to pursue systematically unfair policies. Federalism does not prevent national majorities from legislating on legitimately national matters in ways that deeply and adversely affect some regionally concentrated minority.

Calhoun believed that none of the ordinary constitutional checks on majority rule were sufficient to prevent the majority from systematically oppressing the minority. Calhoun's proposed remedy was to replace majority rule with consensus, or what he called the principle of the concurrent majority: to give every key "portion or interest" in the community veto rights over collective decisions, thus ensuring only those laws and policies that genuinely benefited all parts of the community. He sought deliberately to remodel the

U.S. Constitution into a consensus system of government. He did not believe a consensus requirement would produce anarchy, deadlock, or minority domination. He argued on the contrary that it would be more energetic, effective, fair, and truly inclusive than government based on majority rule.

Calhoun himself attempted persistently to put his consensus theory into practice in his actions as a regional and national leader. This work will critically examine his political theory in historical context, for the specific problems he attempted to solve and the specific minorities he sought to defend—above all the minority of slave-owning Southern planters—shed important light on the theory itself. I will also explore some more recent political arrangements that resemble what Calhoun recommended: in Northern Ireland and the former Yugoslavia, where minority veto/consensus models of government were instituted; and in South Africa, where it was seriously proposed but rejected in favor of majority rule.

I will argue on the one hand that Calhoun's critique of majority rule cannot be easily dismissed and should be taken seriously precisely by those most committed to democracy based on majority rule. On the other hand, I argue that Calhoun's sustained attempt—in theory and in practice—to add a new category to the list of practicable forms of rule ultimately fails. Government by consensus rule is neither effective nor just. It is certainly *possible* to create political orders where every key interest can block collective decisions. But such governments tend to be ineffective, better at preventing common action than achieving common goods, and privilege strategically placed minorities rather than produce genuine consensus. The mechanism of minority veto falls even further from its intended goal—the good of the entire community—than does the mechanism of majority rule.

But the attraction of the consensus theory remains, and it will continue to be a temptation to constitutional architects in deeply divided societies when all other options, including majority rule, are painful ones. Sometimes troubled political communities deliberately choose between majority rule and the minority veto/consensus model of government. South Africa faced such a choice in the early 1990s. So did the United States in Calhoun's time. The title of this book reflects that fundamental choice.

Origins of a Theory

To understand Calhoun's political theory we should begin with the particular events that first occasioned it. In 1828 the U.S. Congress passed, on a close and regionally polarized vote, a highly protective tariff, subsequently denominated the "Tariff of Abominations." The bill extended high protection to (among other items) domestically produced iron, hemp, molasses, finished cotton manufactures, and both raw and finished wool. The bill was strongly supported in New York and Pennsylvania, for which manufacturing was a key economic interest, and in Kentucky, which produced hemp. It was bitterly opposed in the cotton-planting South, whose economic interest lay in free international trade. High protective tariffs raised planters' cost of production and diminished the purchasing power of British textile manufacturers, their chief customers. Southerners were convinced that all benefits of the tariff went to the North, while the burdens fell exclusively on the South; its effect, they believed, was systematically to transfer southern wealth to northern pockets.[2]

There was every reason to believe that this "abominable" tariff could be repealed through the ordinary democratic process. The vote had been close in both chambers. The tariff law contained glaring contradictions that demanded revision soon. Southern congressmen had deliberately voted to make the tariff worse, in the mistaken hope this would kill the bill. All of these circumstances promised a different result in the next round.

The "Tariff of Abominations" owed its existence to a majority vote. According to standard democratic theory, the remedy, for those strongly opposed to a law, is to assemble a majority of their own to repeal it. But that was not the conclusion drawn by one key participant-observer in the event: John C. Calhoun, at that time vice president of the United States, a cotton planter from South Carolina, and one of the chief political leaders of the age.

The 1828 tariff and the politics surrounding it convinced Calhoun that majority rule itself was subject to an inevitable process of degeneration into despotism and required a radical cure. He first formulated that cure in 1828 in his *South Carolina Exposition* (keeping his authorship secret). He reworked and extended his political and constitutional theory, applying it to new issues, above all the growing division over slavery, until his death in 1850. His cure for the perceived pathologies of majority rule is set forth in two posthumously published works: *A Disquisition on Government,* which presents his diagnosis and cure in universal terms, and *A Discourse on the Constitution and Government of the United States,* which applies that diagnosis and cure to the particular circumstances of the United States.

Calhoun's radical cure was to replace majority rule with a consensus model of government, whereby all key "portions or interests" affected by legislation possess formally guaranteed veto rights. The only way to prevent "any one interest, or combination of interests, from using the powers of government to aggrandize itself at the expense of the others," he wrote in the *Disquisition,* is to "give to each division or interest, through its appropriate organ, either a concurrent voice in making and executing the laws, or a veto on their execution."[3] He called this the principle of the "concurrent majority." The "majority" part of Calhoun's "concurrent majority" applied *within* each portion or interest; thus within South Carolina, matters could be decided by majority vote. *Among* differing interests, in the community as a whole, the decision principle was "concurrence": i.e., unanimity, not majority rule.

Within the federal framework of the United States, Calhoun sought to implement the minority veto/consensus principle through nullification: giving each state the right (as he puts it in the *Exposition*) to declare an act of legislation "void within the [state's] limits"; this act of nullification would not only bind citizens of the nullifying state, but also oblige the federal government to suspend enforcement of the law.[4] Thus under Calhoun's proposal a national tariff law (or any act of legislation) would have to achieve not only a majority in both houses of the U.S. Congress (as required by the Constitution) but would also have to be supported—or at least not actively opposed—by majorities in every state. (A tariff fiercely opposed by an entire section of the country, for example, would clearly fail this requirement.) The state alone was judge of whether and when nullification was justified. The only limit Calhoun placed on a state's power to nullify federal law was the following: if three-quarters of the other states, in conventions called for the purpose, passed a constitutional amendment affirmatively rejecting a single state's nullification of a federal law, the nullifying state would either have to rescind its nullification or peacefully secede from the Union.

For Calhoun, consensus was not merely a *goal* to be aimed for; it was a *requirement* for government action. He did not believe that such a decision rule would produce deadlock or anarchy, but instead insisted it would "unite the most opposite and conflicting interests, and . . . blend the whole in one common attachment to the country."[5] Its purpose was not merely negative—to prevent action in opposition to one group's interest—but positive: to facilitate deliberation and the creation of a true common good.

Though he argued that states possessed a constitutional right to secede, secession was precisely what Calhoun hoped to prevent. Nullification was designed as an alternative to secession for a deeply alienated, regionally concentrated minority. Calhoun genuinely believed that if the South uncompromisingly invoked its self-proclaimed right to nullify federal law and threatened to secede if its demands were not met, this would ultimately strengthen the Union. Nullification would force North and South to come to consensus and to recognize and act upon their true common interests—which in Calhoun's view included their common interest in sustaining the institution of slavery.

Calhoun's Political Career

Calhoun's theory grew directly out of his political experience, and in turn his political leadership was shaped by his theory as it developed over time.

He was born in South Carolina in 1782, in the closing years of the Revolutionary War.[6] He received his university education at Yale, as a Jeffersonian among ardent Federalists, and at Tapping Reeve's Litchfield Law School in Connecticut. After returning to South Carolina he was elected to Congress in 1810 and distinguished himself as an ardent nationalist and war hawk during the War of 1812. He served as President James Monroe's Secretary of War from 1817 to 1824 and in that capacity worked persistently, under difficult budgetary constraints, to preserve an effective peacetime military establishment.[7] During this period he supported a mildly protective tariff whose revenues would fund federally sponsored internal improvements (i.e., roads and canals) and favored broad construction of the constitutional powers of Congress.[8] As Secretary of War Calhoun was responsible for Indian Affairs and his policy toward Indians was generous by the standards of the age.[9]

Calhoun was an early candidate for president in 1824 and 1828 but ended up serving two consecutive terms as vice president, first under John Quincy Adams (1825–1829) and then under Andrew Jackson (1829 until Calhoun's resignation in 1832). Then he became U.S. Senator from South Carolina, a position he held to the end of his life (except for a brief interlude as secretary of state, 1844–1845). As vice president Calhoun became a chief political opponent of both of the presidents under whom he served. In Adams's case it was the supposed "corrupt bargain" between Adams and Henry Clay that inaugurated Calhoun's opposition, followed by a dispute over Calhoun's handling of Senate debate and finally by differences over the tariff and other matters of national policy.[10] In Jackson's case the animosity was fueled by Calhoun's criticism of Jackson's conduct during the Seminole War in 1818, and the Peggy Eaton scandal, which tore apart Jackson's cabinet in 1829.[11]

CHAPTER ONE

Calhoun's secretly authored *South Carolina Exposition* of 1828 was the first sustained constitutional argument for the right of a state to nullify federal law. South Carolina senator Robert Hayne, in the famous Webster-Hayne debates of 1830, gave voice to Calhoun's constitutional views at a time when Calhoun himself still maintained public silence.[12] Calhoun's *Fort Hill Address* of 1831 first set forth the nullification doctrine publicly in his own name. He then put the theory into practice in 1832, when after Congress passed another protective tariff Calhoun publicly urged South Carolina to nullify the tariff and took active leadership of the movement.[13]

On 24 November 1832, South Carolina declared the 1832 and 1828 tariffs to be "null, void, and no law"; prohibited any state or federal official from enforcing "the payment of duties imposed by the said acts within the limits of this State"; forbade any appeal to the U.S. Supreme Court; and imposed a test oath requiring South Carolina office holders to swear to uphold nullification.[14] Calhoun actively supported all of these provisions, including the test oath.[15] The test oath was fiercely opposed by a Unionist minority in South Carolina who considered it "wanton, cold-blooded tyranny" by the South Carolina majority.[16]

President Jackson made clear he considered nullification to be treason and disunion and was determined to suppress it; Calhoun denied that the federal government had any constitutional power to use force against a sovereign state.[17] A potentially violent showdown was averted through Henry Clay's compromise tariff of 1833. Calhoun helped persuade South Carolina "fire eaters" to accept the compromise and rescind the Ordinance of Nullification.[18] The United States was thus spared (for a generation) the prospect of armed confrontation between the federal government and the state of South Carolina. Calhoun was convinced to the end of his life that the 1833 compromise demonstrated the practicality of nullification, and that by standing up for principle South Carolina had halted a national slide toward corruption and despotism.[19]

Calhoun believed compromise was appropriate on the tariff. On slavery, the issue that preoccupied him from the early 1830s to the end of his life, he utterly rejected compromise—this despite the centrality of compromise to his consensus theory of government. On 6 February 1837, arguing that antislavery petitions must not be permitted even to enter the doors of Congress, Calhoun warned: "If we concede an inch, concession would follow concession—compromise would follow compromise, until our ranks would be so broken that effectual resistance would be impossible. We must meet the enemy on the frontier."[20] The antislavery position, whether it proposed immediate or gradual abolition, was wholly illegitimate, indeed criminal in Calhoun's view, and must be entirely shut out of politics if the Union was to survive. Slavery in his view was not merely an evil to be tolerated; it was a "positive good" to North and South alike.[21] Congress, he argued, had no power to restrict slavery in the District of Columbia or in federally owned territories; it was unconstitutional for Congress even to discuss such restrictions.

Calhoun used his brief term as President John Tyler's secretary of state in 1844–1845 to work for the annexation of Texas as an additional slave state. He returned to the Senate during President James Polk's administration and, unlike many southerners, had reservations about the Mexican War because he feared the vast new territories acquired in the war would worsen the sectional conflict over slavery.[22]

Calhoun's principal target in the last years of his life was the growing Free Soil movement, which proposed to leave slavery alone where it existed but prohibit its spread to new territories. The opening shot of this battle was the Wilmot Proviso of 1846, which provided that "neither slavery nor involuntary servitude shall ever exist" in any territories acquired in the Mexican War.[23] The proviso passed the House of Representatives, indicating majority support in the United States as a whole, but failed in the Senate where slave and free states were equally represented.

Calhoun, fatally ill, had someone read out his final speech in the U.S. Senate on 4 March 1850. In it, Calhoun denounced the Compromise of 1850. That compromise (which passed in final form after Calhoun's death) included the admission of California as a free state, prohibition of the slave trade in the District of Columbia, and a stronger fugitive slave law. The admission of California especially alarmed Calhoun because it disrupted the free state/slave state balance in the Senate and thus removed the South's last check on antislavery legislation. He insisted that, for the Union to survive, northern states had to promise to return fugitive slaves and to suppress the abolitionist societies active within their borders.[24] He also proposed a constitutional amendment designed to "restore to the South in substance the power she possessed of protecting herself" before the sectional balance was disrupted. The amendment would have inserted Calhoun's consensus model directly into the Constitution by creating a dual executive, with one executive representing the North and the other the South, and "requiring each to approve all the acts of Congress before they become laws."[25] It is unclear whether Calhoun's final speech was a last desperate attempt to save the Union, or an epitaph on a Union he considered already dead and a signal to the South that secession was inevitable.[26]

The Case for Majority Rule

In order to understand Calhoun's rejection of majority rule we should first clarify the case *for* majority rule: not absolute, unchecked majority rule, but majority rule disciplined by constitutional checks. In the *Disquisition* Calhoun drew a stark contrast between what he called "the numerical, or absolute majority" which "regards numbers only" and governs by ignoring the interest of the minority; and the "concurrent, or constitutional majority" which "regards interests as well as numbers" and governs according to the "united sense . . . of the entire community."[27] Calhoun here stated the alternatives in polarized form: either unlimited majority rule or true consensus.

But no responsible democratic theorist calls for the unchecked rule of the majority in all things. The laws and constitutions of all modern democracies—including the American democracy Calhoun considered defective—prescribe limits on what majorities can do. The real question is whether it is possible even for constitutionally limited democracies to slide toward the kind of absolute majoritarianism Calhoun feared. So we should first ask how constitutionally limited majority rule—of the kind Calhoun considered inadequate protection—ordinarily guards against majority tyranny.

A usefully succinct summary of the limited-majority-rule model comes in Abraham Lincoln's First Inaugural Address of 1861, which itself sought to refute a Calhoun-influenced full-state-sovereignty interpretation of the U.S. Constitution. "A majority, held in restraint by constitutional checks, and limitations, and always changing easily, with deliberate changes of popular opinion and sentiments, is the only true sovereign of a free people."[28] Lincoln further argued that the only alternatives to majority rule of this kind were minority rule or anarchy.

Several elements in this passage deserve attention. First, this is a formulation for *checked and limited* majority rule, not unchecked majority rule. This is not a prescription for unrestrained rule by what Calhoun called "the numerical majority."

Second, however, Lincoln's formulation *is* in the end a version of majority rule, not a prescription for unanimity (which Lincoln ruled out as impossible). According to Lincoln, the majority, so long as it respects the constitutional rules, must in the long run have the final power of decision, the right of sovereignty. In endorsing majority rule Lincoln definitely did not mean that the majority was always right, that the voice of the people was the voice of God. He merely meant there was nowhere else that a free people could safely place this final power of decision.

Third, the passage speaks of *deliberate* changes of popular opinion and sentiments. This presupposes some process of deliberation rather than immediate, unreasoning action. One of the functions of constitutionally guaranteed freedom of speech and press is to facilitate precisely this kind of deliberation.

Finally, the passage speaks of a *changing* majority, responding to shifts in popular opinion. The composition of the majority itself can change over time, as fluctuating public opinion causes some voters to shift from the majority to the minority and the erstwhile minority becomes the majority. Individuals may find themselves in the majority at one point in time and in the minority the next (or vice versa). This presupposes that at least some voters, as a result of deliberations mediated by public opinion, may change their political allegiances. No one is eternally "fixed" as a member of the majority or the minority.

What here is supposed to prevent the majority from tyrannizing over the minority? The ruling majority is held in check by constitutionally guaranteed rights to freedom of speech and press and by the minority's right to form political organizations, criticize the governing party, present an alternative political program, and compete in elections. Of course the reigning majority might brazenly ignore constitutional rights and outright silence the opposition. This is a real enough problem; there is no failsafe guarantee against it. But this could happen under any set of constitutional rules, including those proposed by Calhoun. Moreover, even to invoke such a danger is to point, ironically, to one principal strength of the limited majority rule model of government. There would be no point in silencing critics of the ruling party if free speech and free press were having no effect—if voters' loyalties were so absolute that no criticism of the ruling party could sway them.

Under the limited majority rule model it would not be in the majority's own interest flagrantly to violate the rights of minorities and individuals, because, at least in a fluid system of this kind, the individuals and groups who compose the majority may find themselves in the minority in the future. Simple prudence would caution the majority of the moment against pressing its temporary political advantage too far. Thus majorities have an interest in limiting what majorities can do.

The application of this argument to federal systems is somewhat more complicated (and Lincoln's formulation itself emerged out of a crisis in a federal system). Under federalism the limited-majority-rule model depends upon drawing some clear distinction between types of decisions that principally affect the local units (states or provinces), which are to be made by the majority of that state or province; and decisions that significantly affect the entire political community, which are to be made by the majority of that entire political community. This raises the question: which level of government—national or state/province—decides where and how to draw the line between their respective spheres of authority? According to Lincoln's (and also James Madison's) limited-majority-rule formulation, these boundary-drawing decisions would have to be made at the national level, by the national majority or some tribunal deriving its authority from the national majority.[29] Otherwise a minority (the state or province) would be deciding matters affecting and binding the whole.

Thus federalism as such is not incompatible with the limited-majority-rule model outlined above. But the *full* sovereignty of states or provinces, including a state's claim to be final judge of its own constitutional rights and obligations, is incompatible with majority rule on decisions affecting the whole community. Full state sovereignty, as we shall see, was central to Calhoun's consensus theory as applied to the United States.

Calhoun's Critique of Majority Rule

The limited-majority-rule model summarized above has both strengths and vulnerabilities; it depends for its healthy functioning upon a number of preconditions that may or may not hold in practice.

The model assumes that political preferences are not rigidly fixed: that a critical mass of individuals might shift their support from majority to minority or vice versa depending on the arguments and appeals presented to them. If majority and minority never could exchange places—if an individual or group were permanently in the majority or in the minority on every issue of importance—then the deliberative assumptions underlying the limited-majority-rule model would fail. In that case an outvoted group might retain the right to speak but members of the majority would have no reason to listen. It would be impossible for a minority opposition effectively to check the majority and "keep them honest" because nothing the majority party does will cause any significant shift of votes to the minority. The element of deliberation essential to democracy would be lacking, not because of irrationality or impulsiveness on the part of the electorate (which the ordinary constitutional checks are designed to restrain), but because the process of deliberation effectively excludes members of the permanent minority. Members of the permanent majority, without breaking the ordinary constitutional rules, could calmly and rationally pursue policies systematically oppressive to the minority.

A deep and rigid division between majority and minority could occur for a number of reasons: for instance, where voting decisions always followed some ascriptive, prepolitical aspect of the individual—his or her ethnicity, race, language, religion, or so on. In the comparative politics literature terms like "plural" or "segmented" or "deeply divided" are employed to describe societies of this kind.[30]

It should be emphasized: it is not the *existence* of ethnic, religious, racial, and linguistic differences that undermines the preconditions for healthy majority rule, but rather the degree to which those differences *control the political behavior* of both elites and ordinary voters. At the extreme, where members of different groups inhabiting the same territory view one another as foreigners and enemies, majority rule over the whole loses its legitimacy altogether.

But to speak of "divided societies" leaves unanswered the question of how they got that way; this is a static rather than dynamic formulation. Equally important is the way in which *political* decisions can either reinforce or counteract the effects of existing social divisions.

Calhoun's critique of majority rule did not begin with the existence of deep social or cultural divisions. The sectional divisions over the 1828 tariff, for example, were not racial or ethnic or religious but rooted in the kind of distributional conflicts that exist in every modern political community, however homogenous or heterogeneous. Calhoun argued that the political process itself and the actions of government under majority rule would over time inevitably *create* and subsequently reinforce deep and permanent divisions between majority and minority.

Calhoun's most concise argument to this effect came in his 1833 speech on the Force Bill. He dramatized the problem by means of a simple model. Suppose a political community consists of just five persons. The community decides, democratically, by a vote of three to two, to levy a tax on all five members. It then decides, again democratically by a vote of three to two, to distribute all of the benefits of the tax to the majority of three, leaving nothing for the other two.[31] By repetition of this kind of action over time, a selfish majority could systematically transfer to itself the wealth of the minority. Though the form under which it would occur is democratic, and formally the laws apply equally to all, from the perspective of the exploited minority this is no different from being ruled by the most absolute of tyrants.

To this elementary model Calhoun added an analysis of the workings of political parties, in order to explain how a unified majority could emerge in the first place in a diversified society where no single interest initially enjoyed a majority. Put another way: he sought to explain why Madison's solution in *Federalist* No. 10—which seeks to prevent majority tyranny by increasing the number and diversity of interests—cannot work in the long run.

Calhoun admitted that the interests that constitute modern political parties may be very diverse and internally conflicting. But he maintained that strategic coalitions over time would overcome the effects of diversity. "If no one interest be strong enough, of itself, to obtain [a majority], a combination will be formed between those whose interests are most alike;—each conceding something to the others, until a sufficient number is obtained to make a majority."[32] All members of a majority coalition have a common interest in securing "the honors and emoluments of the government" and to this end it is "indispensable to success to avoid division and keep united." To ensure the unity required for victory, a party will "concentrate the control over its movements in fewer and fewer hands" so that in practice a majority party is under the control, not of the majority of the whole community, but of the majority of the majority—at best no more than one-fourth of the community, and probably far fewer.[33]

One might suppose the majority's own internal diversity would moderate its actions once in power, out of fear that some interests in the coalition might defect and the party lose its majority status. Calhoun denied that a majority's uncertain hold on power and the risk of defection prevented it from acting despotically. "On the contrary, the very uncertainty of the tenure, combined with the violent party warfare which must ever precede a change of parties under such governments, would rather tend to increase than diminish the tendency to oppression."[34] The very narrowness and uncertainty of a governing majority would increase the temptation to resort to warlike methods that further reinforce divisions within the political community.

Calhoun did not consider this a merely hypothetical possibility. He believed the political coalition formed in support of the "Tariff of Abominations" proved his point. The interests served by the tariff—iron, hemp, processed cotton, processed as well as raw wool, and so on—were diverse and partly contradictory and would seem to invite defection. But once the political bargain was sealed, all the favored interests united and locked it into place, at the expense of those excluded from the bargain.

In Calhoun's view the same pattern underlay the threat to slavery when antislavery replaced the tariff as the chief source of conflict between North and South. The northern campaign against slavery, Calhoun believed, was caused by an unholy alliance between a northern majority motivated by economic and political self-interest and a small but potent abolitionist minority inspired by religious fanaticism. The abolitionist minority was just large enough to give it leverage in northern states where two roughly equal parties, looking to secure a majority, competed for its support. In this way, Calhoun feared, the workings of party politics would eventually place all three branches of the national government in the hands of a majority fundamentally hostile to the slave-based economy and social order of the South.[35]

Calhoun considered the traditional safeguards against abuse of power in a popular government—responsibility of the government to the governed, freedom of the press, and separation of powers—insufficient to prevent the oppression of a minority by the majority. The right of universal suffrage can prevent the government from oppressing the community as a whole; it cannot prevent one part of the community from oppressing another. Freedom of the press likewise cannot prevent oppression of the minority. Calhoun admitted that the press was a very great power—indeed a dangerous power in the hands of what he considered abolitionist fanatics—but its tendency was not to moderate but "to increase party excitement, and the violence and virulence of party struggles; and, in the same degree, the tendency to oppression and abuse of power."[36]

Nor was any remedy to be found in the constitutional "division of government into separate, and, as it regards each other, independent departments." This may slow the progress of the majority's accumulation of power by inducing "greater caution and deliberation"; but over time nothing prevented the majority from taking control of all of the departments. The only way to prevent the majority's capturing all branches of government, he argued, was "to go one step further, and make the several departments the organs of the distinct interests or portions of the community; and to clothe each with a negative on the others."[37] At that point separation of powers would be transformed into exactly Calhoun's own remedy, the concurrent majority.

Several elements of Calhoun's diagnosis deserve emphasis. First, nothing in the usual constitutional rights and limitations necessarily prevents a majority from abusing its power. Calhoun's scenario presupposes a majority exploiting the normal taxing and spending powers of government, where all laws are formally equal in their application. Freedom of speech and press and the right of political opposition remain undisturbed, but do nothing to restrain an oppressive majority.

Second, Calhoun's diagnosis suggests that entrenched majorities and minorities might come into existence in a political community characterized at the beginning by economic diversity and political fluidity. A political order that was not deeply divided at first may become so over time through the interplay of economic self-interest, political party strategy, and majority rule.

Finally, Calhoun believed that a process of democratic degeneration was not merely possible, but necessary and inevitable, unless prevented by a formal constitutional mechanism giving each portion or interest a veto. "One portion of the community may be crushed, and another elevated on its ruins, by systematically perverting the power of taxation and disbursement . . . That it *will* be so used, unless prevented, is, from the constitution of man, just as certain as that it *can* be so used."[38] Whether such a process *must* occur in the absence of Calhoun's prescribed remedy may be doubted. But he made a plausible argument that it *can* happen, and that the ordinary constitutional checks on majority rule are no proof against it.

Federalism and the Consensus Theory

Calhoun presented his remedy to majority tyranny in general and universal form in the *Disquisition*, which argued that every "portion" or "interest" must enjoy veto rights. As applied to the particular circumstances of the United States, Calhoun's remedy took the form of a specific interpretation of the Constitution whereby every *state*—as an equal member of the constitutional compact—had a unilateral right to block federal laws and policies it considered "unconstitutional, unequal, and oppressive."[39] Calhoun made no essential distinction between these three things: a law that was "unequal and oppressive" to a state or geographical interest was for that reason also unconstitutional.

In a very significant 1827 letter, Calhoun revealed that his minority veto/consensus theory was both logically and chronologically prior to his interpretation of the Constitution. The immediate occasion of the letter was the 1827 Harrisburg Convention of protectionists. Calhoun wrote, "After much reflection, it seems to me, that the despotism founded on combined geographical interest, admits of but one effectual remedy, a veto on the part of the local interest, or under our system, on the part of the States."[40] States, in other words, when nullifying federal law, would act as the agents of some "geographical interest" threatened by national legislation. We find here at once the diagnosis and the remedy that later formed the basis of Calhoun's mature constitutional theory as well as the core argument of the *Disquisition*.

Moreover, it is clear from the letter that Calhoun began with the core idea later expressed in the *Disquisition*—minority veto as a check on the majority—and then interpreted the Constitution to fit that idea, not the other way around. His theoretical starting point was not state sovereignty but the protection of geographically concentrated minority interests; he seized upon the former as a means to accomplish the latter. "It is difficult to conceive, how, peculiar local & minor interests can be secured unless by a negative of the kind; but how far such a negative would be found consistent with the general power, is an important consideration, which I waive for the present."[41] In this last phrase Calhoun admits that he has not yet constructed a constitutional theory consistent with the idea of minority veto; he realizes that its consistency with the constitutional powers of the national government is a problem that still needs to be worked out. Within a year, by the time he drafted the *Exposition* in 1828, Calhoun had developed a plausible-sounding constitutional theory that, through the mechanism of single-state nullification of federal law, put into practice the fundamental idea of minority veto.

One of the purposes behind Calhoun's doctrine of nullification was to vest each state with the power to judge the constitutionality of federal laws. For example, by enacting the protective tariff, Calhoun argued, Congress "pervert[ed] a power, from an objected intended [raising revenue], to one not intended [protecting manufactures], the most insidious and dangerous of all infractions."[42] Setting and collecting tariffs was a power specifically assigned by the Constitution to Congress (Article I, Section 8) and specifically denied to the states (Article I, Section 10). Calhoun could not plausibly claim that the protective tariff was unconstitutional because it usurped some right or power reserved to the states. But a power specifically assigned to the federal government might still be exercised in an unconstitutional manner: there were reasonable arguments on both sides about whether Congress had overstepped its bounds in enacting a specifically *protective* tariff. Calhoun believed that every state had the right to judge, not only the extent of its own reserved powers, but also whether the federal government was exercising *its* designated powers in constitutional ways.

Judging whether Congress has exercised its powers constitutionally is a decision typically made by the federal judiciary. But Calhoun was not willing to entrust the final judgment of constitutionality to the Supreme Court, or to any federal body.[43] The state alone was ultimate judge of its constitutional rights and obligations, and consequently of whether and when nullification of federal law was justified. Thus state court decisions took precedence over federal courts; federal appellate jurisdiction over state courts was in Calhoun's view blatantly unconstitutional.[44] The only qualification Calhoun admitted on each state's right to be final judge of its rights, obligations, and powers was (as noted above) that an act of nullification could be affirmatively overruled by three-quarters of the other states—at which point the nullifying state could exercise its ultimate right of final judgment by seceding.

Under Calhoun's rules it is clear that no federal law or federal court ruling that was seriously opposed by any state (and the economic or social interest that predominated in that state) would ever go into effect. That indeed was exactly Calhoun's aim. But he believed that a federal system based on full state sovereignty and state nullification of federal law was in fact fully compatible with energetic, fair, and effective federal government. In this respect his full-state-sovereignty version of federalism absolutely depended upon the plausibility of his consensus theory of government.

Calhoun's Commitment to Slavery

Calhoun's commitment to slavery must appear to modern readers a glaring inconsistency in his political philosophy. How could a political theorist determined to protect minorities from the ravages of unchecked power simultaneously be a staunch defender of slavery? The fact that slaves were actually a *majority* of the population in Calhoun's home state (while a large minority in the South and the United States as a whole) only heightens the irony.[45] Yet Calhoun himself saw no contradiction between his defense of minority rights and his defense of slavery.

Calhoun did not seek to protect slavery merely because it existed and was difficult to eradicate. He believed deeply in the moral rightness of slavery and its supposed beneficial effects on the United States as a whole. His life's work was a sustained effort to build a foundation upon which *both* slavery and the Union could be preserved, and civil war avoided.

One might address the slavery problem in Calhoun's thought in at least three ways. One is to treat his commitment to slavery, however damnable, as an inessential element of his minority veto/consensus theory of government and to examine that theory on its own terms.[46] For clearly the consensus model of government as such does not logically require slavery. Alternatively one could plausibly enough portray Calhoun's entire political theory, from beginning to end, as an elaborate rationalization for slavery.[47] Finally, one could attempt to deny or downplay the extent of Calhoun's commitment to slavery and even hint that he foresaw some eventual abolition of the institution.[48] The former two approaches are intellectually defensible, if selective; the last is incompatible with the historical record.

My approach here will be to explore interconnections between Calhoun's consensus theory of government and his defense of slavery. On the one hand I do not dismiss the theory itself as merely an elaborate rationalization for slavery; it clearly has resonance beyond slaveholding societies. On the other hand, slavery was an essential component in the *effective functioning* of the consensus model as Calhoun envisioned it.

Under any consensus model of government, the number of "interests" entitled to veto rights must necessarily be limited. It might be possible to secure the ongoing consent of two or three basic interests, but not of ten or fifty. Slavery provides a brutally effective (if transparently unjust) way of drawing this line, of deciding whose interests count *as* interests and whose do not. In the absence of slavery some other method of drawing the line would be required, perhaps equally arbitrary if not equally unjust.

Furthermore, a minority veto/consensus model of government works best if internally each "portion" is relatively homogeneous and characterized by a high degree of shared interest. *Between* the different veto-wielding "portions or interests" (between North and South, for instance) there can be sharp differences of interest; *within* each "portion or interest" (within South Carolina, for instance, or within the South as a section) those differences of interest must be small, otherwise one would have to create additional veto rights for internal minorities and face the danger once again of an infinite regression. Calhoun made absolutely clear that in the American South the institution of slavery and its racial hierarchies created homogeneity of interest and outlook among white citizens that would otherwise be lacking.[49] Political consensus was facilitated by racial solidarity.

Calhoun's critique of majority rule and his defense of slavery had at least one common root: his rejection of individualistic, natural rights–based political theory. Human beings, he argued in the *Disquisition* and elsewhere, are not "born free and equal" but instead are born "subject, not only to parental authority, but to the laws and institutions of the country where born, and under whose protection they draw their first breath."[50] Liberty is not a natural right but a privilege, a hard-won achievement dependent on a long process of civilization. Some people are "prepared for liberty" and some are not, and Calhoun intended his consensus model of government to apply only to those he deemed prepared for liberty. His broader political theory cannot be reduced simply to a defense of slavery, but the two are so interlinked that disentangling them is a complicated operation.

Aims of This Book

This work is intended to accomplish three different goals: first, critically to examine Calhoun's minority veto/consensus model of government; second, to use Calhoun to shed new light on the crisis that led up to the American Civil War; and third, to explore attempts elsewhere to institute Calhoun's consensus model of government, or something like it. The book is intended for, among others, readers interested in political philosophy and democratic theory; the intellectual and political history of antebellum America; the history of slavery and race in the United States; and the comparative politics of modern-day culturally, racially, or ethnically divided societies.

There are a small number of book-length studies of Calhoun's political theory; none of them is adequately critical.[51] A handful of journal articles on Calhoun's political theory are more critically insightful than the books.[52] Calhoun is the subject of a number of good biographies,[53] and of course turns up as a key actor in narrative histories and scholarly monographs on nullification or slavery or South Carolina politics.[54]

What distinguishes the present work is that it takes Calhoun's minority veto/consensus theory seriously as well as critically. Some discussions of Calhoun's thought treat his critique of majority rule seriously but conclude quickly that his solution is unworkable.[55] Ultimately the present work reaches the same conclusion. But it does so by reframing the question: not whether Calhoun's consensus model is *possible*—for systems are clearly possible where one or more strategically positioned minorities enjoy veto rights over collective decisions—but whether and under what conditions this would produce genuine consensus and thus offer a superior alternative to majority rule. I will argue here that it does not, or does so only under very improbable and fragile conditions. The mechanism of minority veto, simply of itself, does not ensure consensus, fairness, or justice and can very well guarantee the opposite.

A reader might fairly ask: what justifies so extensive a study of a figure whose theory one considers unworkable, or workable only in ways that are less fair and just than majority rule? There are a number of ways of answering this question.

The most straightforward answer is historical. Calhoun was a key intellectual and political leader of the antebellum South and for that reason helps us understand the crisis that led up to the American Civil War and why many southern defenders of slavery genuinely believed that a completely uncompromising proslavery policy would save the Union rather than destroy it.

This historical answer simultaneously points to another reason for taking Calhoun's theory seriously: its seductive promise of a consensus-based polity in which no "portion or interest" ever has to give up what it considers most important, yet in which the energy and effectiveness of government is not sacrificed.

Calhoun's consensus model (or something akin to it) has for good or ill entered the institutional "tool box" available to well-meaning leaders and constitutional architects faced with the governance challenges of deeply divided political orders like South Africa, Northern Ireland, and the ill-fated former Yugoslavia. The consensus model seems especially attractive where all other options including majority rule are so obviously unattractive. The minority veto/consensus model also appeals to strategically placed minorities everywhere in the world who want to pretend they advance the common good precisely by uncompromisingly insisting on having their own way. By specifying the (improbable) set of conditions under which a consensus system could work effectively—i.e., enable collective action rather than merely block it—Calhoun's theory provides critical purchase on contemporary proposals to institutionalize a minority veto/consensus system of government.

Finally, Calhoun is worth examining because he sheds light on how far short of its theoretical ideal democracy can fall. No reasonable person would advocate democracy if it meant rule by 51 percent of the population entirely for the benefit of that 51 percent, wholly indifferent to (or viciously inclined toward) the other 49 percent. Calhoun may have been wrong to claim this kind of pernicious democracy was inevitable without iron-clad minority vetoes. But it is disturbing enough to acknowledge such an outcome is possible—on that point Calhoun was right—and that none of the ordinary constitutional processes provide sure guarantees against it.

Chapter Summary

Calhoun's political theory required a radical reinterpretation of the Constitution and of the nature of the federal union, but in a way that exploited tradition wherever possible. That is the theme of chapter 2, which describes how Calhoun used Jefferson's Kentucky Resolutions and Madison's Virginia Resolutions of 1798 to present his own political and constitutional theory as a faithful continuation of the Jeffersonian creed—though Calhoun explicitly rejected Jefferson's natural rights philosophy and his condemnation of slavery. Madison was still alive during the nullification crisis and argued publicly that nullification would contradict the basic principles of republican government by allowing the minority to rule the majority.

At the core of Calhoun's theory of the concurrent majority is an ethic of reciprocity among mutually dependent interests. That is the theme of chapter 3, which examines Calhoun's political economy, and in particular how he conceived the economic interdependence of the different geographic sections of the United States. In his nationalist phase (through the mid-1920s) Calhoun believed that enlightened leadership, acting through the ordinary democratic processes, could achieve this sectional reciprocity. His turn to nullification came when he concluded that reciprocity would have to be forced by giving each geographical interest a constitutionally guaranteed veto.

Chapter 4 examines how Calhoun creatively reinterpreted constitutional text and framing-era history to fit his minority veto/consensus model of government and his full-state-sovereignty version of federalism. In Calhoun's view the high degree of consensus achieved in the process of drafting and ratifying the Constitution ought to be required on a *continuing* basis for all key political decisions—political life as a kind of permanent constitutional convention. The chapter also examines Calhoun's argument that all antislavery agitation was inherently unconstitutional, indeed criminal, because it violated the spirit of equality and reciprocity among states.

Chapter 5 discusses Calhoun's defense of slavery as a "positive good" (rather than merely a difficult-to-remove evil) and the interconnections between his proslavery argument and the broader political theory of the *Disquisition*. Calhoun genuinely believed that slavery based on racial hierarchy was in the common good of the entire United States, North as well as South, because he claimed it provided a safe and stable foundation for republican political institutions. In his defense of slavery Calhoun was caught between two contradictory views of the nature of liberty. He sometimes argued that progress was the fruit of liberty and liberty the fruit of progress, which is difficult to reconcile with his commitment to permanent slavery for the African race in America. At other times he spoke as though liberty for one always depended upon lack of liberty for someone else, a position more obviously consistent with his defense of slavery.

Chapter 6 is a comprehensive critical examination of Calhoun's consensus model of government. The examination raises three fundamental objections to Calhoun's theory. First, where each "portion or interest" possesses a negative on the decisions of the whole, what prevents deadlock or anarchy? Second, what prevents minority veto from becoming in practice minority domination of the majority? Finally, *within* each "portion or interest" where does the minority veto stop, and can any stopping point be justified? Why not an infinite regression of vetoes-within-vetoes? By considering these objections and Calhoun's responses to them we gain a clearer view of the assumptions and preconditions necessary for his consensus model to work as he intended it.

Chapter 7 turns to modern-day "divided societies" where majority rule is problematic and examines some actual or proposed consensus models that resemble Calhoun's. The 1998 Good Friday Agreement for Northern Ireland displays a nearly exact parallel to Calhoun's theory of the concurrent majority. The 1974 constitution of the former Yugoslavia attempted to resolve interrepublic rivalry by means of a consensus rule. In South Africa a minority veto/consensus model was persistently sought by the National Party for a postapartheid constitutional settlement, though ultimately refused in favor of a majority-rule model. Chapter 7 also discusses the contemporary political scientist Arend Lijphart, whose theory of "consociational democracy" bears a close and explicitly acknowledged resemblance to Calhoun's theory, and whose writings were influential among constitutional architects in all three of the countries examined in the chapter. The chapter closes with Lani Guinier's diagnosis of politically entrenched racial divisions in *The Tyranny of the Majority*, which parallels Calhoun's own diagnosis of entrenched majorities and minorities.

The book's conclusion argues that Calhoun's minority veto/consensus model fails to offer a superior alternative to majority rule. The failure of Calhoun's remedy does not, however, entail the irrelevance of his diagnosis. Democracy may indeed be susceptible to serious pathologies for which there is no permanent remedy. Constitutional checks can do only so much; beyond that point the health of democracy irreducibly depends on the politics we practice and the leaders we choose.

TWO

Calhoun and the Legacies of Jefferson and Madison

Calhoun's political philosophy was a response to critical unresolved problems of the American republican experiment. The specifically American setting is obvious in the *South Carolina Exposition,* the *Fort Hill Address,* the *Discourse on the Constitution and Government of the United States,* and many other key writings and speeches. But *A Disquisition on Government* too, though it speaks in universal terms and draws material from the wide sweep of human history, is equally a response to the American political crisis in which Calhoun himself lived and acted. For better or worse, Calhoun's political philosophy was an American product, not some exotic import.[1]

The founding generation left at least two crucial problems unresolved: the disputed sovereignty relationship between national government and states and the continued existence of slavery in a nation committed to ideals of universal equality and liberty. The "second generation" of American statesmen—which included Henry Clay, Daniel Webster, John Quincy Adams, and John C. Calhoun—attempted in different ways to resolve, or at least manage, these explosive tensions.

Calhoun's attempted resolution was perhaps the most radical, in effect cutting two Gordian knots with a single stroke. The sovereignty dispute between federal government and states he unequivocally resolved in favor of state sovereignty: the federal government was, he argued, merely the creation and agent of the sovereign states, and each state, as sovereign, is the final judge of its constitutional obligations. There could be no more talk of divided or partial sovereignty under the Constitution. By asserting full state sovereignty Calhoun sought not only to resolve the constitutional contradictions, but also to put into practice the minority veto/consensus theory of government expressed most fully in the *Disquisition*. He believed that if each state (and the interests it represented) could veto actions of the federal government, only policies truly beneficial to all sections and interests would be put into practice.

Calhoun's response to the incompatibility between slavery and the ideals of the Declaration was equally radical. He rejected the phrase "all men are created equal" outright, calling it a dangerous error that was inserted unnecessarily into the Declaration. He opposed not only the phrase itself but the natural rights, contract-theory political philosophy upon which it was based, and attempted in the *Disquisition* to provide an altogether different theoretical foundation for liberty and republican government.

Calhoun's theoretical move here should be compared with other attempted resolutions of the same contradiction. One could of course recognize the contradiction for what it was and demand that practice conform to ideals: that was the abolitionist response. Few white Americans in the antebellum period were willing to accept the abolitionists' radical consistency on this matter.

A more common way of managing the contradiction was to admit slavery to be a moral and political evil incompatible with the ideals of the Revolution, but assert that for practical reasons the evil could not be soon or easily remedied. That was the approach taken by Jefferson and Madison and many other slaveholders of the revolutionary generation. It was in direct opposition to this way of talking that Calhoun asserted in 1837 that slavery in the American context was not an evil at all but a "positive good."[2]

An alternative resolution to the contradiction was to assert that the phrase "all men are created equal" was intended only to apply to the white race. This is the approach taken by Stephen Douglas in the Lincoln-Douglas debates of 1858: the language of the Declaration, Douglas asserted, was intended to apply only to men of European descent, not to Africans or Indians or any other "inferior" race.[3] Justice Roger Taney in the Dred Scott decision of 1857 resorted to a similar ideological move. Taney's opinion followed Calhoun's constitutional theory in many respects: Taney, like Calhoun, denied that either Congress or territorial legislatures could prohibit slavery in federal territories, the key point in Dred Scott. But, unlike Calhoun, Taney's opinion still granted high authority to the phrase "all men are created equal" and thus (like Stephen Douglas) denied it was intended to apply to the African race.[4]

Calhoun's resolution was more straightforward than Taney's, and as radical as the abolitionists' though in the opposite direction. Recognizing that "all men are created equal" necessarily entailed a condemnation of slavery—by the force of words, whatever may have been the intention of the signers—he rejected the conclusion by denying the premise. But Calhoun did not see himself as turning his back on the American revolutionary and constitutional traditions, but as *fixing* revolutionary and constitutional traditions that could no longer survive in their original form. In this respect he was an earlier counterpart to Lincoln, who also sought to resolve the two key problems (slavery and sovereignty) the founding generation left unresolved. Calhoun's attempted resolution was of course diametrically opposed to Lincoln's on both points.

This chapter examines Calhoun's political and constitutional theory through his engagement with the legacies of Thomas Jefferson and James Madison. Jefferson and Madison were not Calhoun's only influences. There were other American traditions from which he drew, and he was acquainted with key classical and modern works of political theory. But as a rule Calhoun was singularly unrevealing about his theoretical influences. The *Disquisition* does not refer to other works of political theory. One may find in Calhoun's speeches and private correspondence an occasional reference to John Locke, Aristotle, Edmund Burke, Adam Smith.[5] Some scholars have seen in the references to Aristotle and Burke an important key to understanding Calhoun's political philosophy.[6] But the references are too brief and scattered to be of much use in illuminating Calhoun's theory, even if he was indeed influenced by these authors.

Jefferson and Madison are exceptions here because Calhoun was explicit both about what he took and what he rejected in their thought. Jefferson's and Madison's legacies were distinctly double-edged with respect to Calhoun's own purposes. Jefferson was on the one hand the author of the Kentucky Resolutions of 1798, which were the single most important precedent for Calhoun's own constitutional doctrine of nullification. Madison, besides his stature as a framer of the Constitution, penned the Virginia Resolutions of 1798, another key precedent for Calhoun, and in his contributions to the *Federalist* Madison sought to describe how to protect the minority from an oppressive majority—the same general problem Calhoun attempted to solve. On the other hand Jefferson was responsible for inserting "all men are created equal" into the Declaration and at least in the 1780s had attempted to stop the spread of slavery to federal territories, thus providing ideological weapons to the abolitionists and free-soilers of Calhoun's time. Madison himself lived long enough to denounce Calhoun's doctrine of nullification as a perversion of the Constitution and to deny that the Virginia Resolutions, properly understood, gave any support to such a doctrine. Calhoun claimed in turn that Madison's attempt in *Federalist* No. 39 and elsewhere to describe the federal union as "partly national and partly federal" was incoherent, and that Madison's remedy to the danger of majority faction was rendered obsolete by the advent of national, patronage-based political parties.

Calhoun was never a straightforward disciple of any theory or tradition. On the contrary, he always transformed whatever he touched. But it was politically prudent that his innovations appear to be a faithful continuation of an earlier tradition. Even where he explicitly rejected elements of Jefferson's and Madison's legacies (and the American republican tradition more generally), he claimed to be doing so in order better to preserve what remained.

Selectively Appropriating Jefferson and Madison

When Calhoun sat down to draft what became the *South Carolina Exposition* (1828), he asked William Preston, chair of a key committee in the South Carolina legislature, "to obtain and forward me the Kentucky resolutions" because Calhoun had lent out his own copy which had not been returned.[7] Four years later, after Calhoun had perused a recently published edition of Jefferson's writings that included Jefferson's own more radical draft of the Kentucky Resolutions, he remarked that there was such a "striking coincidence" between Jefferson's views and his own, that "I should have been exposed to the charge of plagiarism, were it supposed possible, that I could have previously known what his were."[8] The public revelation of Jefferson's more radical draft provided additional ideological ammunition to South Carolina in its decision to press forward with nullification in 1832.[9]

These two details reveal how Calhoun regarded the relation between his own thought and that of Jefferson. He could be accused of plagiarism, but the accusation would be false because, Calhoun implied, he came up with his ideas independently. By the time he sent for a copy of the Kentucky Resolutions in 1828, he had already worked out the essentials of his own doctrine of nullification. When it became publicly known in 1832 that Jefferson had penned a draft asserting the right of a state "to nullify of their own authority, all assumptions of power by others" (language dropped from the final version of the Kentucky Resolutions), Calhoun had already formulated his own more radical version of the idea. If Calhoun and Jefferson ended up in the same place, Calhoun suggested in denying the "plagiarism" charge, it was only because Calhoun had followed his own train of thought there. This assertion may appear arrogant, but it is almost certainly true and helps us understand the relation between Calhoun's and Jefferson's thought. Their conclusions were similar in some respects; but the closer one examines the reasoning underlying those conclusions, the more differences one notices.

In the *Exposition,* the first systematic statement of his mature constitutional theory, Calhoun argued not only that a protective tariff was unconstitutional, but that a state judging a law unconstitutional has a right to refuse to obey that law within its borders. In constitutional disputes between the federal government and a state, he argued, the state must remain the final judge. That same theory is enlarged upon in the *Fort Hill Address* of 1831 (where Calhoun made public his support of nullification) and the *Discourse on the Constitution,* which was published after his death in 1850.

All three of these statements of Calhoun's constitutional theory draw upon Jefferson for support. In the *Exposition* Calhoun wrote that "it would seem impossible to deny to the States the right of deciding on the infractions of their rights, and the proper remedy to be applied for their correction. The right of judging, in such cases, is an essential attribute of sovereignty." Later in the *Exposition* he quotes from Jefferson's Kentucky Resolutions of 1798, where Jefferson wrote that "the Government created by this compact was not made the exclusive or final judge of the extent of the powers delegated to itself, since that would have made its discretion, and not the Constitution the measure of its powers; but as in all other cases of compact between parties having no common judges, each party has an equal right to judge for itself, as well of infractions as of the mode and measure of redress."[10] Calhoun quoted this passage again in the *Fort Hill Address,* and remarked: "Language cannot be more explicit; nor can higher authority be adduced."[11]

In the *Fort Hill Address* Calhoun observed: "The question of the relation, which the States and General Government bear to each other, is not one of recent origin. From the commencement of our system, it has divided public sentiment . . . The great struggle, that preceded the political revolution of 1801, which brought Mr. Jefferson into power, turned essentially on it." Calhoun then remarks that, though the Virginia and Kentucky Resolutions "con-

Calhoun and the Legacies of Jefferson & Madison   27

tain, what I believe to be, the true doctrine on this important subject," their meaning has been differently interpreted; therefore "I will, in order that my sentiments may be fully known, and to avoid all ambiguity, proceed to state summarily the doctrines, which I conceive they embrace."[12] In short, Calhoun here presents his own constitutional theory as no more than a fuller explication of Jefferson's.

The central principal of that constitutional theory—Calhoun's but presented as an explication of Jefferson's—is:

> That the General Government emanated from the people of the several States, forming distinct political communities, and acting in their separate and sovereign capacity, and not from all of the people forming one aggregate political community; that the Constitution of the United States is in fact a compact, to which each State is a party, in the character already described; and that the several States or parties, have a right to judge of its infractions, and in cases of a deliberate, palpable, and dangerous exercise of power not delegated, they have the right, in the last resort, to use the language of the Virginia resolutions, *"to interpose for arresting the progress of the evil, and for maintaining within their respective limits, the authorities, rights, and liberties appertaining to them."* This right of interposition, thus solemnly asserted by the State of Virginia, be it called what it may, State right, veto, nullification, or by any other name, I conceive to be the fundamental principle of our system, resting on facts historically as certain, as our Revolution itself.[13]

Calhoun's *Discourse on the Constitution* was written much later, when defending the rights of slaveholders had replaced opposition to the tariff as his principal concern. The constitutional doctrine is essentially the same as the one presented in the *Exposition* and the *Fort Hill Address,* though drawn out in greater detail and with explicit attention to the constitutional status of slavery. Once again, Jefferson is enlisted as an ally on matters of constitutional theory. But in the *Discourse* the emphasis is on Jefferson's failure adequately to institutionalize his constitutional principles.

Calhoun once again quotes at length from Jefferson's Kentucky Resolutions—this time from Jefferson's more radical draft—and now contrasts them with Madison's Virginia Resolutions as being "differently expressed, and, in some respects, fuller than the latter." (Madison's explicit rejection of nullification, discussed below, may explain Calhoun's elevating Jefferson over Madison.) Calhoun then goes on to detail Jefferson's failures once in office. The Alien and Sedition Acts, it is true, went by the wayside. But Jefferson "did nothing to arrest many great and radical evils"; he did not elevate state judiciaries from subordination to the federal courts "to their rightful, constitutional position"; and did nothing "towards maintaining the rights of the States as parties to the constitutional compact, to judge, in the last resort, as to the extent of the delegated powers."[14]

Calhoun's complaint, in brief, was that Jefferson once in power did not *institutionalize* the principles set forth in the Kentucky Resolutions. Jefferson, in Calhoun's view, ought to have made nullification a regular and ordinary part of the workings of the federal system. Instead Jefferson's nullification idea remained no more than a one-time response to a particular crisis. Calhoun suggested that the political struggle that brought Jefferson to power in 1801 "was too short to make any deep and lasting impression on the great body of the community" and as a result Jefferson himself came away from it lacking "a just and full conception of the danger."[15]

Calhoun's own narrative of the 1790s located the principal danger to liberty not in the Alien and Sedition Acts, but in the twenty-fifth section of the Judiciary Act of 1789, which made "the judiciary of the United States . . . paramount to that of the individual States."[16] If states were fully sovereign—a premise upon which Calhoun believed he and Jefferson agreed—then state court decisions should take precedence over decisions of federal courts. That is what Jefferson, in Calhoun's view, ought to have fought for if he had truly understood the danger and consistently followed his own principles.

The Jeffersonian Political Tradition

We might of course ask how Calhoun was able to invoke Jefferson's draft of the Kentucky Resolutions as a high constitutional authority in the first place. Jefferson's *draft* of the Kentucky Resolutions went further toward nullification than the version ultimately authorized by the Kentucky legislature, and behind the scenes Madison may have convinced Jefferson to tone down the more extreme statements. Jefferson himself sought to keep secret his authorship of the Kentucky Resolutions. When his authorship was publicly revealed in 1821 Jefferson reluctantly admitted it, but claimed to have only a vague recollection of the matter (and his own more radical draft had not yet come to light).[17] It was the nullification movement itself that elevated to the status of canonical text Jefferson's secret and long-unpublished draft of the Kentucky Resolutions.

It is not immediately clear why a draft of a document possessing no constitutional or legal status, from which the author later sought to distance himself, a draft not fully supported by the state that commissioned it, and even in its more moderate final form not endorsed by any other state at the time, could later be treated by Calhoun and other nullifiers as though it were equal in authority to the Constitution itself and key to understanding the Constitution's true meaning.

In order to understand how the nullifiers' appropriation of the Kentucky Resolutions was possible we must survey the Jeffersonian political tradition from which Calhoun emerged and his own changing relationship to that tradition. Jefferson's name carried enormous weight in antebellum American politics. But it was not principally his authorship of the Declaration of Independence that gave such weight to his name (as is probably the case today). His accomplishments as two-term president were honored, the Louisiana Purchase especially, but this also does not explain his preeminence.

The authority of Jefferson's name arose from his founding a political movement from which every viable political party in Calhoun's time claimed descent. By 1820 there was effectively only one party in the United States, the Jeffersonian Republican party, and all the real political battles of the decade were fought out within that party. By the mid-1830s there were two political parties, the Jacksonian Democrats and the Whigs, both claiming descent from Jefferson (and each accusing the other of betraying Jeffersonian principles).

It was not merely Jefferson's victory in the 1800 election, but how he and his political followers interpreted that victory, that explains the later canonical use of his name. Jefferson saw his election not merely as a change of government but as a second American Revolution against the resurgent forces of monarchism and corruption.[18] The political movements and parties descended from Jefferson, whatever their other differences, all more or less accepted this interpretation of events to such an extent that by the 1820s (except in the Northeast) hardly anyone defended the old Federalist party, and to discredit opponents it was sufficient to associate their policies with Hamilton or some other high Federalist. If the Federalists had remained viable as a political party (not self-destructed during the War of 1812), Jefferson's name might not have carried such weight and Jefferson's draft of the Kentucky Resolutions would have been less useful to Calhoun. It is their connection with the "Revolution of 1800" that gave the Kentucky Resolutions an authority they would otherwise lack.

The Jeffersonian legacy in Calhoun's time was as diverse and internally conflicted as Jefferson himself. One could find a Jeffersonian precedent for practically anything one favored or opposed. Throughout his political career Calhoun referred frequently to Jefferson. This in itself was not remarkable; almost all statesmen of the period did the same.[19] What is revealing is *how* Calhoun invoked Jefferson, in what context, for what purpose. This changed over time and mirrored Calhoun's own principal concerns of the moment.

In the early to mid-1820s, still in his nationalist phase, Calhoun (who was then secretary of war) was often attacked for violating Jeffersonian strict-constructionist principles by supporting strongly national measures like the national bank and federally funded internal improvements. His response in an 1824 letter was to emphasize, not Jefferson's principles, but Jefferson's *actions* as president, which created legitimizing precedents for the policies Calhoun himself supported. Jefferson, despite his 1791 strict-constructionist argument against the Bank of the United States, as president tacitly accepted it and even extended its operations to the Louisiana Territory. In the same letter Calhoun argued against strict construction of the Constitution as leading to insoluble contradictions. He asserted that he fully supported states' rights and the Constitution's "admirable distribution" of powers between national and state governments—without indicating in the slightest that nullification was one of these state rights.[20] In short, it was Jefferson's liberal use of powers as president, not Jeffersonian strict constructionism or the Kentucky Resolutions, that mattered to Calhoun during his nationalist period.

Calhoun's use of Jefferson began to change shortly after that 1824 letter. From late 1824 (when Calhoun was elected vice president) until mid-1827 (when he began to formulate his theory of nullification) the side of Jefferson that Calhoun most emphasized was Jefferson as populist opponent of elite corruption.

Calhoun's concern with corruption was driven by two events connected with the 1824 election, when Calhoun himself was an early contender for the presidency. He was fiercely opposed to the congressional caucus method of selecting presidential candidates, the caucus having selected his enemy William Crawford, and denounced the supposed "corrupt bargain" between John Quincy Adams and Henry Clay (whereby Clay, who finished third in electoral votes, cast his support to Adams during balloting in the House of Representatives and was later appointed secretary of state). These two events led Calhoun, for a time, into a kind of Jeffersonian populism. In an 1826 letter to Andrew Jackson (the immediate victim of the supposed "corrupt bargain") Calhoun spoke of a "scheme . . . to perpetuate power in the present hands, in spite of the free and unbiased sentiment of the country" whereby through "artful management of patronage . . . power can be acquired against the voice of the majority."[21] Calhoun here sounds very much like Jefferson in opposition during the 1790s, though still without any hint of nullification. Calhoun's target here is not yet an oppressive *majority*, but a *minority* frustrating the will of the majority. If power has been acquired in an ill manner, he wrote later in 1826, then "we must recur to first principles; go back to the doctrines of the Revolution . . . [and] the great Republican struggle, which brought Mr. Jefferson into power."[22] In practice this led Calhoun to favor abolition of the caucus system, a constitutional amendment to allow each congressional district directly to select presidential electors, and to support the most popular candidate for president, Andrew Jackson, in the 1828 election.[23]

Through most of the 1820s Calhoun appeared a defender of Jeffersonian majority rule against minority machinations and Jeffersonian virtue against political corruption. It was not until 1827 that he began to give priority to the problem of a majority oppressing a minority, and within a year produced the *Exposition*.[24] Calhoun's shift here appears in retrospect quite radical and sudden. It may have seemed less abrupt a shift to Calhoun himself for two reasons. First, both in his populist phase and after his turn to nullification and minority veto, Calhoun was preoccupied with what he considered to be political corruption. In Calhoun's letters from 1827, when the shift was in process, he readily blended corruption of the "corrupt bargain" variety (frustrating the will of the majority) with a new kind of corruption whereby "one section will be bribed by means flushed from another."[25] The problem of an oppressive majority enters Calhoun's political universe dressed as another corrupt spoilsman.[26]

Second, Calhoun would have seen both his majoritarianism of the mid-1820s and his later minority veto as different applications of the same republican (and Jeffersonian) principle: that those who govern must be held responsible to those they govern. In the *Fort Hill Address*, for example, he asserted that universal suffrage and minority veto were in fact different instruments of the same principle: "to secure *responsibility*, that is, *that those who make and execute the laws should be accountable to those, on whom the laws in reality operate; the only solid and durable foundation of liberty.*"[27]

This was for Calhoun the key principle of the Constitution, the central accomplishment of the Jeffersonian Revolution of 1800, and the real meaning of the American Revolution—not the words "all men are created equal." One may of course ask a question Calhoun himself does not consider: whether a single state unilaterally remaking federal law through nullification exercises a new form of irresponsible power over citizens of other states.

Calhoun and Jefferson Compared

Jefferson's draft of the Kentucky Resolutions, which asserts the right of a single state to declare acts of the federal government "unauthoritative, void, and of no force,"[28] does lend support to Calhoun's doctrine of nullification. Nevertheless there are important differences between Jefferson's theory and practice in 1798 and the theory and practice of nullification formulated by Calhoun.

Calhoun tended to take premises and drive them to relentlessly logical conclusions; his thinking was systematic in a way that Jefferson's never was. Once in office, Jefferson did not institutionalize the abstract principles set forth in the opening and closing sections of the Kentucky Resolutions, focusing instead on eliminating the abuses detailed in the long central section of the document. Calhoun suggested that if Jefferson had fully understood the implications of his own premises, he would have reformed the entire government on the principle of unequivocal state sovereignty.

Jefferson's inconsistencies are not difficult to catalogue. However, in this instance, Jefferson's course of action was not necessarily inconsistent. His political and theoretical starting point was in fact rather different than Calhoun's.

Jefferson in his battle against the Alien and Sedition Acts firmly believed that a national majority was on his side, or would soon come to see things his way. In a 1798 letter to John Taylor of Caroline, who was considering a resort to secession, Jefferson counseled patience: the "reign of witches" would soon pass and reason would prevail.[29] Both he and Madison were convinced that the Federalists were an embattled minority whose rule could be overturned by a democratic electorate—and Jefferson saw the victory of his party in 1800 in exactly these terms. This distinguishes Jefferson's political aims in the Kentucky Resolutions from Calhoun, who treated the majority itself as the problem and sought permanently to prevent a national majority from having its way.

It must be admitted, however, that the language of Jefferson's Kentucky

Resolutions does support single-state nullification, which would indeed allow a minority to block the will of a national majority. This is the most important difference between Jefferson's Kentucky Resolutions and Madison's Virginia Resolutions, which do not support single-state nullification (despite Calhoun's argument to the contrary). There is a large tension between Jefferson's majoritarian political purposes in 1798 and the particular constitutional medicine he administered in the Kentucky Resolutions. Jefferson may have sought principally to win through the electoral process, but he was willing to play with fire along the way.

Even on the level of constitutional theory, however, there are some significant differences between Calhoun and the Kentucky Resolutions. Jefferson's Kentucky Resolutions are not entirely clear whether state nullification is asserted as a *constitutional* right or as a resort to the *natural* right of revolution against a despotic power. The difference is important because if nullification were a clear constitutional right, then it ought to guide the routine workings of the federal system. If instead Jefferson intended nullification as a resort to the natural right of revolution—or at least a threat of this last resort—then it could not and should not be institutionalized. Jefferson's strategy may have been deliberate ambiguity on this point. But at least some passages hint that he is calling on the states to exercise their natural right of revolution. At one point Jefferson writes that, where powers delegated to the national government have been abused, "a change by the people would be the constitutional remedy"; but "where powers are assumed which have not been delegated" the case is different; no state is obliged to submit to "undelegated, and consequently unlimited powers" and in such cases "every State has a natural right in cases not within the compact (casus non foederis) to nullify of their own authority all assumptions of power by others within their limits." Near the close of the document Jefferson writes that the "co-States, recurring to their natural right in cases not made federal, will concur in declaring these acts void, and of no force."[30] The phrase "recurring to their natural right" suggests a resort to revolution, though the qualifying phrase "in cases not made federal" complicates the matter by implying nullification may be a constitutional right after all.

Either Jefferson understood nullification as a resort, or threat to resort, to the natural right of revolution, or he was deliberately hedging on the question of natural versus constitutional right. Neither reading provides a secure foundation for making nullification part of the routine workings of the Constitution, as Calhoun believed Jefferson ought to have done.

The Kentucky Resolutions draw from a contract theory of government, just as the Declaration of Independence does. In the former Jefferson speaks of a "compact among powers having no common judge"[31]—as though the Constitution were the result of a treaty among states hitherto subsisting in complete natural independence of one another.

To a certain degree this way of speaking converged with Calhoun's purposes; he and Jefferson agreed that the federal Constitution resulted from a compact among states. But Calhoun rejected contract theories that presupposed that *individuals* form governments through contract. A compact among sovereign states was, for Calhoun, fundamentally different than a contract among individuals—whereas Jefferson saw these as different manifestations of the same natural right. In the *Discourse* Calhoun rejected the view that an "unorganized mass of individuals"[32] had any right to form itself into a political community or to throw off its established government. Sovereign states may form a federal constitution through a compact, and any member state may revoke that compact at will. But contract theories of government stop at the state line. Calhoun's objection to "unorganized individuals" claiming natural rights links to another difference with Jefferson—slavery.

At the very beginning of the *Disquisition* Calhoun made clear his opposition to contract theories of government based on the assumption of naturally free, equal, independent individuals.

> I assume, as an incontestable fact, that man is so constituted as to be a social being. His inclinations and wants, physical and moral, irresistibly impel him to associate with his kind; and he has, accordingly, never been found, in any age or country, in any state other than the social. In no other, indeed, could he exist; and in no other,—were it possible for him to exist,—could he attain to a full development of his moral and intellectual faculties, or raise himself, in the scale of being, much above the level of the brute creation.

Government was indispensable, but also dangerous because of its liability to abuse; for this reason constitutions have been devised to limit the abuses of government. Government is "of Divine ordination"—meaning that it exists at all times and places, we have no choice in the matter. Thus the origin of government—and of social authority in general—is not any contract or deliberate human decision. Constitutions, which perfect and limit government, are by contrast the fruit of human decision, but they are not contracts either. Constitutions instead result from a long historical evolution that depends upon the level of "civilization and intelligence" diffused among the community.[33]

Later in the *Disquisition* Calhoun reiterates, with greater vehemence, his rejection of natural rights–based contract theories of government. A number of "great and dangerous errors" originate in "the prevalent opinion that all men are born free and equal;—than which nothing can be more unfounded and false." Because "there never was such a state as the, so called, state of nature, and never can be, it follows, that men, instead of being born in it, are born in the social and political state; and of course, instead of being free and equal, are born subject, not only to parental authority, but to the laws and institutions of the country where born, and under whose protection they draw their first breath." Calhoun then proceeds to argue that

> it is a great and dangerous error to suppose that all people are equally entitled to liberty. It is a reward to be earned, not a blessing to be gratuitously lavished on all alike;—a reward reserved for the intelligent, the patriotic, the virtuous and deserving;—and not a boon to be bestowed on a people too ignorant, degraded and vicious, to be capable either of appreciating or of enjoying it . . . Attempting to elevate a people in the scale of liberty, above the point to which they are entitled to rise, must ever prove abortive, and end in disappointment.[34]

Calhoun does not specifically mention slavery here, but—going by parallel passages in his 1848 speech on the Oregon Bill—at least one of his purposes is to refute antislavery arguments based on natural right. In the Senate in 1837 he argued that the body must not even receive antislavery petitions: "This position, that [slavery] was a moral evil, was the very root of the whole system of operations against it. That was the spring and wellhead from which all these streams of abolition proceeded."[35]

And the dangerous view that slavery was a moral evil Calhoun to a large degree attributed to Jefferson's influence—both Jefferson's explicit condemnation of the institution, and the natural-rights language in the Declaration of Independence. In Calhoun's lengthy 27 June 1848 speech on the Oregon Bill, Jefferson is a key figure. The immediate point at issue was a clause in the bill that would have excluded slavery from the territories. Jefferson was invoked on both sides of congressional debate because, on one hand, Jefferson's own 1784 draft ordinance for the Northwest Territories included a prohibition on slavery; on the other hand, the elderly Jefferson had harshly condemned the attempt by northern congressmen to exclude Missouri from the Union because it was a slave state.

The advocates of the proposal to restrict slavery in the territories, Calhoun remarked, "hold up the name of Jefferson in its favor, and go so far as to call him the author of the so-called Wilmot proviso" but "if we may judge by his opinion of [the Missouri crisis] . . . instead of being the author of the proviso, or being in its favor, no one could be more deadly hostile to it." Calhoun then quotes extensively from Jefferson's writing in letters to John Adams and John Holmes during the Missouri crisis that "this momentous question, like a fire-bell in the night, awakened and filled me with terror. I considered it at once as the knell of the Union . . . A geographical line, coinciding with a marked principle, moral and political, *once conceived and held up to the angry passions of men, will never be obliterated; and every new irritation will mark it deeper and deeper.*" Calhoun himself adds that "Twenty-eight years have passed since these remarkable words were penned, and there is not a thought which time has not thus far verified"; he asks: "Can any one believe, after listening to this letter, that Jefferson is the author of the so-called Wilmot Proviso, or ever favored it?"[36]

But Calhoun could not deny there was some truth to antislavery use of Jefferson.

> But I must speak the truth, while I vindicate the memory of Jefferson
> from so foul a charge. I hold he is not blameless in reference to this
> subject. He committed a great error [in 1784] in inserting the provision
> he did, in the plan he reported for the government of the [Northwest]
> Territory . . . It was the first blow—the first essay "to draw a
> geographical line coinciding with a marked principle, moral and
> political." It originated with him in philanthropic but mistaken views of
> the most dangerous character.[37]

Near the end of the speech, Calhoun returns to Jefferson's dangerous, mistaken view. After warning that the slavery question is "the only question sufficiently potent to dissolve the Union," he attacks the natural rights philosophy expressed in the Declaration. If the Union and its system of government should perish, the cause would be traceable to an axiom now repeated on both sides of the Atlantic, that "most false and dangerous of political errors . . . that 'all men are born free and equal' . . . Taking the proposition literally (it is in that sense it is understood), there is not a word of truth in it . . . Men are not born. Infants are born. They grow to be men . . . While infants they are incapable of freedom, being destitute alike of the capacity of thinking and acting, without which there can be no freedom." Calhoun then levels his attack directly on Jefferson. The proposition "all men are created equal" was put forth on a great occasion and thus "fixed itself deeply in the public mind."

> It was inserted in our Declaration of Independence without any necessity. It made no necessary part of our justification in separating from the parent country, and declaring ourselves independent. Breach of our chartered privileges, and lawless encroachment on our acknowledged and well-established rights by the parent country, were the real causes, and of themselves sufficient, without resorting to any other, to justify the step. Nor had it any weight in constructing the governments which were substituted in the place of the colonial. They were formed of the old materials and on practical and well-established principles, borrowed for the most part from our own experience and that of the country from which we sprang.[38]

Notice here that Calhoun rejected two separate, though related, elements of Jefferson's Declaration: the claim that all individuals were equally entitled to natural rights and the claim that governments may be rightfully dissolved when these natural rights are violated. The separation of the colonies from England ought instead to have been justified by reference to "breach of our chartered privileges . . . and well established rights." Moreover, the "new" American governments were not new at all: they were "formed of the old materials and on practical and well-established principles." In effect, the states, at the moment of the break with England, inherited the sovereign authority that had belonged to England, and retained it permanently afterward. Neither the national government, nor the so-called "people of the United States" can divest states of this sovereignty they acquired at the moment of independence. The *states,* as corporate entities, may have reentered a state of natural liberty with regard to one another when they broke the colonial tie; but the *people* of those states—individually and collectively—never ceased for a moment to be fully subject to the authority of one government or another.

It would follow, then, that nothing in the historical record of the American colonies' break with England could justify any rebellion by "unorganized individuals," in the name of their supposed natural rights, against established state authority; nor can national government or the "people of the United States" encroach upon the established authority of states in order to defend those supposed natural rights. The state's vested authority is unimpeachable, both within and without.

Calhoun's style of political thought was thus quite different from Jefferson's. Calhoun could, without distortion, cite passages from Jefferson in support of nullification, and on the danger of making divisions over slavery coincide with a geographical line. But this limited convergence was reached through very different reasoning. Jefferson's version of nullification was grounded in a natural rights theory that Calhoun rejected. As for slavery, in the same letter to Holmes in which Jefferson strongly opposed a federally imposed geographical line separating slave and free territories, he reiterated his condemnation of slavery as a great injustice and hoped for some "practicable" way of abolishing it. Jefferson has been criticized for condemning slavery in the abstract while failing to take practical steps to abolish it. But for Calhoun it was Jefferson's abstract condemnation of slavery itself, not his impractical schemes for abolishing it, that made Jefferson's views dangerous.

In the *Exposition* and the *Fort Hill Address* Calhoun had presented his own constitutional doctrine as no more than a detailed explication of Jefferson's. Once slavery came to the forefront, however, he could not claim Jefferson as a true ally. The best he could do was undermine abolitionists' claim to Jefferson's legacy. By the 1840s Calhoun was markedly more critical of Jefferson, even implying that the author of the Declaration of Independence misunderstood the true character of the American Revolution.

Calhoun's own attempt to reclaim the revolutionary legacy for slavery and state sovereignty, and his conviction that Jefferson's views were dangerously erroneous, suggest an ironic vindication of Jefferson. For if Jefferson added "all men are created equal" *unnecessarily* to the Declaration of Independence—if it really did not advance the task at hand—then Jefferson's own contribution to the cause of human liberty becomes all the more significant.

Madison Enters the Nullification Debate

Calhoun's original term for what came to be called nullification was "interposition," derived from Madison's Virginia Resolutions of 1798, which spoke of the right and duty of the states "to interpose for arresting the progress of the evil." The "evil" for Madison, as for Jefferson, was the Alien and Sedition Acts and, more generally, a "deliberate, palpable, and dangerous exercise" by the federal government of powers not granted by the Constitution.[39] Calhoun's *Fort Hill Address* referred to "this right of interposition, thus solemnly asserted by the State of Virginia" in the Virginia Resolutions of 1798, and called it "the fundamental principle of our system."[40] Calhoun later came to accept and employ the term "nullification" (which comes from Jefferson's Kentucky Resolutions draft). But it is ironic that Calhoun's originally preferred term was supplied by Madison, who soon publicly denounced both Calhoun's doctrine itself and Calhoun's use of the Virginia Resolutions.

Madison's name did not carry as much weight in Calhoun's time as Jefferson's did. Jefferson's birthday was commemorated throughout the United States; Madison's was not. Jefferson was a demigod while Madison remained human. Yet as the last surviving leader of the founding generation, and one who self-consciously preserved the political legacy of his generation, Madison's authority and his arguments could not be easily ignored.[41] During the nullification controversy, when South Carolina sought in vain for support from other southern states, one of Calhoun's correspondents from Georgia informed him that "It is not believed among us that a State can annul an act of Congress within her boundary and remain in the confederacy . . . Mr. Madison's recent exposition of [the Virginia Resolutions of 1798] is highly approved of here."[42]

Though Jefferson's name carried greater weight, on the level of constitutional theory it was above all Madison with whom Calhoun had to engage. Jefferson (now dead) could be invoked; Madison (still alive and writing) had to be answered. Jefferson played no direct role in framing the Constitution, whereas Madison took the lead and shaped the document more than any other single individual. Jefferson nowhere presented a systematic and detailed commentary on the Constitution as Madison did in the *Federalist*, his *Report of 1800*, and numerous other writings and speeches. Calhoun's own central works of constitutional theory—the *Exposition*, the *Fort Hill Address*, and the *Discourse on the Constitution*—are more comparable in their comprehensiveness and detail to Madison's constitutional commentary than to Jefferson's scattered remarks. In a sense all of Calhoun's political and constitutional theory, including the minority veto/consensus model of government set forth in the *Disquisition*, is a response to Madison's constitutionalism and to Madison's own very different diagnosis and remedy for majority tyranny.[43] The elderly Madison's response to nullification conveniently highlights the wider differences between Madison's and Calhoun's political thought.

Madison was the last surviving Founder able to bear direct witness to the intentions and understandings of those who framed and ratified the Constitution. Constitutional discourse in the 1830s invoked the framers as a common argumentative strategy, in a way not dramatically different from the way we invoke them today. In 2008 it is safe to say, "if James Madison were alive he would support such and such" because there is no chance the real James Madison will appear and dispute one's use of his authority. But that is exactly what the elderly Madison did during the nullification controversy. Madison's entry into the nullification dispute dramatized the very different way in which Madison's and Calhoun's generations—driven by very different passions and interests—thought about and used the language of the Constitution.

Madison's participation in the nullification debate had the ironic effect of dramatizing the differences between Madison's and Jefferson's thought and of publicizing exactly the radical states' rights dimension of Jefferson's thought that Madison had persuaded Jefferson behind the scenes to moderate in 1798. Madison denied that the Virginia Resolutions supported nullification, but the Kentucky Resolutions were a different matter. Madison's response to nullification thus reveals that the fault lines in the Founders' fractured legacy ran not only between Hamiltonians and Jeffersonians, and between free and slave states, but also between Madison and Jefferson despite their political partnership and personal friendship.

Madison's response to nullification highlights the differences between Madison's and Calhoun's diagnoses and remedies for majority tyranny. Madison always insisted that he sought (as in *Federalist* No. 10) "a republican remedy to the diseases most incident to republican government." By "republican remedy" Madison meant one that checked the abuses of majority rule while still preserving majority rule itself as the fundamental principle of republican government. Madison's objection to nullification was that it substituted *minority* rule for majority rule and thus violated republican principle. Calhoun on the other hand denied that nullification amounted to minority rule: nullification, he insisted, replaced majority rule with a third possibility, that of consensus. Madison's own experience with the Articles of Confederation (where a single state could block any significant action) led him to reject any such model of government.

In the *Exposition* and the *Fort Hill Address* Calhoun had interchangeably invoked as precedents for nullification the Kentucky Resolutions of 1798 (authored by Jefferson), the Virginia Resolutions of 1798 (authored by Madison), and the *Report of 1800,* Madison's extensive explanation and defense of the Virginia Resolutions. At least at first Calhoun referred to "the principles of '98" in a way that made no distinction between the Virginia and Kentucky Resolutions or between the constitutional thought of Madison and Jefferson. If anything Calhoun relied more heavily in the *Exposition* on Madison's language than on Jefferson's. He quoted from Madison's Virginia Resolutions to the effect that "in cases of a deliberate, palpable, and dangerous exercise of other powers, not granted by the said compact, the States, who are parties thereto, have the right, and are in duty bound to interpose to arrest the evil, and for maintaining, within their respective limits, the authorities, rights, and liberties appertaining to them."[44] This leaves open what Madison himself meant by "interpose" and how in practice Madison expected states to challenge unconstitutional acts by the federal government.

Madison's initial entry into the tariff/nullification controversy came in 1828 when he addressed the question whether a tariff intended primarily for protection was constitutional. Madison expressed the "confident opinion" that the power in Congress "to impose a tariff for the encouragement of Manufactures" is "among the powers vested in that Body." When the Constitution was drafted and ratified, Madison argued, it was clearly understood on all sides that the phrase "to regulate trade" included encouragement of manufactures. Such was the universal practice of commercial nations at the time, and both those who supported and those who opposed the Constitution agreed that it would transfer to Congress the power to encourage manufactures. The first session of Congress, and every succeeding Congress for the last forty years, had acquiesced in this power, thereby adding to original understanding the force of cumulative precedent. Madison emphasized that his intention was only to address the constitutionality of encouraging manufactures, not the "justice and general good" of such a policy, "for which members of Congress are responsible to their constituents."[45]

Madison's concerns soon turned to the more critical question of a constitutional right of nullification. Madison claimed nullification was fundamentally at variance with the Constitution and the obligations of the compact upon which it was based. He also argued that nullification was not supported by the Virginia Resolutions of 1798, which Madison himself had drafted. In an 1830 letter to Edward Everett, Madison responded to Everett's request for his opinion of "the nullifying doctrine" and "the proceedings of the Virginia Legislature in '98, as appealed to in behalf of that doctrine." Calhoun's authorship of the *Exposition* was not yet public knowledge, but Madison may have already suspected Calhoun's involvement: "The distinguished names & high authorities which appear to have asserted and given a practical scope to this doctrine, entitle it to a respect which it might be difficult otherwise to feel for it."[46]

The point immediately at issue between Madison and Calhoun was whether the Virginia Resolutions of 1798 endorsed the right of a single state to nullify acts of the federal government which that state judges to be unconstitutional. Calhoun interpreted "interpose" to mean single-state nullification. Madison denied that the Virginia Resolutions of 1798 contained "any reference whatever to a constitutional right in an individual State to arrest by force the operation of a law of the U.S." and instead called upon other states "*concurrently* and co-operatively" to remedy the obnoxious laws through "measures known to the Constitution, particularly the ordinary controul of the people and Legislatures of the States over the Govt. of the U.S."[47] The Virginia Resolutions declared the unconstitutionality of the laws, but did not claim the right of a single state to act on that judgment; they appealed to other states to participate in a collective remedy. In short, Madison's Virginia Resolutions were intended, not to thwart permanently the will of a national majority, but to build a national majority to overturn the obnoxious laws in some constitutional manner.

Vesting each individual state with the power, not only to declare the unconstitutionality of a federal law, but to act unilaterally on that judgment unless and until overturned by three-quarters of the other states (which is what Calhoun's doctrine of nullification entailed) would in Madison's view mean giving to the minority the power to impose the law upon the majority and thus "overturn the first principle of free Govt." If each individual state were final judge of the Constitution, this "could not fail to make the Constitution and laws of the United States different in different States . . . & speedily put an end to the Union itself." If nullification meant merely that a single state declared the unconstitutionality of a law, and appealed to three-fourths of the other states to sustain its judgment, "the decision to be without effect during the appeal," then it would be unobjectionable in principle but would add nothing to the regular constitutional provisions for amendment.

But South Carolina (and Calhoun) claimed that a single state's judgment affirmatively overruled the law of the United States unless and until the nullifying state was overruled by three-fourths of the other states. Such a doctrine, Madison wrote, "puts it in the power of the smallest fraction over 1/4 of the U.S. . . . to give the law and even the Const. to 17 States."[48]

Calhoun considered nullification a valid extension of the principle embodied in separation of powers. Madison however denied there was any valid analogy between reciprocal checks among the three branches of the national government established by the Constitution and a single state's nullifying decisions of the national government. "In the case of disputes between independent parts of the same Govt., neither part being able to communicate its will necessarily brings about an accommodation." This is fundamentally different from "disputes between a state Govt. and the Govt. of the U. States . . . each party possessing . . . an organized Govt. . . . and having each a physical force to support its pretensions."[49] Put another way, Madison denied that nullification was a merely negative power like a presidential veto or judicial review; instead it gave armed states the affirmative power to act in dangerous ways.

Madison could not deny the possibility of "an undue preponderance" of power in the national government at the expense of "the rights and powers of the States in their individual capacities." In rejecting nullification Madison had to propose some other remedy. The first resort was the ordinary political process. Madison, like Jefferson, was confident that the Alien and Sedition Acts were "passed in contravention to the opinions and feelings of the community" and for that reason fell at the first election. (This answer might not reassure an embattled minority interest which has the "opinions and feelings of the community" against it, which was Calhoun's central concern.) The next resort was to amend the Constitution. If every constitutional resort failed, there remained the natural right of revolution.[50]

In the *Exposition* Calhoun had argued for a state's constitutional right of secession should its nullification of federal law be affirmatively overridden by three-fourths of the other states. Madison, in response to arguments he was hearing from South Carolina, argued that the remedy of secession could only be justified as a resort to the natural right of revolution—not as a constitutional right.

> If one state can at will withdraw from the others, the others can at will withdraw from her, and turn her, nolentem volentem, out of the union. Until of late, there is not a State that would have abhorred such a

doctrine more than South Carolina, or more dreaded an application of it to herself. The same can be said of the doctrine of nullification which she now preaches as the only faith by which the Union can be saved.[51]

Both secession without permission of the other states and single-state nullification of a national law were in Madison's view violations of the compact upon which the Constitution and Union were based. Madison, like Calhoun, used the term "compact" to refer to the Union, but the two had very different understandings of that compact and the rights and duties it entailed.

A fair reading of the Virginia Resolutions—and Madison's *Report of 1800*, which explained and justified those resolutions—upholds Madison's later denial that they support single-state nullification. Despite Calhoun's invoking the *Report of 1800* as precedent for nullification, its closing section is clearly incompatible with Calhoun's doctrine of nullification. Madison's *Report* affirms a state's right "of declaring the alien and sedition acts to be unconstitutional," of "communicating the declaration to other states," and of inviting other states to "concu[r] in making a like declaration, supported too by the numerous applications flowing immediately from the people." The object of such a declaration would be to lead states to make "a direct representation to Congress, with a view to rescinding the two offensive acts" or, by a two-thirds majority of states, to "propose an explanatory amendment to the constitution."[52] Madison, in other words, allowed a single state to make a verbal declaration that a federal law was unconstitutional, but he nowhere endorsed the right of a single state affirmatively to act on this declaration. All a single state could constitutionally do was sound the alarm and encourage other states to join it in overturning the obnoxious acts through constitutionally prescribed processes. What Madison said in 1830–1831 in his response to nullification is in fact fully consistent with what he had said in 1800.

But this leaves Madison with one major problem: Jefferson's Kentucky Resolutions do seem to support single-state nullification. Madison and Jefferson had disagreed over exactly this issue back in 1798, when the Virginia and Kentucky Resolutions were drafted.[53] By the time of the nullification crisis Jefferson was dead and could no longer explain his meaning. The Virginia Resolutions always referred to "States" in the plural, Madison explains, but "the Kentucky Resolutions being less guarded have been more easily perverted." In another letter he observes, "Allowances . . . ought to be made for a habit in Mr. Jefferson as in others of great genius of expressing in strong and round terms, impressions of the moment." He also pointed out that the nullifiers invoked Jefferson's record only when it supported their case and ignored him "whenever his authority is ever so clearly and emphatically against them." Jefferson, for example, had supported "the powers of the old Congress [under the Articles of Confederation] to coerce delinquent states."[54] Madison hoped to demonstrate that if Jefferson were still alive he would be on Madison's side, not that of the nullifiers, but under the circumstances the best he could do with Jefferson's Kentucky Resolutions was limit the damage. The very differences between his own constitutional views and those of Jefferson that Madison had worked so diligently and with apparent success to moderate in 1798 were now central to a constitutional crisis that threatened the Union itself.

Madison consistently maintained that the union established by the federal constitution was neither wholly "national" nor wholly "federal" but a combination of the two. He made this argument in *Federalist* No. 39 and made it again in 1830 in his reply to the nullifiers.[55] The American people were, for certain purposes, a single national political community and for other purposes a multiplicity of political communities. The existence—for certain purposes—of a single, sovereign American people did not mean that all political power must be consolidated in the national government at the expense of the states. It meant that the American people could deliberately choose how much power to vest in each level of government. "The Constitution was proposed to the people of the States as a *whole,* and unanimously adopted by the States as a *whole.*"[56] Where there is a dispute about where to draw the line between national and state authority, that dispute must be settled by some tribunal that represents the American people as a whole—not by a single state. When he received a transcript of Calhoun's speech on the Force Bill, where Calhoun denied that there existed any American "nation" or any "American people" in the singular, Madison remarked to Senator William Cabell Rives (the latter fresh from his Force Bill debate with Calhoun): "What can be more preposterous than to say that the States as united, are in no respect or degree, a Nation . . . and at the same time, to say that the States separately are completely nations & sovereigns; although they can neither speak nor harken to any other nation?"[57]

In his posthumously published "Advice to My Country" Madison urges "that the Union of the States be cherished and perpetuated" and warns against both the open enemy to the Union, who should be regarded as "a Pandora with her box opened," and "the disguised one" who should be regarded "as the Serpent creeping with his deadly wiles into Paradise."[58]

While he does not name these open and disguised enemies, Madison made clear that the effect of Calhoun's doctrine of nullification would be to "speedily put an end to the Union itself." Calhoun for his part continually insisted that his own purpose was to save the Union, not destroy it. This combination of facts leaves little doubt in which category of enemy the elderly Madison placed Calhoun.

Calhoun's Response to Madison

Calhoun found Madison's 1830 retrospective on the Virginia Resolutions unconvincing. He hinted that Madison's intellectual powers were failing (though there is not the slightest evidence of this).[59] In an 1833 debate with Senator William Cabell Rives of Virginia (who was corresponding with Madison during this period, and whose interpretation of the Virginia Resolutions accords with Madison's), Calhoun accused Rives of degrading the Virginia Resolutions "by explaining away their meaning and efficacy." If the Virginia Resolutions merely asserted the right to overturn abuses of federal power via ordinary political processes, it was too weak a remedy; and moreover it would have been "egregious trifling" to declare so solemnly "what no one had ever denied."[60] Calhoun's reply to Rives is in substance a reply to Madison.

But Calhoun appears subsequently to have realized there were significant differences between Madison's understanding of American federalism and his own. He continued to speak as though the Virginia Resolutions supported his doctrine of nullification—ignoring Madison's own explanation of their meaning—but sharply criticized what Madison said elsewhere about federalism, especially in *Federalist* No. 39.

Calhoun completely rejected the possibility of anything "partly national" and "partly federal." It was all or nothing. In the *Discourse*, explicitly criticizing Madison's *Federalist* No. 39, Calhoun asks: "What can be more contradictious" than "a government partly federal and partly national?"[61] Either each individual state is unquestionably sovereign, and as sovereign retains the right of final judgment, or sovereignty lies in a "consolidated" federal government and states are reduced to the equivalent of counties. "We might just as well speak of half a square, or half of a triangle, as of half a sovereignty."[62] If one was unwilling to vest all political power in the national government—and Calhoun judged that his contemporaries would be unwilling to do this—the only alternative was full state sovereignty.

Both Madison and Calhoun were concerned with the danger of tyrannical majorities under popular governments. One of Madison's principal aims going into the Federal Convention of 1787 was to remedy the "Vices of the Political System of the United States," and one of the chief vices was the danger that the majority would commit "unjust violations of the rights and interests of the minority, or of individuals."[63] In *Federalist* No. 10 and No. 51 Madison famously argued that the greater extent of territory and diversity of interests in the large republic, along with the separation of powers established by the Constitution, would make it more difficult for an unjust majority to acquire and hold power. "In the extended republic of the United States," Madison wrote in No. 51, "and among the great variety of interests, parties and sects which it embraces, a coalition of a majority of the whole society could seldom take place upon any other principles than those of justice and the general good."[64]

Calhoun's construction of the Constitution was also intended as a remedy to the danger of majority tyranny. In the *Exposition* Calhoun quotes the following passage from Madison's *Federalist* No. 51 (though attributing it to Hamilton): "It is of the greatest importance in a republic, not only to guard society against the oppression of its rulers, but to guard one part of society against the injustice of the other part. Different interests necessarily exist in different classes of citizens. If a majority be united by a common interest, the rights of the minority will be insecure."[65] Calhoun immediately adds that "the AMERICAN SYSTEM"—meaning the political coalition behind the protective tariff of 1828—is exactly the kind of majority faction warned against in *Federalist* No. 51. Calhoun obviously believed that he was, in a different time and context, addressing the same general problem that had preoccupied the author of *Federalist* 51 (and also *Federalist* 10, though Calhoun does not specifically mention the latter).

That Madison's and Calhoun's remedies to the problem were radically different is clear from Madison's response to the nullification doctrine. Madison's own explanation of the Virginia Resolutions makes clear that his purpose was to use the states (in the plural) to build a national majority against oppressive federal measures, and thus to replace a bad national majority with a good one. Madison was equally committed to the principle of majority rule a decade earlier when drafting the Constitution and writing the *Federalist*. Because Madison presupposed that one way or another the majority must rule in a popular government, the challenge was to design ways to *slow down* the process by which majorities form, so that, once formed, the majority would act deliberately rather than quickly and passionately. This is what Madison meant by a "coalition of a majority of the whole society" forming only around principles of "justice and the general good." A just and deliberate national majority ceases to be a majority *faction* (factions being by definition unjust).

Calhoun, in contrast, did not believe that majority tyranny could be remedied by making the majority slow-moving and deliberate. On the contrary a slow, deliberate, long-in-forming majority was precisely the greatest danger. "To form combinations in order to get the control of the government, in a country of such vast extent,—and consisting of so many States, having so great a variety of interests, must necessarily be a slow process, and require much time, before they can be firmly united, and settle down into two organized and compact parties. But the motives to obtain this control are sufficiently powerful to overcome all these impediments."[66] Calhoun here argues, contrary to Madison, that extensive territory and great variety of interests will not prevent the formation of oppressive national majorities, but only slow the process of inevitable degeneration.

In Calhoun's view what specifically rendered the Madisonian solution to majority faction obsolete was the emergence of national, patronage-based political parties. In the *Discourse* Calhoun prefaces his diagnosis of the problem by quoting Madison himself from *Federalist* No. 38 to the effect that there may be "errors . . . contained in the plan of the convention" which will not be discovered "until an actual trial will point them out." Calhoun then extends Madison's own point. One of the errors that the framers failed to guard against was that "most corrupting, loathsome and dangerous disease, that can infect a popular government . . . known by the name of 'the Spoils.'"[67] The increased "power and patronage of the federal government"— which for Calhoun was closely connected with the protective tariff and the revenues it generated—had the effect of rendering "the struggle between the two parties more and more intense . . . To secure the desired object, the concentration of party action and the stringency of party discipline were deemed indispensable."[68] Disciplined national political parties organized for the purpose of exploiting the fiscal powers of government gradually reduce the initial political and economic diversity of a large republic (the kind of diversity Madison assumed) to two entrenched interests, a majority and a minority interest. Because these entrenched majority and minority interests were regionally concentrated, the effect of party conflict was dangerously to turn one section of the country against another.

One key difference between Madison's and Calhoun's diagnosis is that for Madison the interests that generate faction (creditors, debtors, farmers, manufacturers, different opinions concerning religion, and so on) already exist in society prior to any action of government. The use of government power may give one of these groups an unfair advantage over another, but government action was not for Madison the principal cause of faction. For Calhoun, on the contrary, the fiscal action of government was itself the principal cause of factional divisions. In the *Disquisition* he argued that "even though it were possible to find a community, where the people were all of the same pursuits . . . and in every respect, so situated, as to be without inequality of condition or diversity of interests," the action of the government itself along with its "honors and emoluments" would suffice to "divide even such a community into two great hostile parties." For as soon as government begins collecting tax revenues and spending them, society is transformed into two fundamental groups, taxpayers and tax recipients, with fundamentally different political interests.[69] (Calhoun does however acknowledge that it would be "nugatory and absurd" simply to return to every individual in disbursements exactly what he had paid in taxes. But his analysis of the fiscal action of government seems to define out of existence any expenditure for truly public goods.)

Calhoun argued that this unequal fiscal action of government would divide even the most homogenous community into two hostile parties. But the more "various and diversified" are the interests in a community, the more "extensive and populous the country" and the "more diversified the conditions and pursuits of its population," the more pronounced will be the unequal effect of government action. For "nothing is more difficult than to equalize the action of the government, in reference to the various and diversified interests of the community." Greater diversity also makes it easier to pervert the powers of government "to aggrandize and enrich one or more interests by oppressing and impoverishing the others."[70]

Notice here that Calhoun has stood Madison's argument on its head. For Madison, because differences of interest arise independently of the action of government, diversity of interest and extensive territory will guard against majority tyranny by preventing any single interest from gaining exclusive control of government. For Calhoun, because control of government is itself the key interest and the principal source of faction, diversity of interest and extensive territory only make the problem worse.

CHAPTER TWO

Calhoun did not argue that the solution was to make the fiscal action of government exactly equal in its effects on all interests and sections, which would be both logically and politically impossible. Nor could he resort, as Madison did, to the distinction between majority factions and enlightened, deliberate, just majorities. Instead the momentum of his argument in this section pushes inexorably toward the minority veto/consensus model, which makes its first appearance immediately following the diagnosis outlined above. The solution was to give to each "interest or portion of the community, which may be unequally and injuriously affected by the action of the government . . . either a concurrent voice in making and executing the laws, or a veto on their execution."[71]

Thus beginning with a diagnosis of majority tyranny that in its general outlines resembled Madison's, Calhoun proceeded via an analysis of faction rather different from Madison's to a proposed remedy radically different from Madison's. Calhoun believed that to insist upon a consensus rule—and, in the American context, upon each state's right to nullify federal law—was to rise above both minority rule and majority rule and achieve a truly just and perfect form of government. Madison regarded Calhoun's proposed remedy as a violation of the fundamental principle of republican government, a formula for minority rule or anarchy or both.

"Innovating Constructions" and Minority Rule

James Madison made two different types of criticism of Calhoun's doctrine of nullification. As the self-appointed guardian of the Founders' legacy, Madison claimed that the "innovating constructions"[72] of the Constitution upon which nullification rested radically diverged from the Constitution as understood by those who drafted and ratified it. He also argued that nullification in practice meant a small minority imposing the law and their own version of the Constitution on the vast majority, thus violating the first principle of republican government.

On the first point Madison was certainly correct: Calhoun's doctrine of nullification, and his whole method of reading the Constitution, would indeed qualify as an "innovating construction." But one must also ask how much fidelity to the intentions of the framers actually mattered to a new generation facing new problems and driven by new passions. The answer is: probably not much, despite the verbal tribute paid to their venerable achievements. Calhoun, for instance, invoked the authority of Jefferson and Madison when it supported positions Calhoun had arrived at on his own, for his own reasons. But when the still-living Madison rejected the use made of his Virginia Resolutions, and when Jefferson's words became a weapon in the hands of abolitionists, Calhoun shifted easily enough from veneration to measured criticism. Neither Madison nor Jefferson, or for that matter any of those who framed the Constitution, could have foreseen the political, economic, and ideological developments to which Calhoun himself was responding. Someone persuaded by Calhoun in 1832 that nullification was the solution to the country's problems would be unlikely to change their mind simply upon hearing that Madison had denounced nullification as a new-fangled doctrine.

However, Madison's claim that nullification amounted in practice to the rule of the minority over the majority is a far more powerful argument, one that taps a deep emotional vein in a republic. Following Calhoun's lead the slave states increasingly insisted during the decades preceding the Civil War that they were entitled to have their way on every federal question. Madison's claim that Calhoun's supposed consensus was in fact a minority imposing its will on the majority helps us understand why white citizens of northern states who cared little for the authority of "original intention," and even less for the rights of blacks, would be willing to fight to the death against what they called "The Slave Power."

THREE

∎

Calhoun's Political Economy and the Ideal of Sectional Reciprocity

Central to Calhoun's argument in the *Disquisition on Government* is the premise that every political community consists of a number of interdependent "portions" or "interests." On the one hand, these interests conflict with one another so that each is tempted to use the powers of government "to aggrandize itself at the expense of the others." On the other hand, their aims converge enough that, where each interest is "truly and fairly represented" and armed with veto rights, "all conflict and struggle between them" may be prevented; the result instead will be "to give a full and faithful utterance to the sense of the whole community, in reference to its common welfare."[1]

Calhoun's consensus model thus presupposes a true common good, above and beyond merely defensive use of veto rights. But the *Disquisition* is vague about this common good and about what defines a "portion" or "interest" (perhaps because no universal definition, valid for all times and places, is possible). Examination of Calhoun's political economy lends substance to the *Disquisition's* generalities.

In applying his theory to the United States, Calhoun was quite specific about what defined the "portions or interests" and what common good united them. The *Fort Hill Address* (1831) argues that in the United States the key differences of interest are "almost exclusively geographical, resulting mainly from differences of climate, soil, situation, industry and production."[2] The common good in the United States required policy that benefited all geographic sections, rather than rewarding one section at the expense of another.

The true statesman was one who practiced an ethic of reciprocity toward other sections rather than seeking selfish short-term gains for his own section. Calhoun believed in this ideal of sectional reciprocity at all stages of his career. His turn from nationalism to nullification in the late 1820s signaled a changed understanding of *how* to realize that ideal.

As a member of Congress in the years immediately following the War of 1812, and as President Monroe's secretary of war from 1817 to 1825, Calhoun strongly supported a system of federally funded internal improvements (national roads and canals), a national bank, and—at least initially—a moderate tariff intended, in part, to protect domestic manufactures that had sprung up during the war. In those years he still believed that elected leaders from each section, acting through the ordinary democratic channels, could and would make short-term sacrifices to pursue policies that in the long run benefit all sections. Calhoun believed his own conduct as statesman exemplified this ethic. His thinking on internal improvements, the bank, and the tariff was interconnected and his overall purpose was to strengthen and harmonize what he then called the American nation.

By the early 1830s his position on all of these matters, including the existence of an American nation, had changed. His own state's generosity toward northern interests in 1816 was repaid, he thought, with an aggressively protective tariff ruinous to southern planters. He continued to believe in the ideal of sectional reciprocity and the possibility of economic policies beneficial to all sections. But he ceased to believe that sectional reciprocity and the common good could be achieved through the regular democratic process; it had to be institutionally forced through the machinery of the minority veto, or what Calhoun called the concurrent majority. He now denied that there existed any such entity as "the American people" or any American nation. He continued to support internal improvements (now in the form of railroads) for connecting the different regions of the country, but realized that improved transportation and communication would not of themselves harmonize the conflicting interests of North and South.

Calhoun was absolutely convinced that low tariffs and the institution of slavery advanced the long-term interest of all sections, including northern states. But he believed majority rule and corrupt party politics would inevitably tempt northern states to employ protective tariffs and antislavery ideology as weapons of economic warfare on the South. In nullifying the protective tariff and staunchly defending slavery, Calhoun argued, South Carolina and the South were not just protecting their own interests but also restoring the political and economic health of the entire United States.

What Is a Nation?

To understand Calhoun's political economy and its changes over time it is essential to consider the meaning of "nation."[3] This elusive but crucial concept established the framework within which more concrete debates over tariff, currency, internal improvements, and so on played themselves out. Perhaps the most fateful difference between early and late Calhoun was precisely his reversal on whether or not there existed an American nation and American people, above and beyond the separate "peoples" of each state.

In 1816, when he supported a moderately protective tariff, a rechartered Bank of the United States, and an ambitious policy of internal improvements, Calhoun spoke explicitly of an American nation. For example his 4 April 1816 speech on the tariff described manufactures as "essential to the independence of the nation" and spoke of the contribution internal improvements made to "the ultimate attainment of national strength."[4] His 4 February 1817 speech in favor of federally funded internal improvements emphasized "the manner in which facility and cheapness of intercourse added to the wealth of the nation."[5] At that time he saw no inconsistency between affirmations of American nationhood, on one side, and federal union on the other.

By the time of his 1833 speech on the Force Bill, Calhoun was denying that there existed any American nation or single American people. His immediate motive was practical: if one granted the premise that "the entire sovereignty of this country belongs to the American people, as forming one great community," then a state would have no more right to resist federal law than a county has to resist state law.[6] If America were a nation, Calhoun conceded, it would be completely legitimate for Andrew Jackson to enforce federal tariff laws upon a recalcitrant state. In order to deny this conclusion Calhoun refused the premise. For the remainder of his life, and especially in his *Discourse on the Constitution and Government of the United States,* Calhoun denied that the people of the United States had ever "merged themselves into one great community or nation," or ever formed "what is called the American people" to whom "allegiance and obedience would be due."[7] From 1833 on Calhoun spoke as though nationhood and federalism were mutually exclusive categories. He had not spoken this way in 1816.

"Nation" and "nationality" are vague terms of uncertain and shifting meaning. The Latin root of the word refers to birth, as though the act of being born unequivocally established one's nationality. But this root comes closer to what we now call race, not nationality, which in contemporary usage is determined more by political loyalties, history, culture, language, and individual choices to immigrate or emigrate. Moreover the idea that one is "born" a member of a particular nation does nothing to resolve the contested question of whether in Calhoun's time that "nation" was a single American state or the United States as a whole: the biological act of birth is indistinguishable in the two cases.

Nationhood is, at least in part, a function of political and economic interdependence—including by Calhoun's own criteria. The presence or absence of an integrated market, convenient means of transportation and communication, a stable common currency, and willingness by all parts and sections to work together to realize common goods and prevent common evils: these elements should be included in any practical, day-to-day definition of what defines a nation. To call one's group a nation—whether defined on the basis of language, culture, shared historical experience, religion, or something else—is simultaneously to demand the practical political and economic benefits of nationhood (and perhaps to deny them to internal minorities not considered part of the nation).

In 1817 Calhoun seems to have included at least three key elements in his vision of an American nation: (1) the existence of distinct, regionally differentiated but economically interdependent "interests" of equal status (northern manufactures, southern plantation farming, western farmers); (2) some means of facilitating political, economic, and intellectual communication between these regionally separated parts—roads, canals, a reliable common currency—to counteract the danger of disunion; and (3) an ethic of political and economic reciprocity, whereby policies benefit all sections equally and no part is sacrificed to the interests of another.

These three things constituted the essence of what Calhoun in 1817 called the American nation. We should ask which of these elements changed enough over the following decades to cause him to retract the designation.

Conquering Space

Calhoun's nationalist political economy was expressed most comprehensively in his 4 February 1817 speech in favor of an ambitious system of federally funded internal improvements designed "to perfect the communication from Maine to Louisiana" and link "the [Great] Lakes with the Hudson River." Calhoun dismissed the strict-constructionist constitutional objections to federally funded internal improvements by arguing that congressional power "to pay the debts and provide for the common defense and general welfare" was not limited to "the powers afterwards enumerated and defined."[8] The magnitude of the task was too great to be left wholly to states or to private initiative.[9]

Calhoun detailed the economic benefits of internal improvements—"the manner in which facility and cheapness of intercourse added to the wealth of the nation . . . Nothing can be more favorable to [increase of wealth] than good roads and canals." He did not mean only that the *aggregate* wealth of the nation would increase, but also that *each* economic interest and geographical section would benefit: "Every branch of national industry, Agricultural, Manufacturing, and Commercial" would be "greatly stimulated and rendered by it more productive." Employing a word, "portion," which later became a key term in the *Disquisition,* Calhoun argued that "every portion of the community, the farmer, mechanic and merchant will feel [the] good effects [of internal improvements]." In wartime, an effective system of roads and canals would better enable the republic to raise revenue and distribute the benefits and burdens of wartime taxation and spending more equally among different parts of the nation.[10]

Of even greater importance than the economic advantages of internal improvements was their effect in counteracting the forces of disunion in a republic as large as the United States.

> But on this subject of national power, what, said Mr. C. can be more important than a perfect unity in every part, in feelings and sentiments? And what can tend more powerfully to produce it, than overcoming the effects of distance? . . . No country, enjoying freedom, ever occupied anything like as great an extent of country as this Republic . . . Let it, said he, be forever kept in mind, that it exposes us to the greatest of all calamities—*disunion.*

Calhoun described both economic and psychological causes that might strengthen or weaken a union as large as the United States.

> Whatever impedes the intercourse of the extremes with this, the centre of the Republic, weakens the union . . . The more enlarged the sphere of

commercial circulation, the more extended that of social intercourse, the more strongly are we bound together . . . Those who understand the human heart best, know how powerfully distance tends to break the sympathies of our nature. Nothing, not even dissimilarity of language, tends more to estrange man from man. Let us then, said Mr. C. bind the republic together with a perfect system of roads and canals. Let us conquer space.[11]

Calhoun's argument for internal improvements exemplified his understanding, at this stage of his career, of what advanced or hindered the national common good, or even threatened the survival of the Union itself. Crucially important was the equal or unequal distribution of economic benefits and burdens among the geographical sections of the United States. Calhoun understood that broadening the internal market and reducing transportation costs would increase aggregate national wealth. But his emphasis was on *equality of benefits* among sections. He believed in 1817 that federally funded internal improvements would indeed benefit all sections and interests. But if it should turn out that the benefits and burdens of this or any other federal policy were not equitably distributed, he would not be able to support it, even if it increased the aggregate wealth of the nation. For Calhoun, even during his most nationalist phase, to benefit the nation as a whole meant to benefit each of its parts.

Here we already have the central goal of his later political theory: where every "portion" or "interest" has a veto, he wrote in the *Disquisition,* the effect will be "to force them to unite in such measures only as would promote the prosperity of all."[12] But in 1817 Calhoun nowhere indicated that state nullification (or any version of minority veto) was necessary to achieve sectional harmony. On the contrary, the "rival jealousy of states" threatened a policy that truly benefited all interests and sections.[13] Only the national government, he believed in 1817, possessed both the necessary means and the necessary impartiality to carry out internal improvements on the required scale.

Another theme echoed in Calhoun's later writings is the tendency of distance "to break the sympathies of our nature." Calhoun observed in the *Disquisition* that human beings were so constituted as to "feel more intensely what affects us directly than what affects us indirectly through others,"[14] an effect magnified by geographical distance. In 1817 Calhoun believed that the facility of intercourse and economic interdependence would counteract the effects of distance and unite the "feelings and sentiments" of fellow citizens from distant parts. Citizens of Maine and New Orleans might see and understand so little of one another as to endanger their coexistence in a common republic; a road from Maine to New Orleans was the obvious remedy. By the late 1820s Calhoun no longer believed that national roads and canals were sufficient to harmonize the divergent sentiments and interests of North and South.

Calhoun never ceased entirely to believe in a national system of transportation, though he came to oppose the use of national authority to achieve it. In the 1830s and 1840s Calhoun hoped for railroads linking the Ohio and Mississippi valleys to South Carolina and Georgia (whose geography precluded any great benefit from canals). By this time Calhoun, shifting his constitutional ground, denied that the federal government had legitimate power to construct internal improvements. Nor could the federal government legitimately raise funds and distribute them to states for this purpose, a policy supported by many Jacksonians. But if a federal surplus existed (justly or unjustly) as a result of the tariff, Calhoun argued that the funds must be distributed to the states, which should then use them to build railroads. These surplus funds, Calhoun argued in 1836, "will afford the means, if properly applied, of opening our connection with the vast and fertile regions of the West, to the incalculable advantage of both them and us" and enable the states, on their own, to construct "a system of rail road communication that, if effected, must change the social, political and commercial relations of the whole country, vastly to our benefit, but without injuring other sections."[15]

Calhoun of the mid-1830s still believed that the entire United States would benefit—or at least would not be harmed—by rail connections between the Mississippi/Ohio river system and the South Atlantic states. But by now he seemed more interested in cementing a commercial alliance between West and South—at the expense, at least politically, of the Northeast—than in benefiting all sections equally as in 1817. And whatever the benefits of railroads, their construction must not be the work of a dangerously powerful national government; in the same letter, Calhoun warned of the danger of antislavery agitation and called for "harmony and concert" among the slaveholding states. Thus Calhoun's 1836 call for southern cooperation in building railroads blended completely with his argument for southern cooperation against the abolitionist threat.

Calhoun supported a moderately protective tariff in 1816. He fiercely opposed the protective tariffs of 1828 and 1832 and generated an entire political and constitutional theory around that opposition. His shift from supporter to opponent of protective tariffs is readily enough explained, for the tariffs themselves changed in magnitude and purpose between 1816 and 1828. What is less obvious but more essential for understanding Calhoun's thought is the change he perceived between 1816 and 1828 in the way sections of the country acted toward one another. He believed that the 1816 tariff was motivated by reciprocal regard for the interests of all sections of the country. The later tariffs were, he insisted, deliberately intended to benefit one section of the country at the expense of another.

The United States had emerged from the War of 1812 with a large war debt; raising funds to service the debt was one purpose of the 1816 tariff. Equally important goals, however, were assisting the manufactures that had sprung up during the war (and the embargo that preceded it) and securing a domestic market for American farmers, who had suffered from the wartime disruption of foreign trade. These mutually reinforcing goals could be justified on grounds of national defense: it was uncertain whether peace would endure, therefore it was risky to depend entirely on foreign suppliers for finished goods and foreign buyers for agricultural goods.[16] The tariff of 1816 provided for 25 percent duties on imported cotton and woolen goods (a low rate compared to later tariffs) until 1819, after which the rate was supposed to drop to 20 percent. It also set a minimum valuation of 25 cents a yard on coarse cottons, which began as a modest protection but became progressively more restrictive as the price of cotton goods fell over the next decade.[17]

In his 4 April 1816 speech on the tariff bill Calhoun called for a "degree of protection" to "our cotton and woollen manufactures" and spoke of the need to give "adequate encouragement" to "those infant establishments." He emphasized "the disinterestedness of his situation": he was not himself a manufacturer, nor from "that portion of the country supposed to be peculiarly interested" in protecting manufactures; the South was agricultural and its immediate interest lay in selling high and buying cheap. But what was at stake here was "the security of the country."[18] Peace was uncertain; security required "moneyed resources" and markets that were not vulnerable to war. Southern producers of cotton and tobacco were seriously hurt by wartime disruption of foreign markets, so they too had a stake in the policy.

Calhoun argued that economic growth was a product of sectional inter-dependency; thus protection would benefit all portions of the country. "Nei-ther agriculture, manufactures, nor commerce, taken separately, is the cause of wealth; it flows from the three combined, and cannot exist without each . . . When separated entirely and permanently, they perish." Calhoun himself raised and answered the laissez-faire counterargument: if the situa-tion of the country was so favorable to the growth of manufacturing estab-lishments, "where is the necessity of affording them protection?" He acknowledged that protection must be temporary: the "fostering care of Government" was needed only until "our manufactures are grown to a cer-tain perfection." But in the meantime their existence must be put "beyond the reach of contingency." If the present manufacturing establishments should fail, and their workmen "dispersed and turned to other pursuits, the country would sustain a great loss" (i.e., loss of human capital, to borrow a twentieth-century term). Calhoun closed the speech with an appeal to national unity and sectional harmony very similar to the one he made in his 1817 internal improvements speech and explicitly connected the two issues. The tariff, Calhoun argued, "is calculated to bind together more closely our widely spread republic. It will greatly increase our mutual dependence and intercourse; and will, as a necessary consequence, excite an increased atten-tion to Internal Improvements." Through this tariff policy, Calhoun observed, "the *liberty* and the *union* of this country were inseparably united." For the greatest of all political dangers was "disunion . . . against it we ought to be perpetually guarded"—here echoing the central point of his argument for internal improvements.[19]

We should note the following about Calhoun's argument for the 1816 tar-iff in light of what came later. First, Calhoun argued that the tariff (along with the internal improvements the tariff made possible) would benefit all interests and all sections of the country. It might not appear in the short-term interest of the South, but it was in their long-term interest—a point under-scored by Calhoun's own "disinterested" support of a measure he considered essential to the survival of the Union. Calhoun would not have supported a tariff in 1816 (or at any other time) that he believed would advance the inter-ests of northern manufacturers at the expense of other interests and sections. In this respect his support for the 1816 tariff is consistent with his opposition to the 1828 and 1832 tariffs, which appealed to explicitly sectional interests and passed Congress by an explicitly sectional vote.

Second, Calhoun regarded protection of manufactures as temporary, not permanent. He understood and, in the long run, accepted the argument that trade should follow natural channels, but made a short-term exception based on the need to develop infant industries, produce skilled workers, and create the infrastructure for a national market. There was no inconsistency—at least in economic reasoning—between Calhoun's early support for a modest, if also protective, tariff that was to diminish over time, and his later opposition to a much higher tariff designed to be permanent. The only permanently and aggressively protective feature of the 1816 tariff was the minimum duty on coarse cottons, which Calhoun later admitted was a flaw in the bill that had "escaped my observation" at the time.[20]

Finally, however, if his economic reasoning remained broadly constant, his constitutional thought clearly shifted between 1816 and 1828. In 1816 Calhoun argued for the tariff in part because of the revenue it raised. But his wider argument specifically emphasized protection and the value of creating national industry and a national market. In 1816 Calhoun did not restrict tariff revenues to paying off the war debt but also considered them a fund for internal improvements and wider national projects. This contrasts with Calhoun's later insistence that tariffs were constitutional only for purposes of revenue, not protection; and only if those revenues were spent on narrowly defined objects.

Violating Sectional Reciprocity

The tariffs of 1828 and 1832 were far higher, more explicitly protective, and more costly to the South than earlier tariffs had been. But what outraged Calhoun more than their direct economic impact was the way they violated the spirit of sectional reciprocity he believed had once characterized national economic policy. In the opening pages of the *South Carolina Exposition* (1828) Calhoun wrote that the committee

> would desire never to speak of our country, as far as the action of the
> General Government is concerned, but as one great whole having a
> common interest, which all the parts ought zealously to promote.
> Previously to the adoption of the Tariff system, such was the unanimous
> feeling of this State, but in speaking of its operation, it will be impossible
> to avoid the discussion of sectional interest, and the use of sectional
> language. On its authors, and not on us, who are compelled to adopt
> this course in self-defense by injustice and oppression be the censure.[21]

CHAPTER THREE

Calhoun extended this point in his 15–16 February 1833 speech on the Force Bill. He opened by lamenting the "deep decay of that brotherly feeling which once existed between these States, and to which we are indebted for our beautiful federal system, and by the continuance of which alone it can be preserved." Later in the speech he reminded his northern and western brethren that "all the Southern States voted with South Carolina in support of the [1816 tariff] bill: not that they had any interest in manufactures, but on the ground that they had supported the war" and felt obligated "to sustain those establishments which had grown up under the encouragement [the war] had incidentally afforded." Calhoun then asks: "Was this example imitated on the other side? Far otherwise."[22]

Thus Calhoun believed there once existed a spirit of sectional reciprocity, exemplified by South Carolina's own support for the 1816 tariff, which by 1828 had been broken through the explicitly sectional policies of the manufacturing states. Calhoun did not believe this spirit of sectional reciprocity could be restored in its original form. Instead he hoped a constitutional mechanism—nullification—would force a sectional accommodation that could no longer occur through the ordinary democratic process.

The 25 percent tariff of 1816 was supposed to have dropped to 20 percent in 1819, but the crash of 1819 created popular pressure for increased protection in the middle and western states—especially in New York, Pennsylvania, New Jersey, Ohio, and Kentucky.[23] New England was divided, but leaning increasingly toward protection as domestic manufacture began to displace foreign commerce. At the same time the crash hurt southern planters, making them less willing than before to support tariffs that raised their costs and brought no direct benefits. The 1824 tariff, which (among other things) increased duties on cotton and woolen goods from 25 to 33 percent, passed on a largely sectional vote. The 1827 tariff bill, which Calhoun, now vice president, defeated with a tie-breaking vote in the Senate, would have kept the general duty at 33 percent but added minimum valuations on coarse woolens—the principal clothing of Southern slaves—in a way that greatly raised the real rates.[24]

The 1828 "Tariff of Abominations," which provoked Calhoun to pen the *Exposition,* raised duties both on manufactured products and on raw materials such as hemp, flax, unprocessed wool, and pig iron required by manufacturers; it was therefore of questionable value even to the manufacturers it was designed to protect. It resulted from complicated, presidential election–oriented politics, further muddled by southern states' strategic decision deliberately to make the bill worse, believing incorrectly that this would ensure its defeat. The bill eventually passed on a straight sectional vote, opposed by the entire South.[25] Calhoun later described the 1828 tariff as "a combined measure, originating with the politicians and manufacturers, and intended as much to bear upon the Presidential election as to protect manufactures."[26]

The 1832 tariff was less "abominable" but more threatening to the South as it was more likely to be permanent. It abolished the system of minimums (which, in addition to disguising the real rates, was difficult to administer) and replaced it with a simple 50 percent ad valorem duty. The high duties on raw materials (hemp, iron, wool) that hurt manufacturers were reduced. According to economic historian F. W. Taussig, "the result [of the 1832 tariff] was to clear the tariff of the excrescences which had grown on it in 1828, and to put it in a form in which the protectionists could advocate its permanent retention."[27]

The 1832 tariff was almost certainly less costly to southern planters, in absolute terms, than the tariff of 1828. But it was the 1832 tariff that led Calhoun and South Carolina to decide actually to press forward with the dangerous step of nullification (as opposed to merely asserting the right, as they had done in 1828). No one believed the 1828 tariff, which pleased no one, would remain permanently on the books, and Calhoun had initially hoped Andrew Jackson would support its complete repeal. In contrast the 1832 tariff, Calhoun complained, was intended "to be a *permanent* adjustment; and it was thus that all hope of relief through the action of the General Government terminated."[28]

In 1828 some public debt remained and it was possible to cling to the pretext that revenue was the object of the tariff. By 1832 the public debt had been paid and a surplus remained. This created in Calhoun's view "the most trying of situations . . . an immense revenue without the means of absorption upon any legitimate or constitutional object of appropriation."[29] (One of Calhoun's fears, as we shall see below, was that a federal surplus would encourage antislavery projects.)

Perhaps most importantly, Calhoun argued that the 1832 tariff, though less *absolutely* burdensome to the South, put them at a greater *relative* disadvantage vis-à-vis the northern states than the 1828 tariff. The 1832 tariff, Calhoun observed, effected "a small reduction in the amount of the duties; but a reduction of such a character, that, while it diminished the amount of burden, distributed that burden more unequally than even the obnoxious act of 1828." By eliminating the provisions of the 1828 tariff that harmed both northern manufacturers and Southern planters, but retaining those provisions that exclusively benefited manufacturers, the 1832 tariff became even more explicitly sectional in its impact than the 1828 tariff.[30]

Here we should note once again Calhoun's ideal of sectional reciprocity and its violation. In strictly economic terms, the 1832 tariff was less burdensome on the South than the 1828 tariff. But because it was *deliberately* more unequal in its distribution of burdens and benefits, it was an even greater violation of the "brotherly feeling" necessary to the survival of the Union.

Locating the Tariff Burden

A tariff policy is indivisible within a federal system like the United States. Tariff rates cannot be set at one level in New York and another in South Carolina without defeating the very purpose of the law. For this reason the U.S. Constitution specifically assigns to Congress the power "to lay and collect taxes, duties, imposts and excises" which must be "uniform throughout the United States" (Article I, Section 8) and specifically forbids any state from laying any "imposts or duties on imports or exports" without the consent of Congress (Article I, Section 10). Tariff policy is inescapably interdependent: whatever policy is decided upon by majority vote in Congress is imposed, for better or worse, on the country as a whole.

It would equally follow that a single state with at least one active international port (like Charleston, South Carolina) nullifying a federal tariff (by ceasing to administer it within its borders) is imposing its own policy on the rest of the country. The interdependencies run in both directions here. State nullification of a federal tariff cannot be justified by invoking the powers reserved to states under the Tenth Amendment; the whole point is to redirect the exercise of a clearly assigned federal power.

Calhoun understood the interdependent character of tariff policy. He never claimed that South Carolina could permanently execute a different tariff policy than the rest of the United States while remaining in the Union. His nullification doctrine, whereby three-fourths of the other states could affirmatively override a single state's nullification of federal law, in effect recognized that a nullifying state exercised power over other states—though it offered a very unlikely limit on that power. A three-fourths majority of states in favor of the protective tariff was out of the question. Thus the intention of South Carolina's 1832 Ordinance of Nullification—and Calhoun's own intention—was unilaterally to remake federal tariff policy, and if the action had been uncontested that would have been its effect.

Yet Calhoun did not see this as a minority imposing on a majority, but rather as substituting a just economic policy for an unjust and selfish one. His critique of the tariff and his proposed remedy (including nullification) consisted of at least four separable types of argument. The first was a specifically economic argument about where the tariff burden fell, and how large that burden was. The second argument focused on the *political* character of the tariff-making process, on what Calhoun believed was a conscious design by some states to gain at the expense of others. The third was Calhoun's own alternative vision of economic policy in the common good of the entire United States, including the good of the manufacturing states pushing the protective tariff. The fourth type of argument concerned the expenditure of tariff revenues, a separate issue from the direct economic impact of the tariff. Calhoun believed that tariff revenues rewarded political corruption and reshaped the political system in pernicious ways that went beyond trade policy. He was especially alarmed about potential use of tariff revenues for antislavery purposes.

Calhoun argued in the *Exposition* that the "burdens [of the protective tariff] are exclusively on one side, and its benefits on the other."[31] He calculated the overall average duty under the 1828 tariff to be at least 45 percent and claimed that this fell entirely on the South.[32] A duty on imports, Calhoun argued, was economically equivalent to a tax on exports, for it was in reality a tax on an exchange: "A duty, whether it be on the imports or exports, must fall on this exchange; and, however laid, must, in reality, be paid by the producer of the articles exchanged." This tax falls "almost exclusively" on the South, because the products of southern plantations constituted by far the largest share of American exports: he estimated that of $53,000,000 of annual U.S. exports, $37,000,000 consisted of southern staples such as cotton, rice, and tobacco. Calhoun denied that the trading partner on whose products the duty was directly assessed (in this case Great Britain for the most part) would bear the entire burden. "We export to import . . . Exports and imports, allowing for the profit and loss of trade, must be equal in a series of years." A protective tariff that diminished European cloth manufacturers' capacity to *sell* goods to the United States at the same time diminished their capacity to *buy* goods—above all southern goods—from the United States; and the U.S. domestic market did not consume more than a fourth of the South's products. Thus southern planters would be harmed even if Great Britain did not resort to commercial retaliation—which Calhoun also feared.

At the same time as the tariff diminished the South's capacity to sell goods on the international market, it raised the price of the goods southerners purchased for consumption or as inputs into production; both imported goods and their domestic substitutes would become more expensive. "The effect on us is to compel us to purchase at a higher price, both what we obtain from them and from others, without receiving a correspondent increase in the price, of what we sell." Southern planters could not raise the price of their exports, Calhoun claimed, because unlike northern manufacturers they were oriented toward a competitive world market that determined price. Thus there was no one onto whom they could shift the increased costs resulting from the tariff.[33]

Calhoun's argument concerned both the *location* of the tariff burden (that it fell principally on exporters, which meant southern planters) and the *magnitude* of that burden, which he claimed "to average at least 45 per cent." This translated into "a reduction of 45 per cent in the prices of our [export] products." Meanwhile northern manufacturers were granted "an advantage of 45 per cent" in their competition with foreign producers.[34] Thus by Calhoun's calculations the burden of the 1828 tariff was very large, it fell principally on Southern export-oriented plantations, and it exclusively benefited northern manufacturers; it was a systematic and deliberate transfer of wealth from one section of the country to another.

There was a connection between Calhoun's high estimate of the tariff burden and his argument for nullification. For a single state to block a national law that deeply affected every section and interest of the country created a crisis in which violence and disunion were possible outcomes; Calhoun himself considered nullification a remedy to be used sparingly. Even if nullification were a constitutional right, it would be imprudent to resort to that right if the tariff's effect on the South were modest—for example, 10 percent as calculated by Calhoun's contemporary Jacob Cardozo, a South Carolina economist who opposed the tariff but also opposed nullification.[35] Calhoun's resort to nullification presupposed he was correct not only about who bore the tariff burden but also about its magnitude.

Calhoun was absolutely sure he was right; he employed terms like "the greatest certainty" and "the clearest proof" to describe his own argument. In fact his argument is persuasive on some points and questionable on others. He was correct to argue that a tax on imports was in effect a tax on an entire exchange and that diminished European exports meant diminished capacity to purchase American products. He was probably correct that a *greater* tariff burden fell on the South than the rest of the country, though it is unlikely that the *entire* burden fell on the South (for all consumers of protected products everywhere in the United States bear some part of the tariff burden). Precise calculations of the impact on one particular region and economic sector are very difficult and depend on several assumptions including the structure of the world market.

But Calhoun's critique of the tariff was not limited to its narrowly economic effects. At least as important was a *political* disposition that Calhoun believed violated the ethic of reciprocity that should guide states and sections in their conduct toward one another. At one point in the *Exposition* Calhoun observed that the manufacturing states' own conduct demonstrated they too believed the South would bear the entire burden.

> That the manufacturing States, even in their own opinion, bear no share of the burden of the Tariff in reality, we may infer with the greatest certainty from their conduct. The fact that they urgently demand an increase, and consider every addition as a blessing, and a failure to obtain one, a curse, is the strongest confession, that whatever burden it imposes in reality, falls, not on them but on others. Men ask not for burdens, but benefits.

Later in the *Exposition* Calhoun pointed to contradictions in the protectionist argument. Advocates of protection tell citizens of manufacturing states that everyone in the state will benefit from *increased* prices—"the capitalist, the farmer, the wool-grower, the mechanick and labourer in the manufacturing States are all to receive higher rates" of wages and profits—then turn around and assure consumers in the southern states that the effect will be to *reduce* prices. Protectionists cannot assure citizens of manufacturing states the entire burden will be shifted elsewhere and at the same time claim that all sections, including the South, benefit from protection: "One or the other argument—that addressed to us, or that to the manufacturing States—must be false."[36]

Calhoun here used a kind of political shortcut to establish the location and magnitude of the tariff burden. In strictly economic terms this was a weak argument. The fact that northern manufacturers *claimed* everyone in their state would gain from protection, and the entire burden shifted elsewhere, does not make it so. But Calhoun had a stronger argument about the political bad faith of manufacturing states toward their southern compatriots. If to convince doubters in their own state, protectionists argued that all burdens would fall on other states, then this violated Calhoun's principle of sectional reciprocity. This was unjust from Calhoun's perspective even if his argument was not entirely persuasive in economic terms. Calhoun claimed, in effect, that manufacturing states were politically indifferent to the welfare of southern planting states—in contrast to the spirit of reciprocal concern Calhoun believed his region had shown after the War of 1812.

Whatever the accuracy of Calhoun's calculations about the tariff burden, southern planters (and Calhoun himself) genuinely *believed* its effects were ruinous and persistently communicated this to their northern compatriots. Advocates of protection nevertheless pushed through the 1828 and 1832 tariffs on slim majorities in the face of intense opposition. Even one who rejects Calhoun's conclusions might admit the tariff legislation that provoked him was not the model of a healthy democratic process.

Free Trade, Protectionism, and the Common Good

Calhoun believed that he and his own state, in nullifying the 1828 and 1832 tariffs, were motivated by something quite different than the selfishness of the manufacturing states. Throughout the *Exposition* and in other writings Calhoun set forth what he believed was the true common good of the whole United States, not merely the special interest of his own state or section.

In order to understand the common-good argument Calhoun made in reply to the protectionists, it is helpful to recall the protectionist argument he himself had made in 1816. For the arguments advanced by Henry Clay and others in favor of a protective tariff in the late 1820s and early 1830s were broadly similar to those Calhoun himself had made in 1816: the need to create an American manufacturing sector and to secure a domestic market for American agricultural products.[37] Calhoun had conditionally supported both of these goals in 1816; by 1828 conditions (as well as Calhoun's own thinking) had changed. In 1816 the prospect of renewed war, and the consequent disruption of international markets, were central to Calhoun's support for a protective tariff. By 1828 the risk of war with Great Britain had receded and its importance as a market for southern staples greatly increased. Rather than fearing cessation of world trade, southerners by 1828 took a world market for granted. If in 1816 Great Britain had still appeared a great danger, by 1828 northern economic interests—and increasingly, northern opposition to slavery—made the north appear to many southerners a greater threat than Britain or any other foreign power.[38] Thus Calhoun in 1828 no longer sought to create a domestic market as an *alternative* to the world market.

He did not, however, deny the value of developing a domestic market for southern staples *in addition* to the world market, and he hoped and expected the American market for southern products would expand over time. "A great, natural and profitable commercial communication would exist between us without the aid of monopoly on their part, which, with mutual advantage, would transfer a large amount of their products to us, and an equal of ours to them, as the means of carrying on their commercial operation with other countries."[39] Nor did Calhoun renounce the substantive goal of creating an American industrial sector. What changed was his understanding of how this should occur.

In 1816 (as noted above) Calhoun had accepted a version of the infant-industry argument for protection. In 1828 he still conceded in principle that it may be "wise . . . in many instances to afford protection to the infancy of manufacturing establishments." But now he rejected the premise that industry cannot develop in the United States without protection, advancing a kind of geographical-determinist argument in place of the infant-industry argument. The northern states, he now claimed, would have been forced in any case to turn to manufacturing because their agricultural products were uncompetitive in either foreign or home markets. "The question, then, is not, whether those States should or should not manufacture, for necessity, and the policy of other nations had decided that question, but whether they should, with or without bounty." It was in the interest of both North and South that northern states turn to manufactures. It was in the interest of northern states to manufacture with a bounty, and to secure higher prices; while it was in the interest of southern states that northern states manufacture without a bounty, and sell at lower prices. This explained the fierce sectional clash of interests over the tariff.[40]

But for both political and philosophical reasons Calhoun could not allow clash of interests to be the final note. He needed to argue for the possibility of reconciliation and common interest in the long run. His consensus model of politics could not work otherwise, and he would be violating his own ethic of sectional reciprocity if he failed to make such an argument.

In the *Exposition,* after noting the conflicting interests of North and South, Calhoun turned around and asked, "in tracing the effects of the [protective] system, whether the gain of one section of the country be equal to the loss of the other." He answers no; that in fact the protective system "destroys, much more than it transfers. Industry cannot be forced out of its natural channel without loss and this, with the injustice, constitutes the objection to the improper meddling of the government with the private pursuits of individuals, who must understand their own interest better than the Government can for them."[41] Calhoun here rejects a zero-sum understanding of the economic relations between North and South: gains for one section do not necessarily equal losses for the other. Instead, through a policy of protection, total losses exceed total gains. Conversely, when economic activity is allowed to follow its "natural channel" total gains exceed total losses.

Calhoun couldn't deny that removing protection would cause short-term loss for manufacturers, but argued those losses could be limited and compensated by long-term gains. Reduction of tariffs would work to the advantage of manufacturers in the long term: "If low duties would be followed by low prices, they would also diminish the costs of manufacturing; and thus the reduction of profit would be less in proportion than the reduction of prices of the manufactured article."[42] Calhoun developed this point in the *Fort Hill Address* of 1831, where he argued that dismantling the protective system "should be made with the least possible detriment to the interests of those, who may be liable to be affected by it . . . To effect this, will require the kindest spirit of conciliation, and the utmost skill." But "if judiciously effected, it will not be without many compensating advantages . . . It will . . . tend to harmonize the manufacturing with all the other great interests of the country, and bind the whole in mutual affection." Moreover, "*It will cheapen production* . . . Every reduction will, in fact, operate as a bounty to every other branch, except the one reduced; and thus the effect of a general reduction will be to cheapen, universally, the price of production." Manufacturers' profits would fall somewhat, but not as much as tariff duties and prices; so that on balance everyone benefited. Calhoun here sought to demonstrate that he was truly on the side of manufacturers, not against them. And most important of all, his policy would harmonize the manufacturing interests with "all the other great interests of the country, and bind the whole in mutual affection."[43]

Calhoun here combined both Adam Smith–type language about the collective benefits of allowing *individuals* freely to pursue their economic interests and the somewhat different claim that each *section* of the country—each "portion or interest" to use the terminology of the *Disquisition*—stood to gain, or at least not seriously to lose, from a policy of free trade. In the latter respect Calhoun's free-trade argument differed from the standard utility-maximizing version of that argument set forth in modern-day economics textbooks. It is possible for an economic policy to produce greater aggregate gains—measured in terms of the welfare of the greatest number of individuals—without benefiting all geographical sections of the country. From the standpoint of standard economic theory what counts is the aggregate increase, not its geographical distribution. But from the perspective of Calhoun's political theory, what counted was that *each geographical section,* each "portion or interest," benefited from a policy; failure to reach this result endangered a union as large and diverse as the United States. This is a more difficult accomplishment than realizing greater aggregate gains without regard to their geographical distribution. Calhoun was able to employ the language of individuals and aggregate gain when it was useful, but the core of his argument remained the ideal of sectional reciprocity.

Calhoun's free-trade argument illustrated in concrete form the kind of true common good he believed could emerge from a minority veto/consensus model instead of majority rule. He never forgot that manufacturers, too, constituted a "portion" whose interests must be considered. But if Calhoun's arguments were reasonable and his vision an attractive one, one must also ask why he and his state shouldn't convince the majority to embrace it, instead of imposing it through nullification.

South Carolina's nullification of the tariff was not merely a defense of local interests, but an attempt unilaterally to remake national economic policy. Calhoun himself explicitly understood the act in those terms. He never seriously considered the danger that a state driven by bad economics and bad motives might nullify good laws. Instead Calhoun assumed that a nullifying state, like his own state, did so for good reasons and with a clear vision of the common good.

Tariff Revenues and Political Corruption

Calhoun was even more alarmed by the way in which tariff revenues might be spent than by the tariff itself. He believed the availability of vast tariff revenues corrupted all aspects of the political system, far beyond the immediate sphere of trade policy. He insisted that in nullifying the tariff South Carolina had not merely challenged one bad law but stopped the spread of political corruption itself.

The immediate impact of a tariff is distinguishable from the expenditure of the revenues it generates. In principle tariff revenues could be spent in ways that benefit those sections of the country negatively affected by the tariff itself, thus moderating its impact. Calhoun himself had envisioned this kind of equalizing effect when he supported the 1816 tariff: the South would not immediately gain from the tariff but would profit from the roads, canals, and fortifications funded by tariff revenues. But he believed the *political* alignments and motives behind the 1828 and 1832 tariffs guaranteed that the unequal sectional impact of the tariff itself would be powerfully reinforced in the expenditure of its revenues.

Calhoun's attack on the tariff and tariff politics merged into an all-embracing critique of "corruption" in the American political system. Corruption is an important and extremely expansive theme in Calhoun's thought; he saw it nearly everywhere and in diverse forms. One species of corruption was the political-economic snowball effect, whereby economic interests become subject to political bargaining; and those political bargains then reshape economic life in ways that reward the bargainers at the expense of everyone else. In this way Calhoun blended the traditional republican fear of parasitical "placemen" living off the spoils of politics with a modern understanding of the macroeconomic effects of government interventions into markets.[44] Calhoun described this process at length in his 15–16 February 1833 speech on the Force Bill:

It is the very nature of monopolies to grow. If we take from one side a large portion of the proceeds of its labour, and give it to the other, the side from which we take must constantly decay, and that to which we give must prosper and increase. Such is the action of the protective system . . . And this is the real reason . . . that all acts for protection pass with small [majorities], but soon come to be sustained by great and overwhelming majorities. Those who seek the monopoly endeavor to obtain it in the most exclusive shape; and they take care, accordingly, to associate only a sufficient number of interests barely to pass it through the two houses of Congress . . . In a short time, however, we have invariably found that this [small majority] becomes a decided majority, under the certain operation which compels individuals to desert the pursuits which the monopoly has rendered unprofitable, that they may participate in those which it has rendered profitable. It is against this dangerous and growing disease that South Carolina has acted [in nullifying the tariff]: a disease, whose cancerous action would soon have spread to every part of the system, if not arrested.[45]

Calhoun's target here was not merely the economic impact of one tariff law, but what he believed was a pernicious, self-reinforcing political-economic process recurring over time.

Whether the protective tariffs of 1828 and 1832 actually set in motion this kind of political and economic snowball can be debated, but the dynamic Calhoun described is possible. Yet one must also ask: if this is the disease, how is nullification (or any version of minority veto) the cure? "Portions or interests" wielding veto rights might use them to *prevent* better policy and reinforce the kind of corrupt alliances Calhoun feared. The relation here between disease and cure is accidental at best.

Tariff Revenues and Antislavery Projects

Calhoun was worried above all that tariff revenues would be spent for antislavery purposes. This represented in his view the epitome of political corruption. The supposed antislavery-corruption nexus reinforced in turn the connection Calhoun saw between political virtue and the institution of slavery. Slavery was "the most safe and stable basis for free institutions in the world."[46] He made this case publicly and in detail beginning in the late 1830s, but the underlying ideas were already present during the tariff controversy. In an 1830 letter Calhoun wrote:

> I consider the Tariff act as the occasion, rather than the real cause of the present unhappy state of things. The truth can no longer be disguised, that the peculiar domestick institution of the Southern States, and the consequent direction, which that and her soil and climate have given to her industry, has placed them in regard to taxation and appropriations in opposite relation to the majority of the Union, against the danger of which, if there be no protective power in the reserved rights of the States, they must in the end be forced to rebel, or submit to have their permanent interests sacrificed, their domestick institutions subordinated by Colonization and other schemes, and themselves & children reduced to wretchedness.[47]

It is possible, of course, to oppose protective tariffs and fear political corruption without defending slavery. But in Calhoun's mind these things were inseparably linked, and nullification was the remedy to all of them.

The "Colonization and other schemes" Calhoun referred to in this letter is the plan of the American Colonization Society, which proposed gradually to phase out slavery by purchasing slaves and removing them to Africa or some other part of the world. In 1830 the radical abolitionism of William Lloyd Garrison had not yet emerged. Colonization was the most conservative and establishment-friendly way in which to oppose slavery in the United States; the idea was supported by Thomas Jefferson, James Madison, and Henry Clay, who was one of the Colonization Society's key leaders and—not coincidentally—a leading advocate of the protective tariff.

Compensated emancipation would be expensive, and only the federal government could raise enough money. In 1827 the American Colonization Society petitioned Congress (unsuccessfully) for funds.[48] This coincided with the campaign for a higher tariff, with Henry Clay playing a leading part in both efforts. In 1831 (subsequent to the Calhoun letter quoted above) the colonization issue became central to the debates in the Virginia Assembly over the future of slavery. In the wake of the Nat Turner slave uprising, many Virginians saw slavery as a dangerous institution and were willing genuinely to consider the compensated-emancipation-with-colonization proposal. This position lost by a close vote in the Virginia assembly, the last serious debate over slavery in any southern state.[49]

Calhoun was absolutely opposed to colonization, and indeed any policy, however conservative and gradual, that presumed slavery to be an evil. In his view the Virginia debate underscored the danger of tariff revenues and the uses to which they could be put. In his 15–16 February 1833 speech on the Force Bill, Calhoun denounced colonization as one of the "corrupt" purposes for which tariff revenues could be used. This was a "powerful reason" why South Carolina's nullification of the tariff "could not have been safely delayed." Now that the public debt had been nearly paid off, he observed, the tariff would soon generate a large annual surplus the disposition of which would "become a subject of violent and corrupt struggle." Tariff revenues would create

new and powerful interests in support of the existing system, not only in those sections which have been heretofore benefited by [the tariff], but even in the South itself. I cannot but trace to the anticipation of this state of the treasury the sudden and extraordinary movements [for the emancipation and colonization of slaves] which took place at the last session of the Virginia Legislature, in which the whole South is vitally interested. It is impossible for any rational man to believe that that State could seriously have thought of effecting the scheme to which I allude by her own resources, without powerful aid from the General Government.[50]

Calhoun made no attempt here to answer the arguments advanced in favor of emancipation-with-colonization. He spoke as though the unconstitutionality and dangerous folly of such a policy were obvious. Only the corrupting influence of tariff money could explain why so destructive a policy could have been seriously considered by a slaveholding state.

Manufacturing, Agriculture, and Slavery

"Corrupt" use of tariff revenues to emancipate slaves was part of a much broader set of linkages Calhoun saw between the tariff controversy and slavery. In the 1830 letter quoted above Calhoun observed that slavery put the South "in opposite relation" with regard to "taxation and appropriations" than the majority of the Union. He suggested that the South's very different mode of production made it a target for hostile tariff legislation in the first place.

Calhoun described at least three ways in which the protective tariff threatened slavery: first, tariff revenues could be used for antislavery purposes (as noted above); second, the negative economic effects of a protective tariff were magnified in a slave-based economy; and third, the economic conflicts stirred up by the tariff could trigger a politically motivated attack on slavery by the North.

In the *Exposition* Calhoun discussed the impact of a protective tariff on a slaveholding economy. Anticipating the argument that the South could adjust its economy to take advantage of the tariff by producing agricultural goods for the home market, Calhoun replied that this was no solution because the home market "cannot consume a fourth of our products." That would leave the South no option but to turn to manufacturing, and this would be an especially difficult adjustment for an economy based upon a "peculiar" form of labor: "Forced to abandon an ancient and favourite pursuit, to which our soil, climate, habits and peculiar labour are adapted, at an immense sacrifice of property, we would be compelled, without capital, experience, or skill, and a population untried in such pursuits, to attempt to become the rivals, instead of the customers of the manufacturing States."[51] Calhoun similarly observed in the *Fort Hill Address* that the "great and peculiar agricultural capital [of the South, meaning slave property], cannot be diverted from its ancient and hereditary channels, without ruinous losses."[52]

Calhoun himself had observed how the merchant capital of New England shifted from commerce to manufacture during the period of the Embargo and the War of 1812, when loss of foreign markets forced economic activity into new channels. In a slave economy it was more difficult, though not impossible, to reallocate labor and capital in response to changed incentives. For an owner of a plantation, slaves represented a massive sunk investment compared to the ease with which free labor and financial capital can move to take advantage of new opportunities. In a free labor market, labor "allocates itself," whereas slave labor can be reallocated only through purchase or other administrative arrangement made by slaveholders. Free labor power could be purchased by the month whereas slave labor required a long-term investment. For this reason any major reallocation of resources, and especially reallocation from agriculture to manufacturing, was difficult in a slave society; it would not be easy for the South to turn the tariff to its advantage or limit its losses.

Calhoun did not, however, consider the turn to manufacture impossible, and he was prepared seriously to consider it as a fallback option—so long as it could be done with slave labor. In the *Exposition*, after describing the difficulties the South would face in turning to manufacture, Calhoun speculates on what might follow if the South were successful in this effort:

> But on the contrary, if our necessity should triumph over their capital and skill, if instead of raw cotton, we should ship to the manufacturing States cotton yarn, and cotton goods, the thoughtful must see, that it would inevitably bring about a state of things, which could not long continue. Those who now make war on our gains, would then make it on our labour. They would not tolerate, that those, who now cultivate our plantations, and furnish them with the material, and the market for the products of their arts, should, by becoming their rivals, take bread out of the mouths of their wives and children. The committee will not pursue this painful subject, but, as they clearly see, that the system, if not arrested, must bring the country to this hazardous extremity, neither prudence, nor patriotism, would permit them to pass it by, without raising a warning voice against a danger, of so menacing a character.[53]

In other words, the South could turn to manufacturing if forced; but this would signify deep divisions in the United States, perhaps the unraveling of the Union. A decade later, at the height of the antislavery campaign in Congress, Calhoun encouraged a Philadelphia manufacturer to move south and establish a cotton manufacture in the South, presumably employing slave labor.[54] It is unclear whether Calhoun had much faith in the success of this and similar projects, given his own analysis of the obstacles to southern industrialization; but his willingness to endorse it in 1838 suggests that he believed the "hazardous extremity" he had spoken of in 1828 was coming closer. Calhoun may have reasoned as follows: as long as the South remains in the Union, southern industrialization is costly and unnecessary; better to specialize in agriculture and sell products to northern manufacturers and on the world market. But if the South is forced to secede in order to protect slavery, it would have to develop an industrial base; thus Calhoun wanted to keep that option alive.[55]

Note what Calhoun was and was not saying about slavery and industrialization. He did *not* assert that it was impossible for a slave society to industrialize on the basis of a slave labor force; he clearly considered it possible. But he admitted it would be very difficult, with painful adjustments all around, and that it would heighten rather than diminish the sectional conflict between North and South. Southern industrialization was also unnecessary within a Union characterized by sectional reciprocity and a mutually beneficial division of labor. Calhoun predicted that if the South were to industrialize while remaining within the Union and become a rival to the North, the North would retaliate politically by attacking slavery; Northerners would not allow slave laborers to "take bread out of the mouths of their wives and children." (Notice Calhoun assumes here that southern factories would employ slave labor.)

Here Calhoun expressed a view that was to become increasingly prominent over time in his speeches and writings: that antislavery agitation was principally a tool of economic warfare by the North against the South. What Calhoun feared was a pernicious blending of northern antislavery sentiment with northern economic self-interest. The reasoning went something like this: first, the North adopts a protective tariff out of immediate, if short-sighted economic self-interest; attacking slavery need not be a motive initially. (There was little national discussion of slavery in 1828 when Calhoun penned the *Exposition*.) But if, contrary to northern expectations, the South took advantage of protectionism by establishing slave-based manufacturing that effectively competed with northern free-labor manufacturing, the North would then seize upon antislavery agitation as the weapon of choice in what was essentially economic warfare. In this way moral opposition to slavery on the part of the northern public (which Calhoun took for granted) would provide northern politicians a pretext to pursue policies of sectional economic advantage they could not otherwise justify.

Calhoun was not claiming there was some inherent, irrepressible conflict of economic interest between North and South. On the contrary he still insisted that the true long-term interests of northern manufacturers and southern planters were in harmony. In the passage from the *Exposition* quoted above, where he feared a damaging economic rivalry between North and South, Calhoun at the same time stressed that such rivalry was unnecessary and avoidable: slave laborers "now cultivate our plantations, and furnish [the manufacturing states] with the material, and the market for the products of their arts." There was a natural harmony of interest between northern manufacturers and southern slave owners—an already significant domestic market for manufactured goods that promised to expand without the artificial stimulus of the tariff.

Calhoun believed in this true harmony between southern planters and northern industry not only in 1828 but for the rest of his life, even as the slavery dispute worsened. In an 1847 speech in Charleston Calhoun asserted that the crusade against slavery coming from the North "does not originate in any hostility of interests. The labor of our slaves does not conflict with the profit of their capitalists or the wages of their operatives . . . On the contrary, it greatly increases both." (The vehemence and frequency with which Calhoun made this argument in the speech suggests that his South Carolina audience was skeptical about any shared economic interests between North and South.) The sectional conflict, in Calhoun's view, resulted instead from an alliance between a small number of "rabid fanatics" (i.e., the abolitionists) and a much larger number of political partisans with an intense interest in winning elections and enjoying the resulting "honors and emoluments of government" who needed the small abolitionist vote to provide their margin of victory.[56] This was a broader version of the antislavery/political corruption nexus Calhoun first asserted in the late 1820s with respect to the protective tariff and the revenues it produced.

In the *Disquisition* Calhoun claimed that, no matter how many and how diverse were the interests in a society, sooner or later a coherent and disciplined majority party would emerge and rule at the expense of the minority unless that minority possessed a guaranteed veto.[57] Calhoun's argument that permanent and rigidly entrenched majorities and minorities *must* eventually result from majority rule is not convincing. It was not, however, implausible that deep divisions were inevitable between a free labor, manufacturing-oriented majority and a slavery-based, agricultural, export-oriented minority. Whether the cause of conflict was the pathology of majority rule, as Calhoun believed, or the pathology of slavery, is of course another question.

Banks, Currency, and Southern Unity

On the related questions of national currency and the Bank of the United States, as on internal improvements and tariffs, Calhoun began as a strong nationalist and moved away over time, without quite renouncing his faith in sectional harmony and reciprocity.

Calhoun had been the chief sponsor of the bill to recharter the Bank of the United States in 1816. His argument in his 26 February 1816 speech on the bank was closely connected with support for internal improvements and the tariff. The national bank would create stable currency which, like roads and canals, would bind the parts of the nation into a harmonious whole. Calhoun based his constitutional defense of the bank on Congress's Article I power "to coin money" and "regulate the value thereof," which Calhoun interpreted flexibly as the power and duty "to give a steadiness and fixed value to the currency of the United States." This constitutionally essential function had been undermined by the proliferation of unsecured paper money of wildly fluctuating value, issued by private banking institutions with no responsibility to the public. It was essential that Congress reassert its "right of making money, an attribute of sovereign power" by rechartering the Bank of the United States. (Notice that for Calhoun in 1816 sovereignty inhered in the nation and the national government, a position he would later renounce.)[58]

Calhoun remained a supporter of the bank, at least publicly, throughout the tariff and nullification crisis and supported the extension of its charter in 1832. In late 1833 President Andrew Jackson, without authorization from Congress, began removing federal deposits from the Bank of the United States and placing them in selected state banks ("pet banks" his critics called them) with the aim of killing what he regarded as a powerful, corrupt, and dangerously political institution. Calhoun, making common cause with the Whigs, argued that it was Jackson who was usurping power, using the bank for political purposes and furthering corruption by his high-handed transfer of deposits to politically favored state banks.[59]

By 1837 the Second Bank of the United States was dead, its deposits removed and its charter expired, and the country was experiencing a financial panic that Calhoun claimed to have foreseen as a result of irresponsible and corrupt fiscal and banking policies. The Whig remedy was to resurrect the bank, and Clay and Webster expected Calhoun's support. Instead Calhoun came out in opposition to both a resurrected Bank of the United States and continuation of Jackson's "pet bank" policy, in favor of a third option: an independent federal treasury, which would issue and regulate currency but not engage in the business of banking.

Calhoun's first argument against rechartering the bank was that whatever the merits, "it is utterly impracticable, at present, to establish" another Bank of the United States after the old one had been destroyed. But he was opposed to a new national bank even if it could be resurrected. He blamed the current panic on the protective tariff and the enormous revenues it generated. "Countless millions were thus poured into the Treasury beyond the wants of the Government," which led to "a corresponding expansion of the business of the banks." Calhoun did not blame the bank for either the speculative frenzy or the subsequent collapse; nor did he blame the state banks, who simply acted as any bank would act under the circumstances. The crisis "rose out of the action of the Government." But Calhoun now argued against a resurrected bank, because *any* connection between government and banks, whereby the notes of a single bank (e.g., the Bank of the United States) or of a selected group of banks ("pet banks") were accepted as currency, harbored the same risks.[60]

Even if it had not caused a financial panic, this connection between government and banks should be condemned for the "vast and corrupting influence" it fueled, as banks courted legislatures to grant the charters required for this profitable business. "This gives a control to the Government which grants such favors, of a most extensive and pernicious character . . . until the whole community must become one contaminated and corrupted mass."[61]

Calhoun proposed instead to create "some stable and safe medium of circulation," a responsible paper currency issued by the federal government.[62] This currency would better fulfill the role that bank paper played in the past, while eliminating at one stroke the centralization of power, conflict of interest, and corruption resulting from the connection between government and banks. It would also eliminate the tendency of powerful banks to exert their political influence in favor of high tariffs: "The bank, when united with the Government, is the natural ally of high duties and extravagant expenditure."[63] Once banks and government were separated, however, "the whole banking interest will become the antagonist, instead of the ally, of high duties, extravagant expenditure & heavy surpluses."[64]

Calhoun's argument was reasonable on its own terms and refreshingly undogmatic on the subject of paper money. But Calhoun also explicitly linked his proposal to a perceived threat to slavery. At the same time he was publicly breaking with the Whigs on the bank, Calhoun was at the height of his counterattack in Congress against antislavery agitation (see chapters 4 and 5). In private letters written before the public break, Calhoun explained he could no longer make common cause with the Whigs on the bank, because on all other issues, including slavery, their principles were so different from his. "On what grounds can we compromise? How can the consolidation party and the anti-consolidation; the abolition and anti-abolition, the retrenchment, and the expenditures parties compromise?"[65] He insisted that "I am not of the same party with [Daniel] Webster and others, and do not intend to go into any move, that may be controlled by abolitionists, consolidationists, colonizationists."[66] (Calhoun saw no essential difference between an "abolitionist," a term usually applied to figures like William Lloyd Garrison, and a "colonizationist," which would include establishment figures like Henry Clay, Daniel Webster, and William Henry Harrison.)

In his 3 November 1837 Edgefield Letter Calhoun explained and justified his opposition to the bank and his break with the Whigs (or the National Republicans as Calhoun called them). To have resurrected the bank would entail "the indissoluble union of the political and money power in the hands of our old political opponents, whose principles and policy are so opposite to ours, and so dangerous to our institutions [meaning the institution of slavery] as well as oppressive to us." He added that opposition to the bank "would also give us the chance of effecting, what is still more important to us, the union of the entire South."[67]

Calhoun did not see the perceived threat to slavery as a separate, independent reason to oppose the restoration of the bank. In his thinking northern economic power, corruption, and antislavery formed an indissoluble whole. Nor should we interpret Calhoun's call for a "union of the entire South" as a renunciation of his idea of common good and reciprocity among all sections of the United States. As in his rejection of the protective tariff and support for free trade, Calhoun was convinced that his opposition to the bank and support for an independent treasury were in the interest of the entire United States. He likewise genuinely believed that protecting the institution of slavery was in the true common good of the entire United States.

The ideal of sectional reciprocity and faith in a common good that transcended sectional self-interest informed Calhoun's political thought at all stages of his career. It was central to his nationalist vision in the years following the War of 1812. It shaped his critique of the protective tariff of 1828 and the reasoning behind his argument for nullification. It exemplified the consensus model of government outlined in his posthumously published *Disquisition*. How he sought to realize this ideal of reciprocity changed radically—Calhoun came to believe it could not be achieved through the normal democratic process—but the overall goal remained broadly the same.

Calhoun never changed his conviction that the United States was composed of distinct, regionally differentiated, economically interdependent "interests" of equal status. To the end of his life he continued to believe that the fundamental economic interests of North, South, and West were compatible. This was an important element of his defense of slavery, which he argued was in the economic as well as political interest even of those states that chose not to practice it.

There were three key elements to Calhoun's nationalist vision of 1816–1817: the existence of regionally differentiated but economically interdependent interests of equal status; the facilitation of communication between these regionally separated interests; and an ethic of reciprocity in each section's political and economic conduct toward one another. In 1816 Calhoun spoke of an American people and an American nation. Which of these elements changed to lead him to retract that designation?

Calhoun's views on the first element never changed: even as he denounced the North for its allegedly economically motivated attack on slavery he continued to insist (in the face of growing southern skepticism) that the economic interests of North and South were fundamentally compatible. His views on the second point, how to facilitate communication and connection between the geographically distant parts of the United States, changed somewhat but not dramatically. In 1817 he wanted roads and canals linking distant regions of the United States constructed and funded by the federal government. In the 1830s he still supported "internal improvements" in the form of railroads, but no longer carried out directly by the federal government. In 1816 he believed that a stable national currency was necessary and that a Bank of the United States was the best way to accomplish it. In 1837 he still insisted on national currency but now favored an independent treasury instead of a national bank. His shifts here reveal a growing commitment to limit the power of the federal government in economic life but do not explain his reversal on the existence of an American nation.

The crucial shift occurred with respect to the ethic of sectional reciprocity. If the various sections of an extended political community act toward one another with mutual regard for one another's key interests it makes sense to speak of a single nation. Where sections treat one another like foreigners it does not. In his nationalist phase Calhoun believed this ethic of sectional reciprocity existed and that the leaders of each section (following his own example) could, through the ordinary democratic process, put sectional interests aside and realize the national common good. By the late 1820s he concluded that northern political and economic interests had destroyed this ethic, it could not be restored on its old foundations, and only a formally guaranteed minority veto could force political leaders to reach sectional accommodations. To put it another way: he concluded that the various sections of the United States would act like foreigners toward one another unless constitutionally forced to behave otherwise. This certainly weakened Calhoun's earlier faith in an American nation.

Antislavery agitation, in Calhoun's view, raised the violation of sectional reciprocity to a far higher level. Calhoun predicted in 1837 that this would in time produce between the two sections of the Union "a hatred more deadly than one hostile nation ever entertained towards another" and if the trend were unchecked, "we must become, finally, two peoples."[68] Even where there exist national roads and railroads, a national currency, and true economic interdependence between sections (in which Calhoun never ceased to believe), there could not be a nation—he implied here—where the different parts of the country regard one another with "deadly hatred."

This puts a rather different slant on Calhoun's argument, in his constitutional writings, that no American nation ever had or ever could exist. One gains a rather different picture from study of his political economy as it changed over time. From the perspective of his ideal of sectional reciprocity the conclusion must be, not that an American nation *never* existed, but that in Calhoun's view it *no longer* existed because of northern states' willful pursuit of policies that threatened the essential interests of the South.

CHAPTER THREE

FOUR

■

Calhoun's Constitution, Federal Union, and Slavery

Near the end of his posthumously published *Discourse on the Constitution and Government of the United States* Calhoun argued that if the Union were to be saved, "it is indispensable that the government of the United States should be restored to its federal character. Nothing short of a perfect restoration, as it came from the hands of its framers" could avert the twin dangers of tyranny and disunion. But Calhoun made clear that the "restoration" he had in mind was actually a reconstruction of the Constitution, to correct problems the framers did not foresee: "It is a great error to suppose that they could better understand the system they had constructed, and the dangers incident to its operation, than those who came after them." For this reason, even if it were possible to restore the Union as intended by its framers, this would not be a sufficient remedy.[1]

It was, above all, the free states' attempt to ensure future dominance by preventing new slave states that in Calhoun's view created this constitutional crisis. Once the slave states lost their de facto veto in the U.S. Senate, they lost the last remaining check on a national majority hostile to the future of slavery and, Calhoun believed, could no longer safely remain in the Union. Calhoun's proposed "restoration" was designed to enable slaveholders safely to remain in the Union. Economically motivated, patronage-based mass political parties and the abolitionist "spirit of fanaticism" had deeply alienated southern states in ways that could not be remedied merely by "restoring the government to its federal character;—however necessary that may be as a first step." He continued: "What has been done cannot be undone . . . The nature of the disease is such, that nothing can reach it, short of some organic change,—a change which shall so modify the constitution, as to give to the weaker section, in some form or another, a negative on the action of the government." He then proposed, among other things, the institution of a dual executive, each representing the interests of one of the two great sections of the country and each enjoying a veto over actions of the other.[2]

In other words, the only remedy to the crisis was explicitly to incorporate into the Constitution the principle of the minority veto, the "concurrent majority" set forth in the *Disquisition on Government*. The actual U.S. Constitution contained a number of restraints on the action of the majority, and Calhoun pointed them out. But ultimately all the ordinary constitutional checks had proved insufficient. What mattered to Calhoun were not constitutional mechanisms themselves but the *result*: did they, or did they not, guarantee the minority "portion or interest" a permanent veto over decisions of the majority?

In this respect the actual U.S. Constitution was a kind of imperfect first approximation of what Calhoun considered a truly adequate constitution. The actual Constitution contained vetoes and "concurrent majorities" of various kinds (e.g., the "concurrent majority" of House and Senate required to pass legislation), but there was no direct correspondence between the constitutional checks and the actual, "organic" interests of society—as there was in the case of the English and Roman constitutions. The Senate can kill legislation passed by the House, the president can veto legislation passing both chambers, the Supreme Court can declare legislation unconstitutional, but nothing guarantees that the same majority interest won't ultimately control all three branches of government. Calhoun argued that a consolidation of all three branches in the hands of the same majority was certain to occur over time unless prevented—and the Constitution itself did not prevent it. There was nothing in the existing Constitution to guarantee the slaveholding interest a permanent veto over policies hostile to slavery.

Thus Calhoun's purpose in the *Discourse* was not merely to explain the Constitution but to fix it. In the *Disquisition*, Calhoun contrasted the "numerical" majority with the "concurrent" or "constitutional" majority, the words "concurrent" and "constitutional" meaning the same thing.[3] But "constitutional" in the sense of guaranteeing each organic interest veto rights over collective decisions is not the same as "constitutional" in the sense of consistency with the text of the U.S. Constitution—for by Calhoun's own admission, the Constitution failed to guarantee a veto to each organic interest.

To put it another way: for Calhoun, in some respects the Constitution was constitutional, and in other respects it was not. His goal was to make the Constitution constitutional, as he understood the term.

Challenging the Traditional View

Calhoun's constitutional commentary ranged quite widely, and the present chapter does not attempt to be comprehensive. Previous chapters have examined Calhoun's views on the tariff and a state's supposed right to nullify federal law within its borders.

This chapter focuses instead on two interrelated themes that preoccupied Calhoun in the last fifteen years of his life: the fundamental character of the American union, and constitutional protections for slavery. Calhoun understood the union as a partnership of equal, fully sovereign states making collective decisions according to a unanimity rule; the federal government was the mere agent of this partnership. A state nullifying federal law within its borders (e.g., South Carolina's refusal to collect tariff duties in 1832) exemplified this principle. But from the late 1830s Calhoun pushed a much broader version of the unanimity rule to address problems that nullification itself couldn't reach. Slave states had an enormous stake in decisions about whether slavery would be restricted in federal territories and the District of Columbia, whether new slave states were excluded from the Union, and whether antislavery petitions were permitted in Congress, but none of these perceived threats could be blocked by action *within the boundaries of a state*—i.e., by nullification in its original sense. In 1832 South Carolina could unilaterally nullify the tariff by declaring Charleston an "open port." There was no equivalent weapon at hand for slave states in the controversies that erupted later. Calhoun thus invented new constitutional arguments to give the unanimity rule a new and broader foundation.

My presentation here of Calhoun's constitutional position on slavery differs significantly from the received view, which is something like this: that Calhoun's principal fear was an overly powerful federal government encroaching on the reserved powers of states, and that he sought above all to deny the federal government any power whatsoever over slavery. Thus William Sumner Jenkins in a classic 1935 study described the South's (and Calhoun's) constitutional approach as one of strict construction, keeping the national government to "certain specifically delegated powers, beyond the scope of which the States reserved control over municipal affairs." The federal government must "always remain impartial and neutral upon any question relative to slavery, for upon that question it had no power to act." As long as the federal government possessed no power one way or another over slavery (according to Jenkins's reading of southern theory), the institution was safe; slavery did not need any "positive constitutional sanction."[4] The opponents of slavery, on this view, resorted to expansive readings of the Constitution and even doctrines of higher law, while defenders of slavery took their stand on the actual words and guarantees of the Constitution.

Though there are elements of truth in this picture, on the whole it is inaccurate, at least for Calhoun. Calhoun's construction of the Constitution was anchored neither in constitutional text nor in careful examination of framing-era history; his method of interpreting both text and history was highly selective. He was able strategically to employ strict-constructionist arguments when they served his purpose, but his overall approach cannot accurately be described as strict-constructionist. In this respect he never rejected the broad-constructionist approach of his nationalist years but merely shifted its direction.

More importantly, Calhoun did not in fact take the position that the federal government had no power whatsoever over slavery. His position was that the federal government had no legitimate power to *restrict* slavery or in any way to endanger or morally condemn slavery. He insisted instead that the federal government, acting as the agent of the sovereign states (half of which were slave states) had both the right and the obligation *to give increased support and protection to slavery*—in federal territories, the District of Columbia, in international waters: in short, wherever its legitimate powers touched on the institution of slavery.[5] Jenkins himself admits that "at times" slaveholders demanded positive endorsement and protection from the federal government but suggests they did not understand the implications of an interpretation so "out of harmony with the general strict construction of Congressional powers."[6] At least in Calhoun's case this demand for positive, proslavery federal action was not some inadvertent overshooting the mark, but essential to his thinking.

The received view implies that as long as *federal* power was kept in check, slaveholders were satisfied to remain in the Union. Calhoun certainly feared an antislavery majority in control of the national government; that part of the received view is accurate. But Calhoun's target was not just the federal government. Antislavery actions by fellow states—allowing abolitionist societies to operate within their borders, refusing to honor fugitive slave provisions, bringing antislavery resolutions to Congress—were dangerous enough (and insulting enough) in Calhoun's view to justify secession if they continued unabated, even without antislavery moves by the federal government. Calhoun's reconstruction of Constitution and Union was intended, among other things, to demonstrate to northern states their duty to suppress abolitionist agitation within their borders and to recommit to protecting and supporting the institution of slavery, as (Calhoun argues) northern states did at the Federal Convention in 1787.

Calhoun's reading of the Constitution was coherent only if opposition to slavery was an illegitimate position, devoid of constitutional rights or protections. For if a state opposed to slavery had the same right to veto federal policy that Calhoun accorded to slave states, the result would be an infinite regression of vetoes and end in paralysis, contrary to Calhoun's own insistence on the urgent necessity of federal action. Calhoun conceded that northern states had legitimate interests, but opposition to slavery was not one of them.

Articles of Confederation Still in Force

Calhoun's full-state-sovereignty compact theory of Constitution and union was set forth most fully in the *Discourse,* where his purpose was to restructure the Constitution effectively to address problems its framers could not have foreseen. This reconstruction depended upon a particular interpretation of framing-era history and constitutional text.

Calhoun's reconstruction specifically required three things: (1) a reinterpretation of the relation between the Articles of Confederation and the Constitution; (2) a reinterpretation of certain key constitutional clauses—for instance, the "supreme law of the land" clause in Article VI; and (3) a set of *a priori* background assumptions that controlled and limited all possible readings of constitutional text or framers' intent. These background assumptions included the inherent indivisibility of sovereignty and the nonexistence of "the American people" as a political community. No reading of the constitutional text or framers' intent was acceptable in Calhoun's view if it violated these background assumptions. His strategy was to explode any middle position (like divided sovereignty) and force a choice between the extremes of full state sovereignty and full national sovereignty.

The Constitution, Calhoun asserted in the opening pages of the *Discourse,* was created by "free, independent, and sovereign states" as a "federal" rather than "national" Constitution—Calhoun rejecting as impossible the "partly federal, partly national" characterization set forth in Madison's *Federalist* No. 39. The states "retained, after the ratification of the constitution, the distinct, independent, and sovereign character in which they formed and ratified it."[7]

Such an interpretation is difficult to reconcile with the most obvious difference between the Articles of Confederation and the Constitution: the former explicitly spoke of the "sovereignty, freedom, and independence" of states while this language was conspicuously dropped from the Constitution. If the Constitution is understood as superseding the Articles of Confederation, Calhoun's full-state-sovereignty assumption would be difficult to sustain. Calhoun, however, denied that the Constitution replaced the Articles, insisting instead that *the Articles of Confederation were still in force* and that the Constitution changed only "the superstructure of the system," not its "foundation"—i.e., changed the organization of the federal government, not the nature or location of sovereignty.

To support this assertion, Calhoun repeatedly quoted the Articles of Confederation's declaration that "each State retains its sovereignty, freedom and independence" as though this language were still in the Constitution. Later in the *Discourse,* to furnish "conclusive proof . . . that not a particle of sovereignty was intended to be transferred" from states to national government, Calhoun once again quoted the Articles of Confederation: that "each State retains its sovereignty, freedom, and independence; and every power, jurisdiction, and right, which is not, by this confederation, expressly delegated to the United States in Congress assembled."[8] The disappearance of precisely this language from the Constitution meant, for Calhoun, that full state sovereignty was so obvious it did not require repetition. (In quoting from the Articles to prove the Constitution left state sovereignty undiminished, Calhoun conspicuously assumed what he claimed to demonstrate.)

The Constitution could not be national (either wholly or partly) because there existed no American "nation" nor any "American people" to authorize it.

There is, indeed, no such community, *politically* speaking, as the people of the United States, regarded in the light of, and as constituting one people or nation. There never has been any such, in any stage of their existence; and, of course, they neither could, nor ever can exercise any agency,—or have any participation, in the formation of our system of government, or its administration . . . The whole, taken together, form a federal community;—a community composed of States united by a political compact;—and not a nation composed of individuals united by, what is called, a social compact.

This was not an empirical claim about citizens' subjective degree of attachment to their states versus to the United States. It was an axiomatic and normative claim: an American nation *cannot* legitimately exist; citizens' loyalties are "commanded" by "the State to which they owe allegiance."[9]

Calhoun's argument depended upon the meaning of the word "federal" and the plural term "United States." He argued that to call a union "federal" meant by definition vesting each member with full sovereignty and denying any sovereignty to the government of the whole. If that premise is accepted, Calhoun's conclusion becomes an easy one, because clearly the form of government established by the Constitution remained "federal" in some sense.

To demonstrate that the framers established a "*federal* . . . in contradistinction to *national*" government, Calhoun quotes from George Washington's 17 September 1787 letter (as presiding officer of the convention) submitting the proposed Constitution to the Continental Congress. Calhoun observes that Washington's letter, referring to the government established by the proposed constitution, "calls it, in one place,—'the general government of the Union;'—and in another,—'the federal government of these States.'" From this Calhoun concludes: "Taken together, the plain meaning is, that the government proposed would be, if adopted, the government of the States adopting it, in their united character as members of a common Union; and, as such, would be a federal government. These expressions were not used without due consideration, and an accurate and full knowledge of their true import."[10]

That Calhoun's argument here rests on *a priori* assumptions about the nature of a federal government rather than on Washington's own meaning becomes obvious as soon as one consults the actual letter, where Washington writes: "It is obviously impractical in the federal government of these States; to secure all rights of independent sovereignty to each, and yet provide for the interest and safety of all—Individuals entering into society, must give up a share of liberty to preserve the rest." Washington here clearly indicates that an effective federal government is inconsistent with *full* state sovereignty and clearly calls for states to give up at least part of their sovereignty, admitting that "it is at all times difficult to draw with precision the line between those rights which must be surrendered, and those which may be reserved."[11] The most natural reading of Washington's letter would favor a theory of divided sovereignty. The letter clearly rejects full state sovereignty and by implication also rejects full national sovereignty.

The only way Calhoun could possibly use this letter to support his own position was by first assuming that divided sovereignty is impossible, that the only choice was between full state sovereignty and full national sovereignty, and that "federal" entails by definition the full sovereignty of member states. Once these assumptions are made, Washington's letter becomes by process of elimination an endorsement of Calhoun's position. This detail exemplifies Calhoun's selective use of historical and textual evidence.

Calhoun pointed out that the union as a whole, both in the Constitution and in universal usage of the period, is named "the United States." The government established by the Constitution, he argues, was never intended to be "national," because this would mean the states "divested themselves of their individuality and sovereignty, and merged themselves into one great community or nation." If the states were to lose all individuality and be simply "fused, as it were, into one general mass," then how could one call it "federal"? How could one possibly call it the "United States" if states cease to exist?[12]

In at least one respect Calhoun's argument is indisputable. Neither the text of the Constitution—especially after the Tenth Amendment—nor the history of its framing and ratification, support the centralization of all sovereign powers in a national government, whereby states cease to exist except as administrative units. Even those few framers like Alexander Hamilton who hoped for such a government acknowledged that the Constitution did not create it.

The key strategy of Calhoun's argument was implacably to force matters to the polar opposite conclusion: that the *only* alternative to a fully national government was full state sovereignty in a union where no American "people" or "nation" existed. Calhoun thus excluded from the outset at least two other possibilities: (1) that sovereign powers could be in some manner divided between the central government and the states, each sovereign in its own sphere; and (2) that the people of the United States were sovereign, and through the Constitution delegated certain specific powers to both central government and states. The first of the two alternatives, dividing sovereign powers, is expressed in the *Federalist Papers,* especially in No. 39, and in much of the constitutional commentary following the ratification of the Constitution.[13] The second alternative, a single sovereign American people which chooses to delegate its powers to two different levels of government, was the argument advanced most notably by James Wilson, and at times in the *Federalist*.[14] Both of these alternatives could legitimately be described as "federal" and neither dissolved the individuality of states into some "general mass" incompatible with the name "United States."

Calhoun rejected both of these possibilities from the outset. "Sovereignty is an entire thing;—to divide, is,—to destroy it" he insisted in the *Discourse*.[15] This echoes his Force Bill speech of 15–16 February 1833, where he described the American system as "a union of twenty-four sovereign powers, under a constitutional compact, and not of a divided sovereignty between the States severally and the United States . . . I maintain that sovereignty is in its nature indivisible . . . we might just as well speak of half a square, or half of a triangle, as of half a sovereignty."[16] Calhoun considered full national sovereignty (of the kind Hamilton favored at the federal convention) a logically coherent position, though unsupported by the Constitution, but the divided sovereignty for which Madison argued in *Federalist* No. 39—a government "partly federal" and "partly national"—was simply incoherent: "the one of these ['national' and 'federal'] so excludes the other, that it is impossible to blend them in the same constitution, and, of course, in the same government."[17]

If divided sovereignty was rejected *a priori,* it would follow that framers' intent or constitutional text carried weight only insofar as they did not violate the axiom of indivisible sovereignty. Where framers clearly intended to divide sovereignty, their intentions should be disregarded—as Calhoun made explicit in his criticism of Madison's *Federalist* No. 39 and left to implication in his gloss on Washington's letter. It would likewise follow that any reading of constitutional text that supported divided sovereignty was *a priori* an incorrect reading. Insofar as the Constitution attempted to divide sovereignty (or to vest sovereignty in the American people as a whole), the Constitution was wrong.

Only such a rule of construction can explain Calhoun's interpretation of the "supreme law of the land" clause in Article VI. The full clause reads: "This Constitution, and the laws of the United States which shall be made in pursuance thereof, and all treaties made, or which shall be made, under the authority of the United States, shall be the supreme law of the land; and the judges in every state shall be bound thereby, anything in the Constitution or laws of any state to the contrary notwithstanding." The clause does not necessarily endorse a theory of full national sovereignty, for it does not grant the federal government supremacy over the states in all matters. But it clearly indicates that in some important class of cases, federal law takes precedence over state law and that state courts are obligated to respect this federal supremacy.

In the *Discourse* Calhoun quoted this clause in full, then argued that "it vests no new power whatever in the government, or in any of its departments" (recall that for Calhoun the Articles of Confederation remained in force), claiming instead that "this supremacy is not an absolute supremacy. It is limited in extent and degree. It does not extend beyond the delegated powers;—all others being reserved to the States and the people of the States." The federal Constitution has supremacy over acts of the federal government itself; it does not have supremacy over the states. One might suppose from Calhoun's remark about federal supremacy not extending "beyond the delegated powers" that he conceded the federal government *did* have supremacy in the exercise of powers specifically delegated to it by the Constitution. But he turns around and specifically negates this conclusion: even in cases where a law passed by Congress, "carrying into execution one of the delegated powers, comes into conflict with a law of one of the States," the state law takes precedence if the state persists in opposition and bases its claim on "its reserved powers"—the state itself being the final judge of what constitutes its reserved powers. Calhoun insisted there was nothing in the Constitution that "can possibly give the judicial power authority to enforce the decision of the government of the United States, against that of a separate State, where their respective decisions come into conflict."[18]

Calhoun thus interpreted constitutional text the same way he read Washington's 17 September 1787 cover letter for the Constitution. Certain conclusions (above all divided sovereignty and national sovereignty) were ruled out from the beginning, regardless of their degree of textual support. Once the field of possible readings had been narrowed, constitutional text could then be quoted to support the same premise of full state sovereignty Calhoun assumed from the outset.

Calhoun applied a similar rule of construction to his commentary on debates at the Federal Convention. In both the 1833 Force Bill speech and the *Discourse* Calhoun mentions Madison's proposal in the convention to vest the federal government "with a veto on the acts of the separate governments of the several States, in any form or manner whatever." The fact that Madison's proposal failed meant for Calhoun not merely that the federal government had no constitutional power to veto state legislation "in any

CHAPTER FOUR

form or manner whatever"—a reasonable enough inference. For Calhoun it equally followed from the proposal's failure that *states* retain the power to veto acts of the federal government in all cases whatsoever. "We have thus direct and strong proof that, in the opinion of the Convention, the States, unless deprived of it, possess the veto power, or, what is another name for the same thing, the right of nullification."[19] This conclusion does not follow either from the convention record or from logic, unless one adds the *a priori* assumption of indivisible sovereignty. Calhoun's argument in effect is this: there can be only two possibilities, full national sovereignty or full state sovereignty. Madison's proposed veto on state legislation represented full national sovereignty. In rejecting this proposal, the convention thus consciously decided in favor of full state sovereignty. It follows that states enjoy the right to veto federal law in all cases.

But vesting full sovereignty in the states did not exhaust Calhoun's background theory of the Constitution. Equally essential was the premise that such a system could function effectively, even under conditions of high interdependence among states, rather than leading to anarchy or deadlock. Despite his insistence that the Articles of Confederation remained in force after the ratification, Calhoun did not want an "imbecilic" federal government of the kind that subsisted under the Articles. He wanted the best of both—full state sovereignty, and an effective federal government acting as the agent of the sovereign states.

Calhoun's argument that government can function effectively where each significant interest (or state, in the U.S. context) possesses veto rights was set forth most fully in the *Disquisition*. But Calhoun's desire to combine full state sovereignty *and* effective federal government (of the right kind) was also evident in his constitutional approach to the slavery controversy, to which we turn next.

Threats beyond Boundaries

It was clearly understood that the antebellum Constitution permitted states to practice slavery, and that the federal government had no constitutional power to abolish slavery within a state. (The abolitionist William Lloyd Garrison understood this too, which was why he denounced the Constitution as a covenant with death.) Slavery was a "reserved power" of the states in a way that the tariff clearly was not.

But the threats to slavery that preoccupied Calhoun in the last fifteen years of his life did not involve federal attempts to abolish, restrict, or regulate slavery within a state. That scenario was credible only on an enormously extended timeline, and Calhoun knew that slave states would secede long before federal action of this kind was attempted. (And indeed, South Carolina secessionists in 1860 knew that Lincoln and the Republican Party had no plans to abolish slavery where it already existed.)

What preoccupied Calhoun instead were threats to the stability and future of slavery—an institution he intended as permanent—that proceeded from outside the boundaries of slave states, carrying dangerous effects even without any direct violation by the federal government of the reserved powers of states. These threats included the persistent abolitionist agitation in northern states and in petitions to Congress, possible restrictions on slavery in the federal territories and in the District of Columbia, the difficulty of admitting new slave states into the Union, the increasing unwillingness of free states to cooperate in rendering fugitive slaves, and the attempted use of the federal government to make symbolic moral statements about the injustice of slavery.

Abolitionism threatened slavery even if nothing that abolitionists demanded became federal policy. Heated public denunciations of slavery, even in the absence of antislavery policy, could inspire slaves to revolt—for slaves themselves were not obliged to resist only in constitutional ways—and (more dangerous still, Calhoun believed) instill weakness and moral doubt in slave owners themselves. Prohibiting slavery in federal territories would undercut the South's massive investment in slave property by restricting its portability and market value and in the long run subject slavery to a slow political and economic strangulation (which was exactly the free-soilers' aim). By "packing" the Union with new free states, territorial restrictions on slavery would soon overturn slave states' de facto veto on federal policy via their equality in the U.S. Senate (slave states were already outvoted in the House). Finally, using the federal government to make symbolic statements (like prohibiting the slave trade in the District of Columbia) would send an official message that slavery was wrong and thus that slave states were morally inferior to free states within a union that presupposed the equal moral and political status of all partners. All of these threats (and more) were Calhoun's target.

The threats came from diverse sources and were conveyed in diverse ways. However, what they all had in common was, first, that none of them violated the letter of the U.S. Constitution (and some, like the right of petition, were explicitly guaranteed); and second, that there was little slave states could do about them by direct action within the boundaries of their state or by invoking their reserved powers to run their own state their own way. This is why the received view that slave states' strategy was to rely defensively on the reserved rights of states and holding federal power at bay is so misleading.

The impotence of purely state-level response made these threats to slavery fundamentally different from the tariff-and-nullification problem. One peculiarity of the nullification episode was that the tariff, though a national law, could be effectively nullified by action entirely within the bounds of a single state, if that state possessed a major international port. Had South Carolina's action not been challenged by President Andrew Jackson, the state would have been successful in unilaterally remaking a national policy through purely in-state action. The threats to slavery summarized above did not have this particular, indeed accidental, form. (The one exception here was that slave states could and did directly halt the conveyance of "seditious" mailings within the boundaries of their states, an episode noted below.)

Calhoun's challenge as a constitutional thinker in the last fifteen years of his life was somehow to reformulate his understanding of the Union as a joint partnership of equal, fully sovereign states (a theory first developed to justify nullification) in a way that enlisted the authority of the Constitution against threats to slavery that could not be resisted through nullification or any other unilateral state action. Specifically, Calhoun sought a constitutional formula that would:

1. make it a clear duty of the federal government positively to support and strengthen the institution of slavery, not merely refrain from interfering with it—yet do so in a way that respected the full sovereignty of states;
2. clearly prohibit the federal government from restricting slavery or threatening its stability;
3. make clear to northern states their duty, as members of the federal partnership, not to engage in or tolerate any action by or within their state that threatened slavery; and
4. guarantee the slaveholding interest a veto on potentially hostile acts of legislation, administration, or judicial decision, instead of depending any longer on the unreliable de facto veto of equality in the Senate.

On 19 December 1837 Senator Benjamin Swift of Vermont presented to the U.S. Senate an antislavery memorial from the Vermont legislature, which opposed "the annexation of Texas or the admission of any other slave State to the union, affirmed the power of Congress to abolish slavery in the District of Columbia and the Territories and to abolish the slave trade between States." Calhoun responded that "Vermont has struck a deep and dangerous blow into the vitals of our confederacy." The time has come, he asserted, to determine "whether we are longer to remain as one united and happy people, or whether this blessed Union was to be dissolved by the hand of violence."[20]

This was not the first antislavery statement brought before Congress, and from their first appearance in 1836 Calhoun had argued that even to present antislavery resolutions or petitions was unconstitutional (despite the explicit guarantee of the First Amendment), indeed criminal, and they must not be received by Congress. "Show these fanatics, by a decided refusal, by shutting the door in their face, that they have nothing to hope by agitation, and they will soon cease to agitate," he had argued on an earlier occasion.[21]

But the Vermont resolutions presented, from Calhoun's perspective, an entirely different kind of problem than earlier resolutions. They proceeded, not from individuals or private antislavery societies, but from the legislature of a "sovereign" state. For this reason Calhoun, according to his own constitutional principles, could not easily deny the state's right to bring them before Congress.

Moreover these resolutions were constitutionally sophisticated. They did not propose to interfere with slavery within the boundaries of any existing state, which would have been clearly unconstitutional. But Article I does give Congress the power "to exercise exclusive legislation in all cases whatsoever" over the federal district and to "regulate commerce . . . among the several states"; Article IV gives Congress the power to admit new states and to "make all needful rules and regulations" for federal territories. Thus by a kind of *antislavery* strict-constructionist, states' rights reading of the Constitution, the "sovereign" state of Vermont could justify bringing to Congress resolutions proposing the abolition of slavery in the District of Columbia and the territories and the abolition of the interstate slave trade and opposing the annexation of Texas.[22] In other words, antislavery activists sought to beat the slaveholders at their own states' rights, strict-constructionist game.

Federal power over the District of Columbia was probably the strongest of the three constitutional claims upon which the Vermont memorial was based, because the text of the Constitution specifically gives Congress exclusive power over the District, there is no corresponding state power over the District to compete with it, and as a practical matter regulations concerning slavery in the District had to be made one way or another; federal neutrality here was impossible. Using the interstate commerce power to ban the interstate slave trade was a greater stretch because of the difference between regulation and prohibition, but the Constitution did give Congress power to ban the *international* slave trade after 1808, and this precedent might plausibly be extended to the domestic trade. The Vermont memorial did not base its antislavery proposals on Article IV's guarantee to preserve in every state a "Republican form of government" as some abolitionists did (defining slavery as an anti-republican practice); this required a more expansive construction and a clear break with historical intention and precedent. Vermont instead based its antislavery resolutions on the strictest and most explicit constitutional grounds, including its right as a "sovereign state" to make its views known.

It was this that, in Calhoun's view, raised the sectional crisis to a new level and justified open threats of secession. In response to this employment of states' rights in opposition to slavery, Calhoun on 27 December 1837 introduced six resolutions on "Abolition and the Union" that articulated in most comprehensive form his joint-state-compact theory of the Constitution and Union.

In doing so he built on the constitutional ideas he had formulated during the nullification era. In the *Fort Hill Address* of 1831 Calhoun had argued that the federal government was merely the creature of the sovereign states, deriving its powers from "a compact between sovereigns [meaning the states], and partaking . . . of the character of a joint commission."[23] The six resolutions Calhoun introduced in 1837 in response to Vermont likewise presupposed that the Constitution and Union resulted from a joint commission among fully sovereign states. But the actual problems raised by the Vermont memorial were very different from those posed by the protective tariff. South Carolina could, in theory, nullify the federal tariff by actions taken entirely within the territory of the state. But no action taken within South Carolina could guarantee the rights of slaveholders in the federal district, admit new slave states to the union, or prevent Vermont and other states from bringing antislavery resolutions to Congress.

Moreover, the tariff was a federal law and the nullification debate could thus be framed as federal power versus states' rights. Vermont's introducing antislavery resolutions to Congress, in contrast, was not a federal action (except insofar as the forum itself, the Senate, was a federal body). On any matter other than slavery Calhoun would have admitted—on states' rights grounds if nothing else—the Vermont legislature's right to bring resolutions to Congress.

In his response Calhoun did not attempt to demonstrate that Vermont's reading of constitutional language was mistaken, or to answer the state's argument in any way. His purpose instead was to demonstrate the unconstitutionality of Vermont's bringing such resolutions to Congress at all. This was not a question of federal power versus states' rights, but of what Calhoun considered the proper mode of conduct by one sovereign state toward its partner states. Calhoun himself admitted that these resolutions "came from a sovereign State, a party to the constitutional compact, which had a right to enter our doors, and he could not, therefore vote against their reception"; yet, "as a Southern man, representing in part the slaveholding States, which were grossly insulted by the resolutions, he could not vote for their reception."[24] Calhoun's six resolutions were designed to constitutionally prohibit states from doing what he had just admitted they had a constitutional right to do.

Calhoun did not debate constitutional text but invoked principles he regarded as higher than any text. His first resolution asserted that in adopting the Constitution, the states acted "as free, independent, and sovereign States" (here quoting the language of the Articles of Confederation, as though they were still in force) and that each state "by its own voluntary assent, entered the Union with the view to its increased security, against all dangers, *domestic* as well as foreign."[25]

His second resolution reaffirmed the standard antebellum constitutional doctrine that "the States retained, severally, the exclusive and sole right over their own domestic institutions." This meant that any "intermeddling . . . with the domestic institutions and police" of a state by the federal government, or by other states "under any pretext whatever, political, moral, or religious" was unconstitutional.[26] This relatively uncontroversial resolution did not, however, directly address the problem at hand, which was not interference within a state, but antislavery resolutions directed precisely to matters falling outside the jurisdiction and territory of any individual state.

Calhoun's third resolution made the key strategic innovation in his argument. "That this Government was instituted and adopted by the several

CHAPTER FOUR

States of this Union as a common agent . . . and that, in fulfillment of this high and sacred trust, this Government is bound so to exercise its powers as to give . . . increased stability and security to the domestic institutions of the States that compose the Union; and that it is the solemn duty of the Government to resist all attempts . . . to weaken or destroy such institutions, instead of strengthening and upholding them, as it is in duty bound to do."[27] Note that Calhoun here transformed the *negative* obligation of noninterference in the second resolution into a *positive* obligation on the part of the federal government to "strengthen and uphold" the institution of slavery.[28]

That this was a significant move came across during debate. When a Senator from Michigan proposed to amend Calhoun's third resolution "slightly" by limiting it to the negative duty of noninterference, instead of the positive duty to give "increased stability and security" to slavery, Calhoun refused to accept the amendment and emphasized once again the duty "both of the General and State Governments" not merely "to avoid conflict" but "to uphold reciprocally the institutions of each other."[29]

Calhoun's fourth resolution asserted that when the Constitution was adopted, slavery was recognized "as constituting an essential element" of the Constitution, and that "on entering into the constitutional compact," every state accepted "the most solemn obligations, moral and religious" to protect and defend the institution of slavery. For any state—like Vermont—to attack slavery thus signified a "manifest violation of the mutual and solemn pledge."[30]

Calhoun's fifth resolution targeted the proposal to abolish slavery in the District of Columbia by making it morally and constitutionally equivalent to a direct attack on slavery within a state. "That the intermeddling of any State or States, or their citizens, to abolish slavery in this District, or any of the Territories . . . would be a direct and dangerous attack on the institutions of all the slaveholding States."[31]

Calhoun's sixth resolution stated that the Union "rests on an equality of rights and advantages among its members; and that whatever destroys that equality, tends to destroy the Union itself"; and that "to refuse to extend to the southern and western States any advantage which would tend to strengthen, or render them more secure, or increase their limits or population by the annexation of new territory or States . . . would be contrary to that equality of rights and advantages which the Constitution was intended to secure alike to all the members of the Union, and would, in effect, disfranchise the slaveholding States."[32] Again the issue was not mere noninterference, but a positive obligation of the federal government to strengthen slavery by allowing it to expand. To prohibit slavery in the territories, or refuse to admit a new slave state while continuing to admit new free states, would make slave states unequal partners in the compact and was thus inherently illegitimate.

During the debate on his resolutions, Calhoun explained that he based his resolutions not on constitutional text but on "the higher elements of our system, and the necessary relations arising therefrom."[33] He meant there were certain clear and absolute truths deducible from the inherent nature of a federal union of equal states—truths of authority superior to constitutional text itself. Later in the same debate he added: "His object was to place the question on no particular portion of the Constitution, but on its general character and structure, which he thought was much stronger, and much less liable to be disputed."[34] Thus a constitutional interpretation apparently grounded in the text of the Constitution—as Vermont's resolutions were—was inherently illegitimate, Calhoun argued, if it contradicted the "general character and structure" of the American Union.

The idea that the Constitution should be interpreted in accordance with "higher elements" is famously associated with antislavery New York senator William Seward. On 15 March 1850, denying any constitutional obligation to return fugitive slaves, Seward declared that "there is a higher law than the Constitution" that regulates interpretation of that document's "noble purposes."[35] Defenders of slavery denounced Seward and his "higher law." But Calhoun was making higher-law arguments long before Seward, and for precisely opposite purposes.

Calhoun warned fellow senators that "if the resolutions should be rejected, he would consider it as throwing down all constitutional barriers in the way of the abolitionists" and a sign to the South that it could not safely remain in the Union. In other words, a vote against his resolutions was a signal to the South to secede from the Union. Calhoun said that "his first and greatest desire was to preserve the union; but if that was impossible, then (and he would boldly avow it) his next most ardent desire was for the South to save itself."[36] (Thus congressional debate on Calhoun's six resolutions cannot be regarded as a model of unconstrained deliberation.)

Calhoun upbraided southern members who accused him of unnecessarily inflaming the slavery controversy with his counterattack. It was a mistake, Calhoun answered, for southerners simply to insist on the unconstitutionality of abolitionism, deluding themselves that they could remain "entrenched quietly behind the ramparts of the Constitution." The whole point, Calhoun said in a private letter written during this debate, was "to carry the war into the non slaveholding States. There the disease originated, and there it ought to be met."[37] This demonstrates again the implausibility of the received view that Calhoun's constitutional strategy was merely defensive, based on strict construction, states' rights, and limited government, satisfied to keep the federal government neutral on slavery. Every single element of Calhoun's six resolutions contradicts that received view.

Suppressing Abolitionist Publications

Calhoun made clear that states' duty to uphold one another's institutions meant northern states must suppress the abolitionist societies active within their borders. In 1836, in response to resolutions sponsored by a senator from Maine stressing the federal government's mere negative duty not to interfere with slavery where it existed, Calhoun called attention to the existence of the Maine Abolitionist Society. "He held the existence of such a society to be as dangerous to the South as an abolition newspaper; and he thought if the State could suppress the one, it could suppress the other. He hoped that in time public sentiment would be such at the North as to put down all such societies."[38] Calhoun did not quite claim the federal government, on its own authority, could suppress abolitionist societies in a free state against the will of that state; this would be a transparent violation of his constitutional principles. He meant instead that Maine had a constitutional obligation, as a member of the federal partnership, on its own authority to suppress activities within the state that endangered other members of the federal partnership. The federal government then had in Calhoun's view the right and duty to assist the state in suppressing abolitionism.

This anticipates what Calhoun said in closing the final speech of his life (4 March 1850), which summarized the conditions under which the South would remain in the Union. Though some concerned federal policy (e.g., the rights of slaveholders in federal territories), equally important were free states' obligations faithfully to fulfill "the stipulations relative to fugitive slaves" and "to cease the agitation of the slave question."[39] By "cease the agitation of the slave question" Calhoun meant northern states' obligation to suppress the abolitionist societies operating within their borders.

Calhoun believed not only that all states, slave or free, had an obligation to suppress abolitionism, but also that the federal government had an obligation to cooperate with the states in suppressing it. He made this argument clearly in his "Report on Incendiary Publications" of 1836.[40] The issue arose when abolitionists began mass mailing antislavery literature to southern states. (In fact the literature was immediately seized and destroyed and thus never delivered in the South.) President Jackson and his postmaster general, Amos Kendall, called for a federal ban on the mailing of "incendiary" literature.[41]

Calhoun opposed a federal law prohibiting incendiary literature. Invoking the Virginia and Kentucky Resolutions against the Sedition Act, he argued that under the First Amendment the power to suppress dangerous literature was reserved to the states. There is no substantive defense of freedom of speech anywhere in Calhoun's discussion of the First Amendment, in contrast to Madison's response to the Sedition Act. That abolitionist speech and writing must be suppressed Calhoun took as indisputable; the question was *who* had the power to suppress it. Calhoun opposed Jackson's proposed federal law because, by creating a federal power to prohibit incendiary literature, it would simultaneously enable the federal government to judge what was or was not incendiary. This "would be virtually to clothe Congress with the power to abolish slavery, by giving it the means of breaking down all the barriers which the slave holding States have erected for the protection of their lives and property."[42] In other words, Congress could attack slavery by permitting the transmission by U.S. mail of literature that slave states judged to be dangerous.

Calhoun's argument on incendiary publications as described thus far might seem a straightforward states' rights argument restricting the power of the federal government. Under the antebellum Constitution nothing prohibited states from restricting freedom of speech, press, religion, or anything else in the Bill of Rights, which at that time only bound the federal government. But in Calhoun's interpretation of the First Amendment there was a twist. The federal government had no *independent* power to judge and suppress "incendiary" publications. But once a state judged something to be dangerous and decided to suppress it, it was, Calhoun insisted, the obligation of the federal government fully to cooperate in that suppression. "The right to protect her internal peace and security belongs to a State," Calhoun observes, and "the general Government is bound to respect the measures adopted by her for that purpose"—but he then adds, "and to co-operate in their execution, as far as its delegated powers may admit, or the measure may require." (The last five words make clear that Calhoun wanted the fed-

CHAPTER FOUR

eral government to go *beyond* its "delegated powers" if necessary to assist a state in suppressing abolitionism.) He makes the point again: the federal government is bound "not only not to violate" the suppressive measures of the states, "but, as far as practicable, to co-operate in their execution." In "cooperating" with state authorities to suppress incendiary publications, the federal government could legitimately press into service "the powers of Congress over the mail, and of regulating commerce with foreign nations and between the States."[43] So the federal powers Calhoun wanted employed to suppress abolitionist literature were quite extensive and not limited to suppression within the boundaries of the particular states whose laws it was upholding— for Calhoun specifically wanted this federal suppression power exercised in interstate and international commerce.

Thus Calhoun's response to "incendiary" publications exactly paralleled his later response to Vermont's antislavery memorial. In both cases he used states' rights and state sovereignty as his starting point but ended up far beyond mere federal noninterference with slavery, instead demanding the federal government actively use its extensive powers to protect and reinforce the institution of slavery. In Calhoun's view using federal power to suppress "incendiary" literature and speech did not violate the principle of state sovereignty, because the federal government made no independent judgment but merely helped carry out the suppressive agenda of a sovereign state.[44]

To repeat a point made earlier: Calhoun did not consider his full-state-sovereign version of federal union to be a formula for weak or ineffective government. He believed it was possible to have the best of both: a federal government prohibited by states' veto rights from enacting measures that benefited one section at the expense of another, but able energetically to carry out measures that had the support of all members of the state partnership. In Calhoun's view, federal suppression of abolitionist speech and literature— at the direction of those states with the most to lose—was one of these energetic measures in the good of all.

The problem with this picture is that some members of this sovereign partnership were not only unwilling to cooperate in suppressing abolitionist speech, but gave such speech their positive endorsement—as Vermont did in bringing antislavery resolutions to Congress. Here Calhoun ultimately fell back on what he regarded as the inherent ethical obligations of a partnership. Not only the federal government, but northern states themselves, had positive constitutional obligations to give increased security to the institution of slavery. Constitutional text (the basis for the Vermont resolutions) had no authority if employed in ways that contradicted the spirit of the partnership that authorized the Constitution in the first place. Vermont had violated those obligations and thus would bear some responsibility if southern states were forced out of the Union.

Calhoun's denial that even a sovereign state could bring antislavery resolutions to Congress puts in perspective his own commitment to states' rights. Calhoun genuinely believed in the principle of states' rights, but he believed there were restrictions on how they could legitimately be deployed. States' rights were legitimate if used to protect the essential interests of states, as Calhoun insisted was the case when South Carolina nullified the federal tariff. But using states' rights as a shield behind which to mount attacks on fellow states, as Calhoun accused Vermont of doing, was illegitimate. In the end, for Calhoun protecting slavery was a higher principle than states' rights.

Calhoun's response to the Vermont memorial demonstrates how completely his understanding of Constitution and Union presupposed that slavery was morally right and opposition to slavery morally wrong. Calhoun used the theory of the Union as a joint state partnership to argue that slave states retained veto rights over disposition of joint property—i.e., the territories, the federal district, and the operations of the federal government itself. But what was to prevent *free* states from exercising comparable veto rights over policy *permitting* slavery in federal territories? Or from demanding federal cooperation in enforcing free state laws that permitted abolitionist speech? Or from nullifying fugitive slave laws just as South Carolina had nullified the tariff? If opposition to slavery had the same veto rights as support for slavery, the result would be an infinite regress of vetoes over federal policy. Calhoun's state partnership theory of the Constitution worked only if it was understood that opposition to slavery was an illegitimate position, one deserving no constitutional protection, much less veto rights. That indeed was the whole point of his response to the Vermont antislavery memorial.

Secession and Nullification

Calhoun prefaced his six resolutions of 1837 with a secession threat should northern states refuse to accept the principles set forth in the resolutions. In the final speech of his life, 4 March 1850, he likewise issued a set of demands that northern states must meet if slave states were to remain in the Union. These requirements were (1) that the North must concede to the South "an equal right in the acquired territory" (i.e., that slavery be legalized in all federal territories); (2) that northern states faithfully fulfill "the stipulations relative to fugitive slaves"; (3) "to cease the agitation of the slave question" (suppress abolitionist organizations, as noted above); and (4) to accept a constitutional amendment that "will restore to the South in substance the power she possessed of protecting herself, before the equilibrium between the sections was destroyed by the action of this Government."[45] He meant here his proposal for a dual executive, one for each of the great divisions of the United States, each having veto power over federal policy.

That Calhoun reinforced his proposed reconstruction of the Constitution with secession threats could be seen as bullying. Calhoun himself saw secession threats as a principled move, a re-creation of the deliberative conditions of the original Federal Convention of 1787 (a theme examined below.) The general function of secession in Calhoun's political and constitutional theory deserves examination.

Calhoun argued that states had an unqualified constitutional right to secede from the Union. The right of secession was integral to Calhoun's state-compact theory of federal union, and also to his understanding of redress options short of secession, including constitutional amendments and single-state nullification. If states were fully sovereign, then each individually retained the "high sovereign right . . . to change or abolish the present constitution and government at their pleasure."[46] For a state to secede was in effect "to abolish" the constitution for itself.

Calhoun did not base the right of secession on constitutional text nor attempt to show that those who drafted and ratified the document understood it to include that right. Instead he grounded his argument on the assumption of full state sovereignty and on what he considered the inherent logic of the process by which the Constitution was ratified. During the ratification debate it was clearly understood that the Constitution was binding only on the states that ratified it; if for instance North Carolina or Rhode Island had withheld ratification, neither those states nor their citizens would be bound by the Constitution.[47] From the fact that any state could have chosen not to join the union in the first place, Calhoun claimed it logically followed that each state that has joined can exit when it chooses.

That each state could have chosen not to ratify the Constitution and thus stayed out of the union in the first place is fairly straightforward. But that a right *not to join* the partnership in the first place logically entails a right *unilaterally to exit* the partnership once established is another question and does not automatically follow. From the premise that each state initially had the right to join or stay out, two possibilities follow: that the "contract" is one in which this right is retained (Calhoun's reading), or that the contract is such that this right is relinquished and the nature of the relationship transformed by the act of ratification itself. Either type of "contract" is possible (both in private contracts and in political federations). Some federations include an explicit right of secession; some explicitly forbid it, or subject it to qualifications. The U.S. Constitution—like the Confederate Constitution of 1861— is silent on the question.[48]

Calhoun argued that silence in this case entailed presence. "That the States, then, retained, after the ratification of the constitution, the distinct, independent, and sovereign character in which they formed and ratified it, is certain: unless they divested themselves of it by the act of ratification, or by some provision of the constitution."[49] In other words, the right of secession—and all other attributes of state sovereignty—remain unchanged, Calhoun argued, unless there were explicit provisions to the contrary in the Constitution. That the Constitution was silent on secession thus meant the right of secession remained, unaltered, as a continuation of the original right not to join.

In response one might argue that silence entails the absence of the right. For the Constitution to have included an unconditional right of secession at a time when the overriding need was to "form a more perfect union" would have been counterproductive and sent the United States down a very different path of political development; therefore the presumption could be against such a right unless it is explicitly affirmed. One can, perhaps most plausibly of all, argue that silence on this point indicated the framers were themselves not of one mind on the issue and tacitly agreed not to press unnecessarily so fateful a question.

Whether Calhoun's reading was "correct" in the face of the Constitution's silence is ultimately an unanswerable question. It is more productive to ask *how secession functions* in Calhoun's political and constitutional thought, and how his view of secession compared with other types of secession arguments.

In Calhoun's constitutional theory, the right of nullification was logically derived from the right of secession. If a state had a constitutional right to secede, it followed that it could not be forced to obey any federal law it did not consent to, which is exactly the foundation for Calhoun's right of nullification *within* the Union. Recall that for Calhoun, if a state's decision to nullify federal law was affirmatively overridden by three-fourths of its fellow states, the nullifying state still reserved the right to secede. The assumption here is that individual states never relinquished a particle of their sovereignty, neither to the federal government (in any of its branches) nor to other states (no matter how large the majority). Even a constitutional amendment passed by three-fourths of the states could not override the sovereignty of a dissenting state, on Calhoun's reading, for secession was the final proof of sovereignty.

This is clear from Calhoun's discussion of the transition from the Articles of Confederation, which explicitly required that all changes in the Articles have unanimous support, to the Constitution, which can be amended by a three-fourths majority of states. In Calhoun's view, there was no essential change: the requirement of unanimity remained. The Constitution did not replace the unanimity principle, but merely "modified" it: the states "did not intend, by [the provision for amendment by three-fourths of the states] to divest themselves of the high sovereign right (a right which they still retain, notwithstanding the modification,) to change or abolish the present constitution and government at their pleasure"; sovereigns "may, by compact, modify or qualify the exercise of their power, without impairing their sovereignty." Calhoun went so far as to argue that the three-fourths amendment provision was a departure from correct principles, explicable only by the "pressure of very trying exigencies" under which the convention acted when it drafted the Constitution.[50] Thus neither the ordinary three-fourths majority required for constitutional amendment, nor Calhoun's own after-the-fact "jury" of three-fourths of the states passing judgment on an act of nullification, had any real authority over an individual state; each state's sovereign right to "alter or abolish" the Constitution, at least for itself, remained unimpaired throughout.

An alternative and probably more common view in Calhoun's time was that *secession* was justified, but *nullification* was not. William Rawle's *A View of the Constitution of the United States of America* (1829) endorsed a constitutional right of secession. But Rawle specifically rejected any right of nullification, instead taking the view that if a state chose to remain in the Union, it was obligated to obey federal laws.[51] The same view was expressed by William Drayton, a South Carolina Unionist, during the nullification debate in 1831. A state objecting to an "obnoxious law" can endeavor to repeal that law through ordinary procedures, Drayton argued, or it may secede from the Union; but "there are no other alternatives remaining": a state cannot suspend the operation of a law while remaining in the Union.[52]

For Calhoun, the right of secession was a normal and continual element of the Constitution, and through nullification (a kind of mutation of the right of secession) shaped the operation of government powers at every point in time. For Rawle and Drayton in contrast, secession, even if it was a constitutional right, was separate from all other constitutional processes: a mere right of exit.

Both views encounter problems. Calhoun's view invites the objection that one cannot be both in and out of the Union at the same time and that a right to *exit* a political community does not confer a right unilaterally to *alter* the Constitution and laws of that community so long as one remains within it. The view of Rawle and Drayton encounters a different problem: if nullification is prohibited (but secession allowed) this implies a legitimate federal power to enforce federal law against a recalcitrant state. But as soon as enforcement was attempted, the state could shift ground and declare itself to have seceded (perhaps with the expectation of reentering later on better terms) in which case federal enforcement is prohibited. Neither type of secession argument (secession and nullification, secession without nullification) is free of contradictions.

There were thus at least three possible positions: neither nullification nor secession was constitutional (Madison's position)[53]; both nullification and secession were constitutional (Calhoun); secession was constitutional but nullification unconstitutional (Rawle and Drayton). Contrary to what is sometimes asserted, there was no consensus in Calhoun's time about whether there existed a constitutional right of secession.[54]

To argue for a *constitutional* right of secession is, at least in principle, quite different from resorting to the *natural* right of revolution, as American colonists did in 1776. A constitutional right of secession would entail not only the seceding member's right to leave, but a constitutional obligation on other members not to contest secession and peacefully allow partition of the country. The American revolutionaries did not argue that the British constitution authorized their secession, nor did they expect Britain to let them go in peace.

In practice, however, the distinction between claiming a natural and constitutional right of secession is less clear-cut, because even those who claim secession as a constitutional right may know it will be opposed by force and that their claim is no better than the army backing it up. This was true of the Confederate secession of 1860–1861 (with secessionists themselves ambiguous on whether they were invoking a constitutional or natural right[55]). It was also true for Calhoun, whose threats of secession were accompanied by assurances of southern states' willingness to fight: "We shall be as well prepared and as capable of meeting whatever may come as you." He furthermore predicted that "if forced to resist, the weaker section [meaning the South] would prove successful, and the system end in disunion, is, to say the least, highly probable."[56]

So in arguing for a constitutional right of secession, Calhoun was not foolish enough to assume northern states would accept that argument. But he knew that belief in the constitutionality of secession—a well-prepared legal case—would give southerners a better conscience about secession and fortify their will to defend it by arms, if and when secession became necessary to protect slavery.

It is worth noting that South Carolina's 20 December 1860 Ordinance of Secession and accompanying Declaration of Causes of Secession closely followed the constitutional case for secession Calhoun had prepared, with respect both to the right of secession itself and the particular grievances listed as justifying secession. The Ordinance of Secession was a literal un-signing of the Constitution, a formal repeal of South Carolina's ratification of the Constitution on 23 May 1788, exactly following Calhoun's understanding of ratification as a revocable act. The list of grievances likewise closely followed Calhoun, and (like Calhoun in his response to the Vermont antislavery memorial) placed as much emphasis on the current practices of northern states (refusing to honor the fugitive slave law, tolerating abolitionist societies, allowing escaped slaves to vote) as on hypothetical future acts of the federal government. The first grievance detailed in South Carolina's Declaration of Causes is that "fourteen of the States have deliberately refused, for years past, to fulfill their constitutional obligations" to return fugitive slaves; furthermore these states "have enacted laws which either nullify the Acts of Congress or render useless any attempt to execute them." The next major grievance is that these same states "have permitted open establishment among them of societies, whose avowed object is to disturb the peace and to eloign [remove, carry off] the property of the citizens of other States," meaning abolitionist societies encouraging fugitive slaves. Another major grievance was that some northern states gave citizenship to "persons who, by the supreme law of the land, are incapable of becoming citizens," meaning persons of African descent. These grievances concern action by individual states, not by the federal government, and Calhoun prepared the case for all of them. Only well into the document is the election of Lincoln mentioned. This was the final straw, but the document asserts that secession was justified as early as 1852, long before Lincoln's election.[57]

Even though Calhoun endorsed a right of secession and prepared a legal and moral case for that eventuality, secession was precisely what he hoped to avoid and what his entire political and constitutional theory—both in the *Discourse* and in the *Disquisition*—was intended to render unnecessary. The very purpose of providing veto rights to an outvoted minority *within* a political community was to make it safe for the minority to remain in that community. Even if by the end he considered secession inevitable, it signified the failure, not the success, of his efforts as political leader and political theorist.

Calhoun seems to have believed that a well-framed secession argument, backed by willingness to fight, would accomplish the best of both objectives: it would increase the probability that an attempt at secession would succeed and at the same time make secession unnecessary because so serious a signal should force the northern states to change their ways. In the very same breath Calhoun called upon the South "to rise up, and bravely defend herself" and claimed that "this period is favorable" for settling the crisis that endangered the Union.[58]

Calhoun genuinely believed that the right of secession—and the threat to use it—contributed to the effective functioning of a consensus-based system of government. He wrote in the *Disquisition:* "When something *must* be done,—and when it can be done only by the united consent of all,—the necessity of the case will force to a compromise;—be the cause of that necessity what it may."[59] Giving each "portion or interest" a formal right of veto, Calhoun's favored mechanism, was intended to create exactly this decision condition. But a right of secession under conditions of deep interdependency (where all parties would be deeply hurt, as Calhoun recognized) would accomplish the same thing. In either case—the danger of anarchy because of a minority veto, or the danger of disunion because of secession—"the necessity of the case will force to a compromise," just as in the deliberations of a jury. Thus there was for Calhoun a close connection between the right to nullify (a version of the minority veto) and the right to secede. In both cases, Calhoun believed that asserting the right and threatening to use it would improve the political process itself and thus make actual resort to nullification or secession unnecessary.

Calhoun's stated purpose was to "restore" the Constitution "as it came from the hands of its framers."[60] But by "restoration" Calhoun did not mean fidelity to original text or original intention. His interpretation of the Constitution owed more to a particular background theory than to either text or precedent. His proposal for "restoring" the original Constitution was to create a dual executive, one for the North and one for the South, each armed with unqualified veto powers over all acts of legislation and administration. This would have radically restructured the entire federal government in ways not only remote from the Constitution itself, but also from anything proposed at the Federal Convention or during the ratification debate.[61] The connection between Calhoun's proposed dual executive and his own political philosophy is crystal clear. How it supposedly restores the Constitution to its original form is more puzzling.

The mystery disappears, however, as soon as one realizes that what Calhoun sought to restore was not the *product* of the Federal Convention (the Constitution itself) but the *process* that he believed guided its deliberations. The central idea of Calhoun's political philosophy, the unanimity requirement (or what he called the principle of the concurrent majority) can be compared to a kind of permanent constitutional convention in which all key decisions require consensus.

The Constitution itself nowhere requires unanimity as a decision rule and requires supermajorities only in exceptional cases. (And even where the Constitution requires a two-thirds vote this does not guarantee a permanent veto to any particular "portion or interest" as Calhoun demanded.) But the deliberations of the Federal Convention did display a genuine effort to achieve consensus among geographical sections and between large and small states. For a majority of states to have forced provisions deeply opposed by a minority of states would have been self-defeating, because the outvoted states would have exited both the convention and the Union (and such an outcome seemed possible on more than one occasion during the deliberations). The effort to achieve consensus wherever possible ultimately produced a Constitution agreed to by every state and nearly every individual participating in the convention, and ultimately ratified by every state—each one of which could have chosen to remain out of the Union (as North Carolina and Rhode Island did for a time). When Calhoun spoke of restoring the Constitution to its original character, he meant this wider consensus-oriented process, not the mere document.

In the *Discourse* Calhoun observed that deliberations at the Federal Convention were conditioned by the need to secure "the unanimous approval of all, in order to make it obligatory on all, which rendered it indispensable for the convention to consult the feelings and interests of all. This, united with the absolute necessity of doing something, in order to avert impending calamities of the most fearful character, impressed all with feelings of moderation, forbearance, mutual respect, concession, and compromise" and "stamped their work with so much fairness, equity, and justice,—as to receive, finally, the unanimous ratification of the States."[62] Calhoun's argument here applies the same idea, and in similar language, as the unanimous-consent jury model he argued for in the *Disquisition:* "In such cases, compromise among the parties is an indispensable condition to acting, it exerts an overruling influence in predisposing them to acquiesce in some one opinion or course of action."[63] Calhoun believed that the constitutional drafting and ratification process—like juries—demonstrated the workability of unanimity as a decision rule in political life.

The convention made two critical compromises familiar to all students of the period. One was the compromise between large states, which sought representation in both houses of Congress based on population, and small states, which sought equal representation for all states regardless of population. This conflict was resolved in the so-called Great Compromise whereby states were represented proportional to population in the House and equally represented in the Senate. The other crucial compromise was between slave and free states, whereby slaves ("all other persons" in the actual constitutional language) were counted as three-fifths for apportioning representatives in the House and "direct taxes." Free states also agreed not to prohibit the international slave trade before 1808 and to a provision obligating states to return fugitive slaves ("persons held to service or labor"). Many delegates from free states (or more precisely, states in process of abolishing slavery at the time of the Convention) sympathized with Pennsylvania delegate Gouverneur Morris's view that slavery "was a nefarious institution" and that only free men, not property, should be counted for representation. But the delegates from South Carolina—Calhoun's state—replied that "the true question at present is whether the Southn. States shall or shall not be parties to the Union."[64]

Calhoun distinguished the "mutual respect, concession, and compromise" that characterized the deliberations of the convention from the effects of majority rule. If the convention had attempted to decide these two great contested matters on the basis of majority rule (whether majority by population or majority of states) and overruled the minority position, the Constitution would have failed; key states and interests would have refused "to be parties to the Union." The convention instead deliberated under a jury-like rule: the necessity to secure "the unanimous approval of all."

Calhoun was right to insist that simple majority rule could not have resolved either of these two key conflicts. And as a general proposition, constitutional settlements for new or newly constituted political communities often fail unless the groups and interests powerful enough to make trouble are enlisted in support of the constitution. In constitutional settlements it is wise to aim for unanimity, or come as close as possible.

But there is a difference between unanimity as a decision rule in the deliberative process producing a constitution and unanimity as a decision rule under the constitution itself. These unanimous "compacts" (to use Calhoun's term) on representation and slavery were events in the *process* leading to the final document; they are not part of the document itself. The Constitution itself of course contained the specific provisions that resulted from these two compromises. But there is no provision in the Constitution affirming that all key decisions must secure unanimous consent of all states and interests. There are supermajority requirements for confirming treaties, overriding vetoes, and amending the Constitution itself, but no unanimity requirement as under the Articles of Confederation. Even if the framers hoped future decisions would be made in a consensual spirit, there is an enormous difference between encouraging a spirit of compromise, as the framers did, and treating unanimity as a formal decision rule under the Constitution itself, as Calhoun does.

It was exactly this distinction between constitutional process and constitutional product that Calhoun deliberately eliminated. In all of his constitutional interventions—nullification, his six resolutions of 1837, his dual executive proposal—Calhoun sought to make the spirit of unanimity that characterized the Convention into a continual and living principle of the Constitution, applicable to new decisions not treated in the text and capable of overriding the text where necessary. (Of course, both enslaved persons and free citizens who denounced slavery as wicked fell outside the consensus process.)

It is debatable whether these two key compromises—and especially the compromise over slavery—were indeed "compacts" in Calhoun's sense of the word. In his fourth resolution of 1837 Calhoun insisted that at the Federal Convention the northern states had taken on "the most solemn obligations, moral and religious" to protect and defend the institution of slavery. Calhoun here did not merely mean that northern states agreed to certain specific provisions such as the three-fifths clause and the fugitive slave clause. He meant that northern states had taken on positive moral and constitutional obligations that went far beyond mere toleration and noninterference. The difference is important: for by Calhoun's interpretation, northern states were obliged not only to respect (perhaps grudgingly) the specific provisions they had agreed to at a convention two generations earlier, but *here and now*— and in the future—actively to protect slavery from any new threats, including in ways not specified in the document itself; hence the obligation to protect slavery in the territories, the prohibition on restricting it in the District of Columbia, and so on. For it is the supposed "compact," the ethical obligation, that was binding, not the mere text.

The actual recorded debates of the convention do not support Calhoun's claim that northern states saw themselves making a solemn moral and religious obligation to protect and defend slavery when they agreed to the three-fifths clause and other provisions demanded by slave states. Gouverneur Morris's characterization of slavery as a "nefarious institution" and "the curse of heaven on the States where it prevailed"[65] is on the contrary exactly the kind of speech Calhoun sought in the 1830s to ban from public discourse altogether. (In Calhoun's theory it is as if, in agreeing to the three-fifths clause, Morris and other critics of slavery had at the same time agreed forever to cease talking about slavery this way.) John Rutledge, convention delegate from South Carolina, in response to the argument that slavery was "dishonorable to the American character," replied that it was a question of interest, not morality, and that "he will readily exempt the other States" from any obligation to protect slave states against slave insurrections.[66] This exchange likewise contradicts Calhoun's claim that in 1787 the free states promised to uphold slavery against any threat, or that slave states demanded of them any such promise.

But the most striking feature of Calhoun's vision of a permanent constitutional convention is that even if no such promise was made in 1787, it did not matter: the promise could be demanded *now*, in 1837 or 1850. Calhoun's whole response to the Vermont antislavery memorial of 1837 more resembled the opening stages of a constitutional convention than an ordinary legislative debate under an existing constitution. Calhoun's own six resolutions of 1837 rival the Virginia Plan in scope and import—fundamental principles that he believed ought to have been declared in 1787 (and would have if Calhoun himself had been present at the convention). By openly threatening secession if his resolutions were not agreed to, Calhoun in effect sought to reproduce, under changed circumstances, the exit option that every state enjoyed at the federal convention and during the ratification debate. If slave states had not gotten the three-fifths and fugitive slave provisions, they would have halted the process and dissolved the Union in 1787. The terms Calhoun demanded from free states in 1837 and 1850 were different than in 1787 (more demanding, because the threat to slavery had increased), but fundamentally the processes were parallel because the exit option (the threat of not signing in 1787, the threat of secession in Calhoun's time) would force decisions to be made on the basis of consensus. And best of all, the crisis over slavery and the South's threatened secession promised to improve and purify the Constitution, just as the crises faced and overcome in 1787 made the resulting constitution stronger. In his final speech Calhoun insisted that the constitutional changes demanded by slave states as a condition of remaining in the Union, including a permanent slave state veto over all acts of the federal government, "at the same time, will improve and strengthen the Government, instead of impairing and weakening it."[67] For, as he argued in the *Disquisition*, "When something *must* be done,—and when it can be done only by the united consent of all,—the necessity of the case will force to a compromise;—be the cause of the necessity what it may."

To this one might reply: sometimes a crisis forces all parties to a compromise, and sometimes not. Some crises end in civil war.

FIVE

■

Calhoun's Defense of Slavery

Calhoun believed that American slavery was just and that all efforts to abolish it were dangerously evil. He was as opposed to schemes for gradual, compensated emancipation as he was to the program of the radical abolitionists and saw no essential distinction between the two.[1] Slavery in the American South was an institution that could and should "exist among us peaceably enough, if undisturbed, for all time." He genuinely hoped to make the Union safe for slaveholders but made clear he would secede rather than allow the rights of slaveholders to be violated.[2]

Calhoun's uncompromising defense of slavery may appear incongruous for a man whose self-described purpose as statesman and theorist was to secure liberty from the threat of unchecked power. But Calhoun himself saw no contradiction. The liberty to own, buy, and sell slaves was in his view a fundamental liberty, at least as important as any other liberties, and under greater threat. If one grants the premise that slaveholding is a fundamental right, there is nothing odd about Calhoun's reasoning. The question is how he justified slavery in the first place.

The question naturally arises: does Calhoun's passionate defense of an abominable institution merit serious and detailed attention? (No such analysis of Calhoun's defense of slavery currently exists.) His *Disquisition on Government* and *Discourse on the Constitution and Government of the United States* clearly deserve serious examination whether or not one ultimately finds them persuasive. But he produced no books or extended pamphlets setting forth his defense of slavery (unlike some of his contemporaries and successors); his proslavery argument is contained in a handful of public speeches and recorded Senate debates. And even if he had published a treatise on the subject, it is doubtful that it would today be taken seriously as political theory.

In my view Calhoun's defense of slavery should be taken seriously for at least two reasons—one reason principally historical, the other theoretical.

Historically Calhoun played a key role in the transition among southern thinkers and political leaders from a "necessary evil" to a "positive good" defense of slavery. Though the individual elements of the proslavery argument he advanced in the 1830s had all been anticipated in one form or another by others, no one previously had made the "positive good" case as comprehensively and forcefully as Calhoun, and none of the predecessors had the national political stature of Calhoun. In his eulogy for Calhoun, Robert Barnwell Rhett of South Carolina credited Calhoun with being the first "great Statesman in the country, who denounced the cant—that slavery is an evil—a curse."[3] South Carolinian James Henry Hammond's eulogy likewise credited Calhoun with leading the fight against abolitionism by proving that slavery was neither a sin nor an evil "since both the white and black races had improved in every point of view under the system."[4] Calhoun's uncompromising defense of slavery helped give antebellum southerners a good conscience about their peculiar institution and reinforced their will to fight for it.

Documenting the historical significance of Calhoun's defense of slavery, however, does not by itself prove it is worth examining as political theory. And, indeed, taken in isolation Calhoun's defense of slavery would not deserve extended theoretical treatment. But what is important is the *interconnection* between his defense of slavery and his broader argument in the *Disquisition* for a consensus-based political order.

Calhoun clearly believed that slavery was essential, or at least very useful, to the effective functioning of a consensus-based political order (keeping in mind that enslaved persons were not parties to the consensus). The proposal to give every "portion or interest" veto rights over collective decisions does not logically require slavery (and perhaps for this reason commentaries on the *Disquisition* tend to ignore slavery). But *effective* functioning of a consensus model requires not merely mutual vetoes, but the capacity to transform potential deadlock into cooperation for the common good. Calhoun believed that slavery made possible a vision of a common good for the entire United States, including those states that chose not to practice the institution themselves.

Calhoun's defense of slavery also raises in especially stark form the question: does the liberty of one individual or group reinforce the liberty of others (at least under the right institutional arrangements)? Or does liberty for some inherently depend upon slavery, or at least lesser liberty, for others?

Calhoun himself appeared to come down on both sides of this question at different times. He clearly rejected the philosophy of natural rights, whereby all men are born free and equal and for that reason entitled to liberty. But at the same time he believed that progress itself depended on liberty and that liberty in turn was the greatest spur to progress. The progress-requires-liberty argument would seem to favor at least a gradual elimination of slavery as a counterpart to social and political progress. Yet Calhoun insisted that slavery for persons of African descent in the United States must be permanent and was deeply hostile to the existence of free blacks in the United States.

Calhoun's insistence on the permanence of African slavery in the United States is more easily reconciled with a somewhat different thesis about freedom. Calhoun argued that slavery was "the most safe and stable basis for free institutions in the world."[5] The idea here is not that the liberty of one reinforces the liberty of another, but the contrary: that "free institutions" for some depend upon slavery for others. If the progress-requires-liberty argument treats liberty as at least potentially capable of universal extension, this "safe and stable basis" argument makes freedom inherently and permanently exclusive.

Eliminating Middle Ground

It was in response to abolitionist petitions to Congress in 1837 that Calhoun declared that slavery as practiced in the American South "is, instead of an evil, a good—a positive good."[6] But Calhoun was not addressing his argument to abolitionists, whose speech and writings he regarded as criminal. He directed his argument against the far more widely held view that slavery was, as Senator William Cabell Rives of Virginia said in response to Calhoun, "a misfortune and an evil in all circumstances, though in some, it might be the lesser evil." It was precisely Calhoun's strategy to eliminate this middle position and force everyone to declare themselves wholly for or wholly against the institution. Senator Rives and others called slavery an evil, yet insisted on protecting the institution against abolitionist attacks. But in fact, Calhoun argued, to call slavery an evil in the abstract was to play into the hands of the abolitionists: "This position, that [slavery] was a moral evil, was the very root of the whole system of operations against it." Calhoun had no patience with men like Rives who condemned slavery in the abstract but defended it in practice. "The gentleman from Virginia [Rives] held it an evil. Yet he would defend it. Surely if it was an evil, moral, social, and political, the Senator, as a wise and virtuous man, was bound to exert himself to put it down."[7]

That Calhoun's principal targets were those who considered slavery a difficult-to-remedy evil is worth emphasizing because scholars sympathetic to Calhoun have often attributed to him exactly the position he was attacking. Clyde Wilson, in his editorial comments in *The Papers of John C. Calhoun* and in other writings, persistently minimizes the extent of Calhoun's belief in the moral rightness of slavery. Wilson portrays a Calhoun who believed in progress, but who understood the "multiple and imperfect America that existed," in contrast to the abolitionists who demanded that society accord with their own ideal vision.[8] This implies that Calhoun recognized slavery as an "imperfection" and merely opposed the utopian manner in which abolitionists sought to remove it. But this contradicts Calhoun's own pronouncements on the subject. Wilson's description of Calhoun resigning himself to a difficult-to-remove imperfection confuses Calhoun's own position with that of Rives. What Calhoun objected to so fiercely was not *how* the abolitionists condemned slavery, but *that* they condemned it. Calhoun saw many imperfections in American society and political life and spared no effort in speaking out and fighting against them; slavery was not one of those imperfections.

In this same 1837 Senate debate Rives accused Calhoun of reviving "the exploded dogmas of Sir Robert Filmer in order to vindicate the institution of slavery in the abstract." To charge Calhoun with supporting slavery "in the abstract" and associate him with Filmer was in effect to accuse Calhoun of supporting autocracy against liberty, and perhaps even of permitting enslavement of members of the white race (for the principal victims of Filmer's absolutist doctrines were white English subjects).[9]

In response Calhoun "utterly denied that his doctrines had anything to do with the tenets of Sir Robert Filmer, which he abhorred" and instead insisted that "he had been the known and open advocate of freedom from the beginning." Calhoun denied that he had pronounced slavery a good "in the abstract" (which would imply that it was good for all peoples and races) and explained instead that slavery "was a good where a civilized race and a race of a different description were brought together." Rather than being good or bad in the abstract, slavery was bad for a civilized race but good for an uncivilized race and essential where circumstances forced a civilized and an uncivilized race to live together. In short, Calhoun's answer to the charge that he supported slavery "in the abstract" was an explicitly racial answer. He was not, he insisted, a follower of Filmer because liberty for the white race was Calhoun's highest concern. "The defence of human liberty against the aggressions of despotic power had been always the most efficient in States where domestic slavery was found to prevail." It was precisely for this reason that slavery was "a great good."[10]

It was also good for the slaves, though Calhoun does not list liberty, patriotism, or courage among its benefits for slaves as he does for their white owners.

> In point of fact, the Central African race (he did not speak of the north or the east of Africa, but of its central regions) had never existed in so comfortable, so respectable, or so civilized a condition, as that which it now enjoyed in the Southern States. The population doubled in the same ratio with that of the whites—a proof of ease and plenty . . . Both races, therefore, appeared to thrive under the practical operation of this institution.[11]

At least as practiced in the American South, Calhoun saw slavery as an engine of social, moral, and political progress. Progress is also an essential theme in his *Disquisition on Government*.

Harmonizing Interests through Slavery

Over the years Calhoun further elaborated upon his argument that slavery was a positive good. His explanation continued to emphasize these two interconnected themes of progress and liberty: progress for both races, liberty for the white race. In a 10 January 1838 speech Calhoun provided what was perhaps his most comprehensive justification for the institution of slavery, pulling together a number of arguments that occur elsewhere in his writings. The speech came in support of Calhoun's own series of resolutions on slavery and the American union (discussed in chapter 4). Calhoun revised the report of the speech and considered publishing it in pamphlet form, so it may be considered an especially authoritative expression of his thinking on slavery:

He saw (said Mr. Calhoun) in the question before us the fate of the South. It was a higher than the mere naked question of master and slave. It involved a great political institution, essential to the peace and existence of one-half of this Union. A mysterious Providence had brought together two races, from different portions of the globe, and placed them together in nearly equal numbers in the Southern portion of this Union. They were there inseparably united, beyond the possibility of separation. Experience had shown that the existing relation between them secured the peace and happiness of both. Each had improved; the inferior greatly; so much so, that it had attained a degree of civilization never before attained by the black race in any age or country. Under no other relation could they co-exist together. To destroy it was to involve a whole region in slaughter, carnage, and desolation; and come what will, we must defend and preserve it.

This agitation has produced one happy effect at least; it has compelled us to the South to look into the nature and character of this great institution, and to correct many false impressions that even we had entertained in relation to it. Many in the South once believed that it was a moral and political evil; that folly and delusion are gone; we see it now in its true light, and regard it as the most safe and stable basis for free institutions in the world. It is impossible with us that the conflict can take place between labor and capital, which makes it so difficult to establish and maintain free institutions in all wealthy and highly civilized nations where such institutions as ours do not exist. The Southern States are an aggregate, in fact, of communities, not of individuals. Every plantation is a little community, with the master at its head, who concentrates in himself the united interests of capital and labor, of which he is the common representative. These small communities aggregated make the State in all, whose action, labor, and capital is equally represented and perfectly harmonized. Hence the harmony, the union, and stability of that section, which is rarely disturbed except through the action of this Government. The blessing of this state of things extends beyond the limits of the South. It makes that section the balance of the system; the great conservative power, which prevents other portions, less fortunately constituted, from rushing into conflict. In this tendency to conflict in the North between labor and capital, which is constantly on the increase, the weight of the South has and will ever be found on the Conservative side; against the aggression of one or the other side, which ever may tend to disturb the equilibrium of our political system. This is our natural position, the salutary influence of which has thus far preserved, and will long continue to preserve, our free institutions, if we should be left undisturbed. Such are the institutions which these madmen [meaning abolitionists] are stirring heaven and earth to destroy, and which we are called on to defend by the highest and most solemn obligations that can be imposed on us as men and patriots.[12]

This passage makes a number of important claims that will guide my analysis of Calhoun's defense of slavery.

First of all, Calhoun defends African slavery as a positive good, rather than continuing the "folly and delusion" that slavery is a "moral and political evil"—an important shift in southern thinking to which Calhoun himself calls attention in the passage. This supposed good of slavery is expressed first of all in terms of the liberty of the slaveholding race: slavery is "the most safe and stable basis for free institutions in the world." Here Calhoun argues, at least implicitly, that the freedom of one group necessarily depends upon lack of freedom for another. Universal freedom is a dangerous error.

Second, the "peace and happiness" and "degree of civilization" of the "inferior" race is included as an additional benefit, though it clearly does not receive as much emphasis as the liberty-for-white-citizens argument. In the southern states the black race "had attained a degree of civilization never before attained by the black race in any age or country."

Third, African slavery in America is of a permanent, not transitional, character. Calhoun asserts that "under no other relation could [the two races] co-exist together" yet also asserts that separation is impossible, from which it follows that slavery must be permanent.

Fourth, Calhoun claims that slavery is good not only for the South but has a "salutary influence" for the entire nation: "The blessing of this state of things extends beyond the limits of the South." The "complete harmony" between capital and labor in the slaveholding section tends to moderate the conflict between labor and capital that afflicts the northern states. The southern states thus can prevent either northern capital or northern labor from committing aggressions against one another. In this way slavery helps to "preserve our free institutions."

Fifth, capital and labor in the South are in complete harmony because the

CHAPTER FIVE

interests of slaves, insofar as persons without rights have "interests" at all, are fully subsumed under the interest of the slave owner, who "concentrates in himself the united interests of capital and labor." The interests of masters and slaves are thus "completely harmonized."

Finally, the complete harmony between master and slave is of a very peculiar and contingent character, however. If not "disturbed" slavery is a source of social peace and stability; but once disturbed the outcome would be "slaughter, carnage, and devastation." Thus the "highest and most solemn obligations" require Calhoun and other "men and patriots" of the South to resist the agitations of "these madmen"—meaning abolitionists.

Exploring or Ignoring Calhoun on Slavery

Now that the essential elements of Calhoun's "positive good" argument for slavery have been laid out, let us turn to Calhoun's *Disquisition* to begin exploring links between his defense of slavery and his political philosophy more generally.

Calhoun's fervent defense of "the peculiar institution" poses peculiar problems for modern-day interpretations of his political theory. Calhoun's fundamental argument in the *Disquisition* was that the only way to prevent one group from exercising tyranny over another is to give every "portion or interest" of society "either a concurrent voice in making and executing the laws, or a veto on their execution."[13] Calhoun insisted the slaveholding minority must have the power to veto decisions of the majority. But slaves themselves were to have no veto rights, nor indeed any rights of any kind.

The simplest solution to this apparently glaring inconsistency is to "bracket" Calhoun's defense of slavery, to treat it as logically independent of his political theory. However important slavery was to Calhoun and the South, the argument would go, this is irrelevant to the theory that political orders can be governed by consensus rather than majority rule. That the particular minority Calhoun sought to protect was the minority of slave owners would, on this argument, be a mere historical accident. Indeed, Calhoun's own minority-veto idea could be employed today to protect the rights and interests of the very racial minority Calhoun sought to keep in slavery.[14]

But Calhoun's defense of slavery was interconnected with his broader political theory in ways that make a clean "bracketing" of slavery impossible. Calhoun's political theory was not necessarily a seamless proslavery web. But to separate Calhoun's theory from his defense of slavery is a slow process, dependent upon an internal critique of his argument. To simply ignore slavery leaves a distorted picture of his theory.

Scholarly commentaries on Calhoun's political philosophy have typically disconnected it from his fervent defense of slavery.[15] On the other side, at least some (though not all) of Calhoun's biographers have recognized his commitment to slavery.[16] And among historians of antebellum America—especially those treating the slavery crisis—Calhoun's key role in the political and constitutional defense of slavery is on full display.[17] But the nature of the historical and biographical works precludes much analysis of Calhoun's proslavery argument in relation to his political theory more generally, and in some works Calhoun's entire political theory is treated as an elaborate rationalization for slavery. My aim here (and in the following chapter) is to explore interconnections between Calhoun's defense of slavery and his broader political theory without reducing the latter entirely to the former.

There are several types of interconnections, negative as well as positive, between Calhoun's defense of slavery and his broader argument in the *Disquisition*. First, there are lines of argument in the *Disquisition* that do not directly endorse slavery, but function to weaken arguments against slavery. The most obvious example here is Calhoun's rejecting the premise that all men are born free and equal and therefore entitled to equal natural rights. Second, there are lines of argument in the *Disquisition* that would seem to condemn slavery if pursued consistently, and that seem glaringly inconsistent with Calhoun's own strong support of slavery. The clearest example here is Calhoun's argument that moral, intellectual, and economic progress is the fruit of liberty, which would seem hard to reconcile with his insistence on permanent slavery for the black race in America. One might ask whether Calhoun himself saw any contradiction, and if so how he believed he had resolved it. Third, there are passages in the *Disquisition* which, though they do not directly mention slavery, closely paraphrase other Calhoun writings and speeches that directly defend slavery. The clearest case here is Calhoun's insistence that certain people are "unprepared for liberty." Finally, Calhoun's description in the *Disquisition* of how exercise of veto rights would force deliberation in the common good closely parallels how Calhoun believed northern states could be persuaded that slavery benefited the entire United States.

The purpose of constitutional government, Calhoun observed in the *Disquisition,* was to "furnish the means by which resistance may be systematically and peaceably made on the part of the ruled, to oppression and abuse of power on the part of the rulers."[18] But he clearly did not intend this principle to apply to slaves, who had by definition no legal and peaceable means of resisting those who ruled them. Even though slavery is not specifically mentioned in the *Disquisition,* the argumentative niche Calhoun elsewhere used explicitly to justify slavery is clearly visible in that work. "It is a great and dangerous error to suppose that all people are equally entitled to liberty," he remarked in the *Disquisition.* "It is a reward to be earned, not a blessing to be gratuitously lavished on all alike," a blessing not to be "bestowed on a people too ignorant, degraded and vicious, to be capable either of appreciating or of enjoying it."[19] Thus everything Calhoun said in the *Disquisition* and elsewhere about protecting liberty against unchecked power was restricted to those "entitled to liberty"; to those deemed not entitled to liberty, an entirely different set of principles would apply. In his 27 June 1848 speech on the Oregon Bill, Calhoun asserted directly that the black race in the South was "utterly unqualified to possess liberty."[20] Thus for Calhoun the black race in the South (and in the North also, as we shall see) fell into the *Disquisition's* "unqualified for liberty" category.

Calhoun's distinction between those who were and were not "entitled to liberty" (or to any checks whatsoever against arbitrary power) suggests some obvious questions. What specific criteria distinguish those entitled to liberty from those who are not? How does this supposed dichotomy originate? Was the supposed status of being "unqualified to possess liberty" the result of circumstances and environment and therefore remediable, or a permanent condition? Did Calhoun believe in inherent racial inferiority?[21]

The argument of the *Disquisition,* on the face of it, would seem to support an environmentalist interpretation of Calhoun's claim about the difference between those prepared for liberty and those not prepared. From the opening pages of the work, Calhoun's argument presupposes a universal human nature apparently applicable to all nations and peoples: that "man is so constituted as to be a social being" yet feels "more intensely what affects him directly, than what affects him indirectly through others." This assumption of a universal human nature does not, however, lead Calhoun to embrace a theory of universal natural rights; he specifically rejects the premise that men are born free, equal, and independent and by that fact alone entitled to certain rights and liberties. On the contrary, he asserts, man has "never been found, in any age or country, in any state other than the social. In no other, indeed, could he exist; and in no other,—were it possible for him to exist,— could he attain to a full development of his moral and intellectual faculties, or raise himself, in the scale of being, much above the level of the brute creation."[22] Liberty is not a natural right but depends upon the actual conditions under which one lives and one's level of moral and intellectual development.

Liberty thus depends on individual and societal progress, and Calhoun makes clear that progress proceeds slowly. This point is underscored by Calhoun's distinction between government and constitution. No society can exist without government: "Like breathing, it is not permitted to depend on our volition. Necessity will force it on all communities in some one form or another." Government of some type, however brutal or arbitrary, will always exist and thus does not depend upon progress. To form an adequate *constitutional* government, however, which will "counteract the tendency of government to oppression and abuse," while remaining strong enough to fulfill the essential functions of government, is "one of the most difficult tasks imposed on man." Thousands of years of progress have been necessary to create the still-imperfect constitutions enjoyed by civilized peoples of the present day. Conversely, individuals or communities who "may be so sunk in ignorance and vice, as to be incapable of forming a conception of liberty" cannot live under anything other than "an absolute and despotic government." Here again Calhoun has prepared a niche in the *Disquisition* for justifying slavery, without actually using the word. Slavery, it would follow, as the most obvious form of "absolute and despotic government," was inevitable for those "sunk in ignorance and vice."[23]

The argument thus far might seem to justify slavery under certain conditions, without obviously presupposing any inherent racial inferiority. Calhoun's observation about the long time span of social and political progress suggests that all races, including his own, existed at one time in a primitive condition that made them unprepared for liberty. Recall that Calhoun's own explicit justification of slavery as a "positive good" was closely related to the theme of progress: slavery was an engine of civilization and progress for both the race of masters and the race of slaves. The argument of the *Disquisition* thus lends support to Calhoun's defense of slavery in at least three different ways: first, by rejecting the theory of natural right; second, by asserting that despotic government is inevitable for those at a low stage of civilization; and third, by making liberty itself dependent on the level of social and political progress.

Yet when examined more closely, the argument of the *Disquisition* falls short of a convincing justification for slavery as practiced in the United States in Calhoun's time. To argue that despotic government is "inevitable" for peoples at the lowest levels of civilization is not the same as claiming that slavery itself is an engine of moral and intellectual progress, which Calhoun's "positive good" argument asserts. To claim that peoples still living under barbaric conditions in primitive parts of the world are unprepared for free government (which even Calhoun's abolitionist opponents would have assumed about pagan Africa) does very little to justify permanent slavery for people of African descent whose ancestors had lived for generations in the United States and thus benefited from the supposedly high level of American civilization. In short: there is a glaring tension, at the very least, between the claim that slavery is inevitable at a low level of civilization (for all races) and the claim that permanent slavery is itself an engine of civilization and progress (for a particular race).

The apparent contradiction becomes even more striking when we examine closely Calhoun's own argument about how moral and intellectual progress proceeds. Calhoun argues at length in the *Disquisition* that liberty, and the right to keep the fruit of one's labors, are indispensable to moral, intellectual, and economic progress. This would seem powerfully to argue that the state of slavery was detrimental to the "progress" and "civilization" of enslaved persons. Nevertheless Calhoun somehow turns progress-is-the-fruit-of-liberty into an argument *for* slavery by equating opposition to slavery with a more general "leveling" impulse that will endanger all progress:

Inequality of condition, while it is a necessary consequence of liberty, is, at the same time, indispensable to progress . . . The main spring to progress is, the desire of individuals to better their condition; and . . . the strongest impulse which can be given to it is, to leave individuals free to exert themselves in the manner they may deem best for that purpose . . . Now, as individuals differ greatly from each other, in intelligence, sagacity, energy, perseverance, skill, habits of industry and economy, physical power, position and opportunity,—the necessary effect of leaving all free to exert themselves to better their condition, must be a corresponding inequality between those who may possess these qualities and advantages in a high degree, and those who may be deficient in them . . . To force the front rank back to the rear, or attempt to push forward the rear into line with the front, by the interposition of the government, would put an end to the impulse, and effectually arrest the march of progress.

He concludes this argument against the leveling impulse by asserting that "these great and dangerous errors have their origin in the prevalent opinion that all men are born free and equal;—than which nothing can be more unfounded and false." Men are not born into any state of nature, but "born in the social and political state; and of course, instead of being born free and equal, are born subject, not only to parental authority, but to the laws and institutions of the country where born, and under whose protection they draw their first breath."[24] This passage from the *Disquisition* is a condensed version of a similar argument in Calhoun's 1848 speech on the Oregon Bill, which is a long defense of slavery.[25]

In short, the entire passage from the *Disquisition* quoted above, in praise of liberty and the freedom of individuals to better their condition, functions among other things as a defense of slavery. It is not only that—it would also apply to social orders that do not practice slavery—but defending slavery is one of its clear purposes. What must strike modern readers, and at least some of Calhoun's contemporaries, as a bizarre conclusion—the liberty to enjoy the fruits of one's labor is the driving force of human progress, and that is why abolitionist agitation is so dangerous—did not appear strange to Calhoun. For in Calhoun's view, one could not attack ownership of slave property without attacking property rights as such, and thus engaging in exactly the kind of leveling and deprivation of the fruits of one's labor that halts moral and intellectual progress. "The first victims [of abolitionist doctrines] would be the wealthy and talented of the North. We of the South are by far the most safe."[26] (It is as though Calhoun believed the subordination of black slave to white master resulted from some previous, perfectly free and fair competition, the unequal results of which must now be protected.)

At one level there is nothing at all peculiar about Calhoun's linking a defense of slavery with the argument that human progress is the fruit of liberty. If the liberty at issue is the liberty of white citizens to use their talents to acquire property, which may very well include property in slaves, then Calhoun's argument makes sense. The southern slave economy was in fact, as recent research has shown, a profitable and competitive mode of production, not a stagnant, backward institution doomed to inevitable economic demise.[27] To insist on the "dangerous error" that all men are entitled to liberty, to deny the legitimacy (even threaten to confiscate) a certain form of property, would directly threaten this fruitful engine of economic progress.

Calhoun's progress-as-fruit-of-liberty argument is puzzling only if one insists that it apply to slaves, which was not what Calhoun intended. No consistency problem would arise if he had merely claimed that progress for the black race was unimportant. But because elsewhere Calhoun justified slavery as an engine of progress for the black race, one is left to wonder why in his view the conditions of progress for one race were so diametrically opposed to the conditions of progress for another. If some elements of Calhoun's argument can be given a race-neutral, environmentalist interpretation, the contradictory assumptions about what produces progress for these two races inhabiting North America suggests something else is going on.

One might attempt to rescue Calhoun's consistency by imagining him encouraging manumission (as opposed to a general emancipation) as a reward for especially intelligent, energetic, and responsible slaves. Thus the hope of individually escaping slavery might stimulate the intellectual and moral progress of slaves. This line of argument would suggest that, as blacks under slavery made moral and intellectual progress, the proportion of free persons of color would increase and the proportion that remained enslaved gradually diminish.

The argument outline above is not illogical. The problem is that it directly contradicts Calhoun's own position on free blacks. He was deeply suspicious of the existence of free persons of color, whom he regarded as both miserable and dangerous and who undermined the ideological foundations of slavery. This requires us to examine Calhoun's position not only on slavery but on race.

Calhoun and Race

In certain respects Calhoun was absolutely clear on matters of race. American slavery was justified because it involved the enslavement of an uncivilized by a civilized race. Calhoun also made clear that white racial solidarity—the common bond among white Americans generated by their feeling superior to blacks—was essential not only to the institution of slavery itself, but also to the health of American democracy more generally (a theme taken up later in the chapter). Calhoun left no doubt that his defense of slavery and his vision of American democracy depended on racial hierarchy.

But on the specific question of the inherent character of the black race,

Calhoun was relatively tight-lipped. In Calhoun's papers one encounters occasional references to Africans as an "inferior race." For example, speaking in opposition to Henry Clay's motion to allow the American Colonization Society to operate in the District of Columbia, Calhoun asserted that "A mysterious Providence [a delicate reference to the Atlantic slave trade] had brought the black and the white people together from different parts of the globe, and no human power could now separate them. The whites are an European race, being masters; and the Africans are the inferior race, and slaves."[28] Here Calhoun referred to Africans as an inferior race, but without further description, and in a way that did not obviously distinguish him from the way nearly all white Americans of his time—whatever their position on slavery—talked about blacks.

In his relative silence on what he specifically believed made blacks inferior, Calhoun contrasted with some other well-known contemporary defenders of slavery. Fellow South Carolinian William Harper's *Memoir on Slavery,* which was published the same year (1837) that Calhoun delivered his famous "positive good" speech, details at length the supposedly inferior character of the race: "the African is an inferior variety of the human race, of less elevated character, and more limited intellect" whose "physiognomy" is clearly "that of a brute when compared to that of the Caucasian race."[29] Calhoun might have thought this way, but for whatever reason he did not speak this way. He merely called the race "inferior" with respect to its degree of "civilization" and moved on without further explanation.

Calhoun's brevity on the subject makes it possible, at least initially, to attribute to him widely divergent underlying assumptions about race. At one extreme, one might hypothesize that Calhoun's characterization of the black race as "inferior" with regard to "civilization" follows the environmentalist approach of the *Disquisition,* which presupposes a universal human nature but then requires thousands of years of social evolution to produce men prepared for liberty. Though it was almost universally assumed by white Americans in Calhoun's time that blacks were "inferior," it was possible to debate whether this supposed inferiority was the result of contingent (and therefore correctible) factors or an inherent fact of nature.[30] If we take the *Disquisition* as our starting point, Calhoun might seem to come down on the side of the environmentalist argument. But as we've seen, the *Disquisition*'s progress-as-fruit-of-liberty argument is impossible to reconcile with Calhoun's commitment to permanent slavery for African Americans except via an unspoken assumption of racial difference.

Calhoun's relative silence can also be given the opposite interpretation: that out of delicacy he refrained from expressing racial views that would have offended even his contemporaries. In this connection we should examine a fascinating anecdote about Calhoun. Josiah Nott (1804–1873), a physician from Mobile, built upon the racial speculations of Samuel Morton of Philadelphia, one of the pioneers in the new field of "racial science," but took Morton's ideas to far more extreme conclusions. In *Types of Mankind* (1854) Nott and coauthor George Gliddon claimed that the white and black races were actually different species, separately evolved, and that the black race (or species) had "not a single civilization, spontaneous or borrowed . . . to adorn its gloomy past" nor had any Negro "ever written a page worthy of being remembered." Nott's writings were controversial even in the South, not because of their routine assertions of racial inferiority, but because the claim of separate origins flew in the face of Biblical authority.[31]

Nott enlisted the authority of Calhoun (by then conveniently dead) in his battles with religious orthodoxy. The "original diversity of races" and the "consequent permanence of moral and intellectual peculiarities" were truths, Nott claimed, that "had long been familiar to the master-mind of JOHN C. CALHOUN; who regarded them to be of . . . paramount importance." Nott claims that in May 1844, when Calhoun was secretary of state and engaged in sensitive diplomatic negotiations with France and England over the annexation of Texas, Calhoun showed Nott's coauthor Gliddon a draft of his "celebrated letter to Mr. King" (William R. King, U.S. Minister to France) of 12 August 1844. Calhoun (the story goes) felt he could not adequately respond to France without being prepared to discuss "the radical difference of humanity's races" and for that reason needed Gliddon's help. Gliddon provided Calhoun with two of Samuel Morton's books, "which Mr. Calhoun studied with no less pleasure than profit" and "soon perceived that the conclusions which he had long before drawn from history [about the radical difference of races] . . . were entirely corroborated by the plain teachings of modern science." Nott then reports subsequent private conversations with Calhoun in which the latter assured Nott of his complete agreement with his "true ethnological science," but that he refrained from endorsing it publicly because of the "inconvenience" it would have created for his diplomatic work.[32]

This story is accepted at face value by some historians.[33] It is not impossible that Calhoun accepted Nott's theory of racial difference but for political reasons kept it to himself, and there is no way to confirm or deny what Calhoun said in private conversations. But the evidence for this particular version of events comes entirely from Nott, who notoriously thrived on controversy. Calhoun's own papers offer inconclusive support for the story and conflict with it on several particulars. What Calhoun wrote about slavery and race in his August 1844 letter to King (for which Gliddon and Nott's racial science was allegedly decisive) was indistinguishable from what Calhoun said in his April 1844 letter to British envoy Richard Pakenham (discussed below), before Calhoun had met Gliddon. Gliddon did send letters to Calhoun expounding on racial science and Morton sent Calhoun his book *Crania Aegyptica* (which "inquired into the social position of the Negro race in the earliest periods of authentic history"). But there is no extant response from Calhoun to Gliddon's racial speculations, and in Calhoun's brief September 1844 letter to Morton, he merely expressed an interest in "Egyptian antiquities" and apologized that the demands of time had prevented him from reading the book.[34] There is no way of knowing from Calhoun's extant papers whether he ever studied Morton's works closely or embraced Nott's own more extreme theory that Africans were a distinct species.

Nott's story provides weak evidence, at best, for Calhoun's own views on race. But there is much stronger evidence from Calhoun's own hand that he believed in the inherent and unalterable inferiority of the black race. This evidence comes across in Calhoun's hostility to free blacks.

Calhoun defended the constitutionality of a South Carolina law, the Negro Seamen Act, passed in the wake of the 1822 Denmark Vesey conspiracy (discussed later in this chapter), "requiring all colored seamen to be seized and jailed while their ships remained in Charleston harbor."[35] The act applied both to colored residents (including citizens) of other American states and to subjects of other nations. The law, which Calhoun acknowledged "came into conflict with our commercial treaty with Great Britain" (who understandably objected to arbitrary incarceration of its subjects), was challenged in federal court by U.S. Attorney General William Wirt but continued to be enforced by South Carolina. Calhoun asserted that the federal government not only had no right to challenge state laws of this kind, but was duty bound "to cooperate in upholding and sustaining them."[36] In 1828 Calhoun had himself helped to draft regulations for the District of Columbia prohibiting "people of color" (including free black citizens from northern states) from frequenting the Capitol or public square "except on necessary business." He maintained that no person of African descent could be a citizen of the United

States, even if the individual was a citizen of the state in which he resided: the U.S. government had "no more to do with free negroes than with slaves."[37]

In 1825 Calhoun expressed his absolute opposition to sending an American representative to the Assembly of American Nations at Panama (which President John Quincy Adams had considered). The problem for Calhoun was that this would entail implicit recognition of Haiti, a participant in the congress. Calhoun phrased his opposition not, as one might expect, as response to the racial massacres that occurred in the early years of Haitian independence, but as a simple objection to allowing a black minister to be accepted as an equal in the nation's capital. His argument against receiving black ministers would apply not just to Haiti but to black citizens or subjects of any nation in the world.

> It is a delicate subject, and would in the present tone of feelings to the South lead to great mischief. It is not so much the recognition simply, as what must follow it. We must send and receive ministers; and what would be our social relations with a Black minister at Washington? Must he be received or excluded from our dinners, our dances and our parties, and must his daughters and sons participate in the society of our daughters and sons? Small as these considerations appear to be they involve the peace and perhaps the union of this nation.[38]

Calhoun realized that slavery in the American South depended ideologically upon a doctrine of racial inferiority that would be undermined by receiving black diplomats as equals in the nation's capital.

Calhoun's most explicit argument to this effect came in his 18 April 1844 letter, in his capacity as President Tyler's secretary of state, to the British Minister, Richard Pakenham. Calhoun supported the annexation of Texas on explicitly proslavery grounds, fearing that an independent Texas might accept British recognition in exchange for abolishing slavery, which Calhoun believed would gravely threaten the stability of slavery in the southern states. Because British policies toward Texas were justified by the claim that slavery was a moral evil (though Calhoun believed the real motivations were economic), he responded with a defense of the rightness and benefits of slavery. Key to his defense of slavery was the supposed misery and degeneration of free persons of color:

The census and other authentic documents show that, in all instances in which the States have changed the former relation between the two races, the condition of the African, instead of being improved, has become worse. They have invariably sunk into vice and pauperism, accompanied by the bodily and mental inflictions incident thereto—deafness, blindness, insanity and idiocy, to a degree without example; while, in all other States which have retained the ancient relation between them, they have improved greatly in every respect—in number, comfort, intelligence, and morals.

Calhoun claimed the 1840 census demonstrated that 1 in every 96 Negroes in free states was deaf, dumb, blind, idiot, or insane, while in slave states the proportion was only 1 out of 672. He claimed that in Maine (a state hostile to the expansion of slavery) the proportion of mentally or physically defective Negroes was 1 in 12.[39]

In the Pakenham letter Calhoun was not merely claiming it would be a mistake to abolish slavery in the states where it still existed; he also suggested the northern states that abolished slavery in the years following the American Revolution had made a mistake in doing so and ought to have retained the "ancient relation." Whatever Calhoun may have believed was the cause of blacks' supposed degeneration in America outside the framework of slavery, one thing is clear: his vision of progress and civilization for Americans of African descent did not include release from the state of slavery.

The controversy over the 1840 census did not end with the Pakenham letter. As secretary of state, in his diplomatic correspondence, Calhoun continued to cite the 1840 census and its supposed proofs of the degenerate condition of free blacks in the northern states. In his 12 August 1844 letter to King, Calhoun repeated the claim that in "the Northern States of our Union . . . statistical facts, not to be shaken, prove, that the freed negro, after the experience of sixty years, is in a far worse condition, than in the other States, where he has been left in his former condition."[40] As secretary of state it was Calhoun's responsibility to respond to congressional inquiries into problems with the 1840 census. His response to the congressional inquiry contains what is probably his single most revealing remark directly on the subject of race.

Calhoun relied on the 1840 census in the Pakenham letter for his claims about the higher rate of "deafness, blindness, insanity and idiocy" among blacks living in free states. But this census contained some obvious flaws that

CHAPTER FIVE

were subsequently pointed out to Calhoun—for example, that the number of insane black individuals listed as residing in several Massachusetts cities was far larger than the total black population of the same cities.[41] In February 1845 Calhoun responded to the congressional request to correct the census errors. In the face of clear flaws in the census, which undermined his argument about the inevitable degeneracy of free blacks, Calhoun simply denied the evidence and restated his argument with increased vehemence. "The correctness of the late Census, in exhibiting a far greater prevalence of the diseases of insanity, blindness, deafness, and dumbness, stands unimpeachable." Calhoun then observes:

Why the fact should be so is a question of deep import. Without undertaking to investigate it, it may be asserted, that the cause, be it what it may, must be deep and durable. None other can account for the uniformity of its operation through so many States respectively, of such wide extent, and placed in such different conditions.

The other conclusion, not less irresistible, is, that so far from bettering the condition of the negro or African race, by changing the relation between it and the European, as it now exists in the Slave-holding-States, it would render it far worse. It would be, indeed, to them, a curse instead of a blessing.[42]

This passage leaves little doubt that Calhoun subscribed to a doctrine of inherent racial inferiority and that this doctrine is crucial to his defense of slavery. Here, as elsewhere, he refrains from speculating on the cause of the African's supposed inferiority ("be it what it may"). But he claims that it must be "deep and durable" and simultaneously at work everywhere, under a wide variety of particular conditions. This is incompatible with an environmentalist explanation of the African's supposed inferiority, because that would entail different results under different conditions. The fact that Calhoun restates the claim in the face of direct evidence to the contrary indicates how deeply he held the view. That he calls the supposed degeneracy of free blacks a matter of "deep import" shows he considered the premise of inherent racial inferiority to be essential, not tangential, to his defense of slavery.

This suggests, in turn, that Calhoun himself realized his rejection of natural right in favor of an evolutionary account of society and government did not by itself provide a strong enough support for slavery. Advocates of the principle "all men are created equal," when they defended slavery, were forced to resort to a doctrine of racial inferiority to restrict the application of the principle. Doctrines of racial inferiority might seem less necessary to Calhoun since he rejected this natural rights philosophy in the first place. But Calhoun's own remark that these racial assertions were a matter of "deep import" suggests that in the end his evolutionary account of society and government failed to justify slavery without a similar ideological patch.

Whites, Blacks, and Indians

One might attempt to defend Calhoun by arguing that, even if he shared widespread assumptions of racial inferiority, he nevertheless genuinely believed in and valued the moral and intellectual progress of the African race under slavery. But when one turns to Calhoun's few attempts to specify the civilizing effects of slavery, what is striking is how vague and limited they are, and how starkly they contrast with his vision of progress for white citizens enjoying the benefits of slavery. "The population doubled in the same ratio with that of the whites—a proof of ease and plenty; while, with respect to civilization, it nearly kept pace with that of the owners; and as to the effect upon the whites, would it be affirmed that they were inferior to others, that they were less patriotic, less intelligent, less humane, less brave, than where slavery did not exist?"[43] In the space of a single sentence, Calhoun here simultaneously claimed that slavery civilized both races and applied quite different criteria of civilization to the two races.

The claim that southern slaves enjoyed a higher standard of living than wage laborers under capitalism was debated in Calhoun's time and continues to be debated; the increase in population among American slaves is undisputed.[44] It is nevertheless striking that for Africans the only specific criteria of civilization Calhoun listed were population growth and "ease and plenty"—both of them questionable markers of moral and intellectual progress. When Calhoun spoke of moral progress for whites as a beneficial consequence of slavery, he mentioned not only population growth and material well-being, but intelligence, patriotism, and courage—qualities dangerous in a slave. Calhoun might have implicitly included Christianization of slaves under "civilization," but if so he did not emphasize it. To make Christianization of slaves a principal argument for slavery was a politically risky defense, one easily turned into an argument against slavery by evangelical-minded abolitionists. Population growth and "ease and plenty" may have seemed to Calhoun less vulnerable to political dispute.

Even more revealing are the criteria of progress and civilization that Calhoun does *not* speak of in describing the civilizing effects of slavery—above all, literacy and other elements of basic education. The slave codes of the South specifically forbade slaves from being taught to read, and South Carolina's slave code was the harshest of all.[45] Calhoun nowhere indicated that this prohibition should be lifted; to do so would be incompatible with his fierce struggle to prevent the circulation of any "incendiary" writings in slave states.[46] If any significant number of slaves were literate, Calhoun's efforts to suppress incendiary petitions, speeches, and pamphlets would certainly fail.

Elsewhere Calhoun clearly indicated that literacy and enjoyment of property rights were essential to the civilization of a "backward" people. When he was President James Monroe's secretary of war, Calhoun was responsible for Indian Affairs, and in that capacity put some thought into Indian education and the terms of coexistence between Indians and whites. In his 1819 "Regulations Concerning the Civilization of the Indians" he wrote: "The plan of education, in addition to reading, writing and arithmetic, should, in the instruction of the boys, extend to the practical knowledge of the mode of agriculture, and of such of the mechanic arts as are suited to the condition of the Indians; and in that of the girls, to spinning, weaving, and sewing." He envisioned this as an educational program leading to economic self-sufficiency and (at least in some cases) citizenship. He proposed that if the Cherokees were willing to "condense their population, take reservations, become farmers and mechanics" they could be "admitted to the privileges of citizens." Calhoun himself sponsored the legal education of a Choctaw youth, James McDonald.[47]

He supported the policy of westward removal of Indian tribes, but insisted that it be done with as much respect for the rights of Indians as possible. During the 1830s he opposed President Andrew Jackson's forced removal of the Cherokees and Jackson's Indian policy generally for creating unnecessary conflict with the Indians because of corruption and incompetence. In 1838 Calhoun opposed a bill designed to crowd a large number of different Indian tribes, from all over the United States, into the same small location in the Southwest. Calhoun argued that it was necessary to consider "what effect it would have on the Indians themselves. He held that all which was done relating to the Indians was an experiment, but he was anxious that we should persevere with it with wisdom and caution, and see if they could be saved and civilized." He went on to imply that Indians were entitled to Lockean principles of self-government.[48] By the 1830s he seemed sadly resigned, however, to the fact that U.S. policy toward the Indians would not be carried out with the benefit of the Indians in mind.

Calhoun's position on civilizing the Indians would not meet modern-day standards of racial and ethnic equality. But what is important here is the contrast between Calhoun's specific vision of civilizing Indians and his almost entirely empty vision of civilizing Africans under slavery. He clearly cared about, and thought about, American Indians; there is no evidence that he cared about or thought about African Americans to an equivalent degree. It may be that Calhoun believed Africans were an inferior race, while Indians were not (this particular double standard being fairly common in the history of American racial ideology).[49] Or he may have regarded the "experiment" of genuinely civilizing Indians as compatible with the interests of the white majority while any experiment in fully civilizing Africans was not. (These explanations are not mutually exclusive.) In any event, if Calhoun's program for the Indians illustrated his own criteria for civilizing a "half-savage race," then Calhoun's vision of the future of African Americans under slavery cannot be described as civilization.

Slavery, Capitalism, and Class Conflict

Calhoun's claims about the "positive good" of slavery for the enslaved race were empty. But his understanding of the positive good of slavery for white citizens was another matter. He had a clearly worked out vision of the benefits—economic, moral, political—of the institution of racial slavery for the United States, North as well as South. And the supposed positive good of slavery was, at least in Calhoun's own thinking, consistent with the *Disquisition*'s description of a common good that transcends the narrow interests of any particular interest or section. (Recall that for Calhoun the slaves themselves had no legitimate "interests" distinct from their owners.)

The most obvious "positive good" of slavery for the United States as a whole was that southern plantations produced products essential to northern manufacture at a crucial point in America's Industrial Revolution. The products of southern plantations, Calhoun observed, "stimulate and render [the North's] capital and labor profitable; while our slaves furnish, at the same time, an extensive and profitable market for what they make." Without the cotton, rice, and tobacco produced by slave labor, Calhoun asks, what would become of Lowell and Waltham, New York and Boston? Calhoun here was speaking in Charleston to skeptical South Carolinians who must have suspected that antislavery agitation originated in irreconcilable differences of economic interest between North and South. On the contrary Calhoun claimed—repeating himself for emphasis—that "the crusade against our domestic institution does not originate in hostility of interests."[50]

But Calhoun's vision of slavery as a positive good for the whole United States was not limited to narrowly economic concerns or mere exchange of products. At least as important was the moral and intellectual progress he believed slaveholding encouraged (and abolitionism destroyed). Recall Calhoun's observation in the *Disquisition* (quoted earlier in the chapter) that "intelligence, sagacity, energy, perseverance, skill, habit of industry and economy" all result from leaving individuals free to better their condition and providing them secure rights to the fruits of their labor. This argument, apparently opposed to slavery, can be turned into a proslavery argument by treating the labor of the slave as a direct extension of the labor of the slave owner. To threaten the institution of slavery, in Calhoun's view, was to threaten an individual's right to the fruits of his labor and thus to endanger the moral as well as narrowly economic benefits of free markets. It was for this reason he insisted that the principal victims of abolitionist doctrines "would be the wealthy and talented of the North."

Calhoun further claimed (in the long passage quoted early in this chapter) that slavery solved the labor problems of capitalism. "It is impossible with us that the conflict can take place between labor and capital, which makes it so difficult to establish and maintain free institutions as in all wealthy and highly civilized nations where such institutions as ours do not exist." The reasoning behind the claim is that the slave owner "concentrates in himself the united interests of capital and labor, of which he is the common representative" and in that way labor relations were "perfectly harmonized." (This perfect harmony depended, of course, on keeping the minds of slaves completely uninfected by abolitionist doctrines, and on repressive regulations preventing slaves from formulating any autonomous interest separate from the state of slavery.)

Calhoun did not mean that northern capitalist enterprises should switch to slave labor. The benefit they got from southern slavery (besides their obvious interest in southern-produced staples) was indirect: the South represented a "conservative power" that could intervene to oppose "aggression of one or the other side" and keep the political system in equilibrium. Because the slave owner owns both capital and labor, there could be no conflict between capital and labor as in the North or in England.

This line of argument has a familiar ring, in part because later proslavery writers (among them James Henry Hammond and George Fitzhugh) developed it in greater detail and took it in new directions. It was this argument that led Richard Hofstadter to label Calhoun "the Marx of the Master Class," meaning that Calhoun anticipated Marx's conception of class struggle in advanced capitalism but proposed slavery rather than proletarian revolution as the solution.[51] The formulation is an intriguing one which, despite the obvious anachronism in naming Marx, highlights one aspect of Calhoun's common-good defense of slavery. But it imports a number of misleading connotations, and misses some of the most important sources of Calhoun's conviction that slavery was a positive good. "The Marx of the Master Class" label implies that Calhoun's defense of slavery originated as a response to the class conflicts of capitalism. To mention Marx is already to imply that conflicts among capital and labor are fierce and ultimately irreconcilable and that one must take sides.

Calhoun, however, belonged to an earlier generation than Marx that predated full development of capitalist class relations. In Calhoun's formative years he was far more concerned with the political health of a constitutional republic than with conflicts between capital and labor. Calhoun's own experience from the tariff battles of 1828–1833 encouraged the quite different assumption that northern labor and capital had *shared* interests and that the principal conflicts of interest were sectional. His remedy against overreaching on the part of any one geographic interest—state nullification of federal law—would be obviously inadequate where the principal conflicts occurred *within* states and regions (as with capitalist class conflict) rather than between geographic sections.

In the last two decades of Calhoun's life capitalist class conflicts became too obvious to overlook. He recognized them but never considered them necessary or functional. Wherever deep differences of interest begin to develop within a single state, as was "perceptible in some of the larger and more populous members of the Union" (he remarked in his 1833 Force Bill speech), this was "the invariable forerunner of corruption and convulsions." Political as well as economic health consisted in reciprocity between sections and harmony within them.[52]

All this is necessary to understand what Calhoun meant in calling slavery a remedy to the class conflicts of capitalism and how he imagined that remedy to work. He clearly did not see himself as siding with northern capital against northern labor, as the "Marx of the Master Class" label would suggest. Calhoun did observe that "it was an inevitable law of society that one portion of the community depended upon the labor of another portion, over which it must unavoidably exercise control." It would seem necessarily to follow from this "inevitable law" that northern white wage laborers were slaves under another name. But unlike some other defenders of slavery, Calhoun did not draw this particular conclusion (which would have entailed endorsing slavery "in the abstract" and thus without regard to race); instead this line of thought led him directly to the importance of racial hierarchy.[53] In Calhoun's view, northern free white wage laborers were fellow citizens of the republic—as well as fellow members of the white race—and their interests deserved consideration.

Calhoun genuinely saw himself, and the slaveholding class in general, as the judicious friend of both northern capital and northern labor, able to intervene to counter the aggressions of either side against the other. It was in this way—by carrying forward an ideal of republican reciprocity that predated fully developed capitalism—that Calhoun imagined slavery would resolve the class conflicts of capitalism. Calhoun was neither pro-capitalist nor anti-capitalism; capitalism was healthy and good as long as its destructive tendencies were moderated by the medicine of slavery.

In examining Calhoun's claim that slavery counteracted the class conflicts of capitalism it is also important to get the chronology right. He did not first notice the problems of capitalism and then decide slavery was a positive good; it was the other way around. The class conflicts of capitalism provided Calhoun with an additional argument for a conviction he had held, on other grounds, long before the labor problems of capitalism were a major issue in the United States. Calhoun's conviction that slavery was a positive good was more deeply rooted in his preoccupation with preserving republican virtue and counteracting the dangerous tendencies of universal (white male) suffrage.

As early as the mid-1820s, during his nationalist phase before his turn to nullification, Calhoun had associated slavery with political health and virtue, in contrast to political corruption and patronage, which he believed posed a grave threat to republican liberty. In an 1826 letter he wrote: "I am deeply impressed with the belief, that there can be no reaction in favour of liberty in the present state of our country, which does not come from the slave holding states, headed by Virginia and sustained by Pennsylvania." Note here that Calhoun first associates political virtue with a slaveholding state, then immediately places a non-slaveholding state (Pennsylvania) in the role of partner and beneficiary of the slaveholding state's virtue. A year later he wrote: "You know, that it [is] almost an axiom with me, that every revolution in favour of liberty in our system, must be effected by the South, and I may add, the South headed by Virginia. There is something in her character well calculated to give an impulse in such a struggle." Calhoun later lost his hope that Virginia would take the lead in this "revolution in favor of liberty," becoming convinced instead that South Carolina would carry the torch, but the interconnection between slavery, political virtue, and liberty he asserted in the 1820s foreshadowed his "positive good" argument for slavery of the late 1830s.[54]

Why did Calhoun consider slavery a source of virtue and a guardian of liberty to the United States as a whole? Lacy K. Ford identifies at least part of the picture in arguing that Calhoun "preferred an economy dominated by independent producers who were free to find markets with neither hindrance nor protection from the government. Ownership of productive property freed those producers from dependency on other men and placed them beyond the reach of scheming demagogues." Ford's explanation is consistent with Calhoun's proslavery perspective of the 1820s in a way that Hofstadter's proto-Marxist characterization is not. Ford sees in Calhoun's political economy "an accommodation between ancient republican ideals and the realities of modern commercial capitalism."[55] Though an admirer of ancient republicanism, Calhoun was neither anti-capitalist nor anti-modern.

The value Calhoun placed on the personal independence of the slaveholder (which Ford emphasizes) is part of the explanation. But we must not ignore the role of race in Calhoun's argument that slavery benefited the entire United States. In Calhoun's 6 February 1837 Senate speech calling slavery a "positive good" (already noted above) he made a revealing remark that is easily overlooked. Calhoun speaks of a "social experiment" in progress, the results of which will not be known for another ten years. At first it seems that the "experiment" Calhoun refers to is racial slavery in the South. But he soon makes clear the experiment he has in mind is democracy itself, which "was going on both at the North and the South." Yet there was a difference: in the North the experiment being attempted was "pure and unlimited democracy" while in the South it was democracy "with a mixed race." (He did not of course mean that both southern races participated in democracy; he meant democracy founded on racial hierarchy.) After stating that it was too soon to pass judgments, Calhoun nevertheless claims that "the results of the experiment had been in favor of the South" and that "its condition would prove by far the most secure, and by far the most favorable to the preservation of liberty." This is the argument that immediately precedes Calhoun's summary judgment that slavery was not an evil but "a good—a great good."[56] Racial slavery was good because it made universal (white male) suffrage safe.

Calhoun was always ambivalent at best about universal (white male) suffrage. He was willing to extend the suffrage only on the condition that safeguards were in place against its risks. In the *Disquisition* he argued that under governments of the concurrent majority, where the "poor and ignorant" were guided by the enlightened elite, one can safely expand the right of suffrage "without incurring the hazard to which such enlargement would expose governments of the numerical majority."[57] In the 6 February 1837 speech Calhoun identified the same problem—the dangers of universal suffrage—but here proposed racial hierarchy rather than constitutional design as the remedy.

Calhoun consistently emphasized the benefits of racial hierarchy for the health of American democracy, North as well as South. His most famous expression on the theme came in his 27 June 1848 speech on the Oregon Bill, where he observes that in the South, "the two great divisions of society are not the rich and poor, but white and black; and all the former, the poor as well as the rich, belong to the upper class, and are respected and treated as equals, if honest and industrious, and hence have a position and pride of character of which neither poverty nor misfortune can deprive them." One of his obvious purposes here is to praise the southern way of life. But he is saying something else easily missed unless one pays close attention to context. In this section of the speech Calhoun had just admitted that full rights for slaveholders in all federal territories would mean the spread of slavery northward, and as a result the "white labor of the North" might have to "mingle with slave labor."[58] Calhoun wanted to reassure white laborers of the North there would be no degradation in this, precisely because they, like poor whites of the South, will enjoy the status of belonging to the upper class in the racial hierarchy. What may strike us today as a cynical deployment of race prejudice was, from Calhoun's perspective, a lesson for northern citizens on the "positive good" of slavery, directly or indirectly, for the entire United States.

Calhoun Compared to Other Proslavery Writers

Calhoun's defense of slavery did not develop in isolation from other proslavery writers. Many of Calhoun's proslavery arguments were echoed by contemporaries, especially in South Carolina,[59] and developed in greater depth by later writers. Yet Calhoun's own particular synthesis remained distinctive, in part because other proslavery writers lacked Calhoun's broader political and constitutional vision. Many comparisons could be made here, but perhaps the most instructive are with Thomas Roderick Dew (1802–1846) of Virginia, William Harper (1790–1847) and James Henry Hammond (1807–1864) of South Carolina, and George Fitzhugh (1804–1881) of Virginia.[60]

Dew, a political economist, published a widely read critique of the Virginia legislature's 1831–1832 debate over emancipation in the wake of the Nat Turner slave uprising. Those Virginians who supported emancipation made it conditional upon slaves being purchased at a fair price from owners and then transported to Africa. The prospect of a large emancipated black population living permanently on American soil was rejected by both sides in the Virginia debate.

Dew calculated the actual cost of colonization and convincingly demonstrated the total "impracticality of sending off the whole of our slave population, or even the annual increase." Dew considered emancipation without deportation to be both more practicable and more likely than the colonization scheme, but then (like Calhoun) pronounced the Negro population to be totally unfit for freedom and (also like Calhoun) invoked scenarios of violence and insurrection that would follow emancipation.

Dew was writing before the turn in southern thinking from a "necessary evil" to a "positive good" defense of slavery. He did not pronounce slavery to be a positive good; he instead conceded it was an evil but weighed its continued existence against what he considered the greater evils of emancipation with or without deportation. He clearly believed the African to be an inferior race—"the Ethiopian cannot change his skin, nor the leopard his spots"—but his economic analysis of the impracticality of colonization did not depend upon racial assumptions.[61]

By narrowing the available options to either continuation of slavery or emancipation-without-removal, Dew's argument prepared the ground for Calhoun and others to argue in the 1830s that slavery was a positive good. Nevertheless what is most striking about Calhoun in comparison to Dew is Calhoun's unwillingness even to acknowledge, much less answer, the arguments in favor of emancipation as Dew did at length. Where Dew carefully examined the assumptions and arguments behind the colonization proposal, and never confused it with the position of the radical abolitionists, Calhoun consistently spoke as though colonizationists and abolitionists were one and the same. The reason was not that Calhoun was intellectually incapable of discerning the difference between Henry Clay and William Lloyd Garrison. But Clay and Garrison were alike on one crucial point: they conceded the abstract evil of slavery, and from Calhoun's perspective this was to give away everything. If he had chosen, Calhoun certainly could have calculated the economic costs of emancipation or responded in other ways to antislavery arguments as Dew did. But it was never Calhoun's purpose to dignify anti-slavery arguments with a direct response. Dew (at least rhetorically) conceded the evil of slavery and responded with practical objections. By declaring slavery to be a "positive good" Calhoun sent the argument in another direction altogether.

William Harper's *Memoir on Slavery* was first delivered as a public address in 1837, the same year as Calhoun's "positive good" speech in the Senate, and there are some obvious similarities between their arguments. Harper's claim that the practice of slavery was "deeply founded in the nature of man and the exigencies of human society" was in the spirit of Calhoun's calling it a positive good rather than an evil. Harper, like Calhoun, explicitly rejected the maxim that "all men are born free and equal" and like Calhoun insisted that all human beings were "born to subjection," that is, to particular historically derived institutions and laws to which they must conform. Also like Calhoun, Harper declared it the right of the civilized to govern the savage and ignorant. Harper's defense of slavery, like Calhoun's, was explicitly a racial argument, but (as noted earlier) Harper was much more explicit than Calhoun in detailing the supposed inferiority of the African race.[62] Like Calhoun (indeed like most defenders of slavery), Harper contrasted the supposedly paternalistic care of the slaveholder with the indifference of capitalists to the misery of wage laborers.

Calhoun was a nationally prominent figure in a way that Harper was not, so even where they said similar things Calhoun's impact was greater. But there are differences, especially where each speaks on matters about which the other is silent. Harper provides, for example, a quite revealing defense of the sexual indulgences slavery enables the master to enjoy;[63] Calhoun never enters such territory at all. On the other side, there is in Harper no equivalent to Calhoun's sustained attempt to demonstrate that slavery is good for the entire United States, North as well as South—an essential component of Calhoun's claim that slavery was a "positive good." Though both Calhoun and Harper rejected the natural rights philosophy in favor of historically derived vested rights, Harper's political theorizing essentially stopped there; there is no equivalent to Calhoun's consensus model of government or his defense of liberty against unchecked power. Nor did Harper appear to hope, as Calhoun clearly did, that his defense of slavery would help preserve the American Union.

Calhoun's faith that his defense of slavery was Union-preserving also distinguished him from his friend and protégé James Henry Hammond, whose defense of slavery in other respects was very close to Calhoun's and who saw himself as continuing what Calhoun had begun. Hammond's famous "Mud-Sill" speech of 1858 claimed that "in all social systems there must be a class to do the menial duties, to perform the drudgery of life" and that the South was fortunate to have found "a race inferior to her own" to perform that function.[64] This was a way of rudely expressing what Calhoun had expressed more politely (in a passage quoted above) when he observed that in the South all white men were members of the upper class and enjoyed the "pride of character" that comes from contemplating a race of slaves beneath them. Hammond was like Harper in his directness about the African's supposed inherent racial inferiority (in contrast to Calhoun's relative reserve in this matter).

Hammond took up Calhoun's claim that slavery was the remedy to the class conflicts of capitalism and developed it much further in his *Letters to an English Abolitionist* (1845).[65] Hammond contrasted the Southern slaveholders' "humane treatment of the fellow-beings whom God has placed in their hands" with the miseries of the English working class, quoting at length from parliamentary reports on the subject. Hammond's calling slavery the "corner-stone and foundation of every well-designed republican edifice" was essentially the same as Calhoun's calling slavery "the most safe and stable basis for free institutions in the world," and for many of the same reasons. Hammond followed Calhoun in arguing that having an enslaved, racially distinct underclass made it safer to institute universal white male suffrage, because all white citizens in a slaveholding society, regardless of their level of education or wealth, "were more deeply interested in preserving a stable and well ordered government, than the same class in any other country." Hammond even borrowed Calhoun's language in speaking of the danger of rule by a "numerical majority."[66]

But in at least one crucial respect Hammond differed from Calhoun. Calhoun's whole defense of slavery presupposed the hope that the American Union could be saved by making it safe for slaveholders. Hammond had given up any such hope even while Calhoun was alive, and this was a central theme of Hammond's long eulogy for Calhoun. In the eulogy, after surveying Calhoun's life and thought, Hammond concluded that Calhoun had "failed in his glorious designs" and that even if all of the constitutional reforms Calhoun recommended had been enacted it would have accomplished nothing to protect the South.[67] For Hammond, Calhoun's heroic efforts to save the Union with slavery ultimately demonstrated the necessity of secession.

Once one recognizes that Calhoun's defense of slavery was intended as good for the Union as a whole and Hammond's was not, many other differences between Calhoun and Hammond, both of emphasis and substance, become visible. Hammond's deliberately rude way of saying things (the mud sill idea, for instance) that Calhoun said politely would follow from Hammond's seeing nothing to lose by employing rhetoric guaranteed to inflame northerners. On an important substantial matter, Hammond, unlike Calhoun, publicly advocated reopening the Atlantic slave trade (a measure impossible if slave states remained in the Union).[68] Hammond also took the attack on northern capitalism much further than Calhoun. Hammond not only called the miserable English working class slaves. He claimed, directly to the face of a northern senator, that "your whole hireling class of manual laborers and 'operatives,' as you call them, are essentially slaves."[69] However logically Hammond's statement might have followed from some of Calhoun's ideas, Calhoun himself would never have said this. His whole political and constitutional project as well as his defense of slavery (not to mention his never-relinquished presidential hopes) required that white northern wage laborers be treated as fellow citizens, not called by the insulting name of slave.

George Fitzhugh's defense of slavery without regard to race represented in one respect the strongest contrast with Calhoun's essentially racial defense of slavery.[70] Yet in another respect Fitzhugh took to its logical extreme Calhoun's claim that slavery remedied the class conflicts of capitalism.

The best entry point to a Calhoun-Fitzhugh comparison is Calhoun's 1837 Senate exchange over slavery with Senator Rives of Virginia (long before Fitzhugh was writing on slavery). Recall that Rives charged that Calhoun's "positive good" defense of slavery made him a follower of Sir Robert Filmer. Calhoun replied that he was on the contrary an "open advocate of freedom" who "abhorred" Filmer's dogmas. Calhoun's reply makes sense only on the basis of a rigid racial separation: one race to enjoy Lockean freedom and protection from arbitrary power, another race to be subjected to arbitrary power. But if patriarchal rule is good for one race, why not for the other? Fitzhugh's defense of slavery was in effect the intellectual trajectory Rives had predicted for Calhoun.

Fitzhugh challenged southern orthodoxy by arguing that "domestic slavery must be vindicated in the abstract, and *in the general,* as a normal, natural, and, *in general,* necessitous element of civilized society, without regard to race or color." Fitzhugh did not exactly call for the legal enslavement of lower class whites. Instead he treated Negro slavery as one specific legal form of a wider "protective" principle that should extend to whites: "To protect the weak, we must first enslave them, and this slavery must be either political or legal, or social; the latter, including the condition of wives, apprentices, inmates of poor houses, idiots, lunatics, children, sailors, soldiers, and domestic slaves." Fitzhugh's defense of "protective" slavery went along with a wholesale rejection of the modern philosophy of liberty, equality, and free competition, which he saw as mere selfishness and brutality. The only remedy to the evils of ruthless capitalism was "to identify the interests of the weak and the strong, the poor and the rich. Domestic slavery does this far better than any other institution."[71]

Calhoun would have regarded Fitzhugh's attempt to decouple slavery from race as politically self-destructive; as an astute politician Calhoun understood as well as anyone that the persistence of slavery in America depended on preserving the racial divide. Unlike Fitzhugh, Calhoun did not reject the philosophy of free competition (at least among whites) and did not idealize European feudalism. He saw both his own political philosophy and the institution of slavery as modern and progressive and fully consistent with current advances in science, economics, and constitutional law. In all of these respects Calhoun was as far from Fitzhugh as it was possible to get.

And yet Calhoun did claim that one of the advantages of slavery was that the slave owner "concentrates in himself the united interests of capital and labor, of which he is the common representative" and that in this way labor and capital are "perfectly harmonized."[72] This was exactly Fitzhugh's point in claiming that the virtue of slavery was "to identify the interests of the weak and the strong, the poor and the rich." Calhoun intended this "perfect harmony" as only one element, segregated by race, in a wider system that also included free competition and defense of liberty (for whites) against arbitrary power. By removing race as the central element Fitzhugh generalized to the whole of society Calhoun's vision of perfectly harmonious subordination.

Abolition Means Enslaving Slave Owners

The obverse of slavery's "positive good" was the radical evil of abolishing it. Calhoun, like many Southerners, typically invoked violently apocalyptic vi-sions of abolition. Under no other relation than slavery, he asserted, could the two races coexist, and to destroy slavery "was to involve a whole region in slaughter, carnage, and desolation; and come what will, we must defend and preserve it."[73] There was some variation in Calhoun's post-abolition scenarios. Sometimes he predicted that if slavery were abolished "we will be compelled to abandon the South & leave it exclusively to the black race." Sometimes, in contrast, he asserted that abolition, by destroying the "benevolence and kindness of the master," would "terminate in the misery and annihilation of the slave." Sometimes he left open which race would come out on top: abolition would lead to "extirpating one or the other of the races."[74]

More complicated scenarios involved not only southern whites and their slaves, but the economic and political power of the North, which would make slaves of the former slave owners. "Be assured that emancipation itself would not satisfy these fanatics—that gained, the next step would be to raise the negroes to a social and political equality with the whites; and that being effected, we would soon find the present condition of the two races reversed. They and their northern allies would be the masters, and we the slaves; the condition of the white race in the British West India Islands, bad as it is, would be happiness to ours."[75] Calhoun here invokes a kind of zero-sum logic: to free the slaves necessarily means making slaves of those who were once free. He presumably did not literally mean southern whites would become the chattel property of former slaves, to be bought and sold at auction. He probably meant that for proud former slave owners to be ruled politically by an alliance of northerners and former slaves was equivalent in its degradation to the humiliation of being a slave. (Calhoun ceased to call slavery a beneficial and comfortable condition as soon as there was any hint of a reversal of places: a slave, he asserted early in his career, is someone who "creeps and licks the dust.")[76]

Calhoun's apocalyptic scenarios appear at first to be modeled on events in the French sugar-plantation colony of Santo Domingo (which became the Republic of Haiti), where a massive slave uprising, inspired in part by the egalitarian doctrines of the French Revolution, culminated in the abolition of slavery and a violent race war. Haiti was very much on the minds of antebellum southerners, and many white refugees from the colony had immigrated to the American South. The Haiti analogy was also politically convenient: if the only alternative to slavery was the slaughter of one or both races, then no one could reasonably expect southerners to allow the institution to be abolished.

But slavery in the American South was so different from Haiti that the precedent was a questionable one. The Haitian uprising occurred where whites were vastly outnumbered by black slaves, during a time when the French government was paralyzed by the turmoil of the French Revolution and incapable of exercising effective authority in its overseas colonies. In the southern United States, the two races coexisted in roughly equal numbers and very unequal power, making a successful slave uprising unlikely without outside intervention. Calhoun himself believed southern whites had nothing to fear from a spontaneous uprising of slaves; it was only "the action of this [federal] Government" taking the side of the abolitionists, and the agitations of the abolitionists themselves, that worried him. If the South were forced into secession, their separation from an interfering federal government and abolitionist agitation centered in the northern states would make them safe from any slave trouble.

A better analogy for Calhoun's own specific fears is the abolition of slavery in the British West Indies in 1833. The British government abolished slavery peacefully, against the will of the slave owners, and as a direct result of the efforts of British abolitionist societies (who were closely linked with abolitionist societies in the United States). The Emancipation Act provided for gradual abolition with a transitional period of apprenticeship, and 20 million pounds paid in compensation to owners. The transitional period and apprenticeship program turned out to be unworkable, and slavery was abolished outright in 1838. The experiment demonstrated that slavery could be abolished peacefully (no race war ensued), but abolitionist hopes that a free black labor force would prove more profitable than slave labor were disappointed. Many former slaves preferred a peasant-like subsistence to the labor discipline of the sugar plantations, and the ultimate consequence was aggregate economic loss for the colony. (Whether the former slaves themselves were better off is of course a different question.)[77]

Calhoun clearly feared that the abolition of slavery in the British West Indies was a precedent for the United States. In 1836, speaking in opposition to congressional reception of abolitionist petitions, Calhoun remarked: "The spirit of abolition was not to be trifled with. It had had its bad effect on one of the most powerful Governments of Europe [Great Britain], and ended disastrously to its colonial possessions."[78] Calhoun claimed the real motive behind Britain's worldwide opposition to slavery was that, having suffered economic disaster by abolishing slavery in the West Indies, Britain now sought to "cripple or destroy the productions of her successful rivals" by "abolishing African slavery throughout this continent."[79] But the condition of whites in the West Indies, Calhoun claimed, was better than it would be for whites in the American South after abolition: in the West Indies the English government was still interested in preserving the supremacy of the white race and would continue to get labor out of emancipated blacks, while in the United States an abolitionist government would insist on racial equality, and there would be no means of forcing blacks to labor.[80]

Calhoun characterized West Indian abolition as a "disaster," despite its having been done peacefully with no race war and with compensation to slave owners. Thus when Calhoun claimed any attempt to abolish slavery in the United States would "involve a whole region in slaughter, carnage, and desolation, and come what will, we must defend and preserve it," he did not quite mean that slavery could not be abolished without slaughter and carnage. He meant that southern slave owners would make war rather than allow slavery to be abolished, under the West Indian model or any other. His assertion here was at least as much a threat as it was a prediction.

No Compromise with Abolitionism

Calhoun's response to the abolitionists was fierce and uncompromising. There could be no dialogue with them; it was "both absurd and cowardly" to reason with them.[81] Their views must not be expressed in the halls of Congress nor sent through the mail. If the union was to endure, abolitionist societies had to be suppressed by the northern states that had allowed them freely to operate. Calhoun went so far as to praise the northern anti-abolitionist mobs that attacked a number of prominent abolitionists in the summer of 1835: he spoke of the "open, manly, and decided course of a large portion of our Northern brethren during the last summer, against the criminal conduct of the fanatics; but he feared it has not checked the disease."[82]

Calhoun described African slavery in the United States as an extremely stable institution if undisturbed, far more peaceful and harmonious than relations between labor and capital in the north; but once disturbed, once its thick protections were breached, vulnerable to complete collapse. He employed some apt metaphors to underscore this point. Arguing that anti-slavery petitions must not be received by Congress, Calhoun urged that "we must meet the enemy on the frontier . . . Break through the shell, penetrate the crust, and there is no resistance within." Elsewhere he used the powder keg metaphor, arguing that "any attack on slavery in this District [of Columbia] or the Territories" was "a direct attack on slavery in the States . . . as much a direct attack as firing a train to blow up a magazine would be an attack on the magazine itself." In the one metaphor slavery is protected behind thick walls, but once the walls crack all is lost; in the other metaphor slavery is a powder keg, safe until the enemy locates the fuse.[83]

Calhoun also understood the "beachhead" strategy of the abolitionists in beginning with the District of Columbia, where congressional power to restrict slavery was most difficult to deny. The abolitionists had no intention of stopping there: "The universal sentiment with the abolitionists was, that abolition in the District was the first step to abolition in the States. Every abolitionist would say so."[84] By denying their right to petition Congress, and denying Congress authority even to discuss restrictions on slavery in the District, Calhoun believed the beachhead could be resisted.

It did not, however, occur to Calhoun that the extreme vulnerability of slavery, once its thick outer protections were breached, constituted any argument against the rightness and benefits of the institution. An opponent of slavery would argue that slavery's voracious need for protection, and its extreme vulnerability once disturbed, demonstrated the unnatural character of the institution. For Calhoun it signified only that the walls must be made thicker, the powder keg more closely guarded.

Calhoun worried about at least three different sources from which threats to slavery could come: from the action of the federal government; from the action of slaves; and from the moral weakness of the slave owners themselves, who might cease to believe in the rightness of the institution. Abolitionism presented threats on all three fronts. The danger that antislavery forces might ultimately take control of the federal government was obvious enough, and most of Calhoun's political efforts and constitutional argumentation of the 1830s and 1840s was intended to forestall this danger. But there remained significant danger on the other two fronts even if antislavery forces were unsuccessful in taking control of the federal government.

In his fierce opposition to reception of antislavery petitions, and in his hostility to free Negroes, Calhoun may have had in mind the 1822 Denmark Vesey slave conspiracy in South Carolina; Calhoun as secretary of war had sent U.S. troops to South Carolina in the wake of the conspiracy. Vesey was a literate free black carpenter and preacher who had read and distributed copies of a speech condemning slavery that Senator Rufus King of New York delivered during the 1820 Missouri crisis.[85] King in condemning slavery had intended no more than to restrict its spread to new territories. But a moral condemnation of slavery, even a limited one, could take on a life of its own among slaves and free blacks who might be inspired by the condemnation and pay no attention to the limitations. Given the suppression of abolitionist writings, speeches, and mailings in the southern states (suppression Calhoun fully supported), the only way abolitionists could broadcast their message to the South—where it could come to the ears of slaves—was to introduce it into published reports of congressional debate and in that way make it available throughout the United States. It is therefore not surprising that Calhoun sought to prevent antislavery arguments from ever being voiced in Congress.

Calhoun did not, however, seem worried about the danger of spontaneous slave uprisings, as long as there was no "disturbance" coming from the federal government or some other state or nation. As long as white men of the South retained their courage and virtue, they had nothing to fear from their slaves. "Nothing but the grossest negligence on our part can put us in the smallest danger."[86] But if they began to doubt the rightness of the institution, they were in danger. At one point during the abolitionist petition campaign Calhoun observed that

> the war is waged, not only in the most dangerous manner, but in the only manner it can be waged. Do they [meaning other Southerners] expect that the abolitionists will resort to arms, and commence a crusade to liberate our slaves by force? . . . The war which the abolitionists wage against us is of a very different character, and far more effective . . . waged, not against our lives, but our character. The object is to humble and debase us in our own estimation, and that of the world in general.[87]

The danger here was that abolitionists might succeed in getting slave owners to doubt their rights, to "humble and debase us in our own estimation." Once this happened, they were lost. This underscores the importance of Calhoun's argument that slavery was a positive good, not merely an unavoidable evil: his central purpose was to provide slaveholders with a good conscience about the institution.[88]

Calhoun's Marriage of Slavery and Liberty

In his 1975 work *American Slavery, American Freedom*, Edmund Morgan famously argues that there was a "marriage of slavery and freedom" in the origins of the American republic and that "slavery and freedom made their way to England's first American colony and grew there together, the one supporting the other." But the interconnection between freedom and slavery Morgan describes is not as ironclad as the book's title suggests. Morgan emphasizes he does not mean "that a belief in republican equality had to rest on slavery, but only that in Virginia (and probably in other southern colonies) it did."[89] The "marriage of slavery and freedom" he describes is not an indissoluble one and depended upon a number of historically contingent factors.

Calhoun's view of the interrelationship of freedom and slavery was much more tightly woven. "The defence of human liberty against the aggressions of despotic power," Calhoun insisted, "had been always the most efficient in States where domestic slavery was found to prevail."[90] Liberty for Calhoun was a rare fruit, available to some only on the condition that it was denied to others. If there is truth in Morgan's characterization of the freedom/slavery interconnection in the American Revolution, that interconnection is a hundred times stronger in Calhoun's political thought. If the American Revolution was partly characterized by a freedom-depends-on-slavery element, it also generated (as Morgan recognizes) a powerful counter-element in its promise of universal liberty, its commitment to "all men are created equal." It was this counter-element, the promise of universal liberty, that Calhoun sought to expel, both from the philosophical legacy of the American Revolution and from the modern world more generally.

To the modern-day reader Calhoun's defense of slavery might appear to be a desperate attempt to fight the tide of history. But this is to read history backwards through the lenses of the Civil War. From Calhoun's own historical perspective, both modern economics and the evidence of thousands of years of history supported the institution of slavery, as opposed to a quite recent, fanatical, and dangerous abolitionist heresy that it was not too late to uproot. In 1850, the year Calhoun died, there was no obvious worldwide momentum in favor of universal liberty and equality. Slavery in the American South was not dying any "natural economic death" (quite the contrary) and elsewhere there was little evidence that emancipation of slaves improved the economy. Calhoun was convinced, for instance, that by 1844 Great Britain realized it had made an enormous mistake in abolishing slavery in its dominions and only persisted in its antislavery policies in a transparent effort to impose the same damage on its competitors. Slavery in Calhoun's view was entirely compatible with modern market capitalism: it was the slave owners who in the United States pioneered the theory and practice of free trade, as opposed to protectionists who inhibited progress and abolitionists who threatened to destroy it altogether. Calhoun would have seen no reason to believe the tide of history was on the side of the abolitionists.

The inspiration and justification antebellum southern thinkers found in the slaveholding republics of the classical world has been frequently commented upon.[91] Calhoun himself described the Roman Republic admiringly in the *Disquisition,* and his claim (noted above) that the defense of liberty "had been always the most efficient in States where domestic slavery was found to prevail" suggests a long historical time line that would certainly have included the ancient republics.

The republics of ancient Greece and Rome were quite comfortable with the notion that their own freedom and power presupposed the denial of freedom and power to others. Neither the Greek nor the Roman republics pretended to liberate those they conquered or held in slavery. Freedom was never supposed to be universal, not even as an aspiration; the freedom of one presupposed the servitude of others. To put this in Hegelian language, the idea of ancient republicanism was that some are free, not all; as opposed to the modern idea, announced in the American and French Revolutions, that all human beings are free. But in Calhoun's view the classical republicans had always been right: slavery was "the most safe and stable basis for free institutions in the world."

The freedom-depends-on-slavery thesis illustrates an implicit zero-sum logic that turns up frequently in Calhoun's writings, especially when slavery is at issue. Recall for instance Calhoun's version of the racial mud-sill theory: for one group (slaveholders, or members of the white race) to feel the pride of being an aristocracy, someone else must be an underclass. Calhoun's abolition scenarios exhibit the same zero-sum logic: if A is slave owner and B is slave, then abolition would mean reversal, B enslaving A.

But some other strands of Calhoun's political theory seem incompatible with the zero-sum logic that underlies his defense of slavery. Calhoun's own argument that progress was the fruit of liberty (and vice versa) undermined his defense of slavery as a permanent institution that also fostered moral and social progress for the enslaved group. Here Calhoun, whether he knew it or not, expressed the Enlightenment assumption that liberty was at least potentially capable of becoming universal—as a goal if not as an immediate entitlement. According to this line of argument the liberty of one is positively, not negatively, related to the liberty of another. Calhoun, as we saw, could only mask the antislavery implications of this argument by making the questionable assumption that progress for the black race results from entirely different and opposite causes.

Calhoun's consensus model of government likewise contradicts the zero-sum logic. Calhoun presupposed that under the right institutional conditions it was possible for everyone to win: by preventing any one interest from ruling, all interests were forced to come to a true consensus, create a true common good. "The concurrent majority . . . tends to unite the most opposite and conflicting interests, and to blend the whole in one common attachment to the country."[92] Here one group's gain is not another's loss; one group's gain is the other's gain. Calhoun's faith in the possibility of win-win political solutions, though excessive, was also impressive.

Calhoun's peculiar blend of zero-sum and positive-sum political logics suggests a fundamental question with implications that extend beyond the specific problems of slavery and race. Does the zero-sum logic of Calhoun's defense of slavery fundamentally contradict the positive-sum logic of his defense of liberty and his theory of the concurrent majority, so that only a doctrine of racial inferiority can bridge the gap? In that case one would classify Calhoun's political vision as positive-sum in essence, but warped into self-contradiction by an unfortunate and context-bound racial doctrine.

Alternatively, and more disturbingly, one might speculate that for Calhoun the positive-sum and zero-sum logics were somehow organically interconnected, such that the mutually reinforcing rights and freedoms of (white) American citizens must be "paid for" by denying these rights and freedoms to someone else. In this case the racial doctrine—or some equivalent means of designating who will be up and who will be down—is much harder to separate from the core of the theory. It was clear which racial group in the antebellum United States would fill the slot of the underclass. But if persons of African descent were unavailable for that role, someone else (whether inside or outside the bounds of the country) would have to take their place as the group deprived of freedom so that others may savor it. This bleak vision of liberty is not limited to slavery in the legal sense, and it neither originated with Calhoun nor disappeared with his death.

Calhoun's thought expresses both of these logics and does not clearly choose between them or reconcile their tensions. He may have been unaware of a tension that seems obvious to us. His defense of slavery is worth examining precisely for what it leaves glaringly unresolved.

And Calhoun's contradictions on liberty were not peculiar to himself but mirror tensions in the modern world and in our modern ideological lenses that have not disappeared. Even a cursory glance at the contemporary global economy shows that free international markets are quite compatible with forms of forced labor that Calhoun would have found natural and unsurprising. Our politically convenient assumption that unrestricted markets, economic growth, and all other important forms of liberty naturally go together is not without its own self-contradictions. Our contemporary American difficulty distinguishing between spreading liberty and spreading empire, and our deployment of universalistic moral rhetoric while rejecting universally accepted codes of international conduct, shows that we are not ourselves clear on whether we value liberty as a universal good or an exclusive privilege.

Calhoun's defense of slavery, considered as straight political theory, is probably his least valuable accomplishment. But his contradictions on liberty, considered as a mirror on America and the modern world, are perhaps more valuable than anything else he said or did.

SIX

■

Calhoun's Consensus Model
of Government

Central to Calhoun's political theory is his consensus model of government, or what he called the principle of the concurrent majority. Each "portion" or "interest" within a political community, he argued in the *Disquisition on Government*, must be given "either a concurrent voice in making and executing the laws, or a veto on their execution." The "one certain mode" by which this can be accomplished is "by taking the sense of each interest or portion of the community, which may be unequally and injuriously affected by the action of the government, separately, through its own majority, or in some other way by which its voice may be fairly expressed; and to require the consent of each interest, either to put or to keep the government in action."[1]

Calhoun did not merely argue that each interest should be consulted and given fair opportunity to make its case to the public. Nor was consensus merely a goal toward which legislators should aim (sometimes achieving it, sometimes falling short). He meant that consensus was a requirement for any political action at all. The consensus rule was to be enforced by guaranteed veto rights.

This was Calhoun's alternative to majority rule, the usual decision-making procedure in popular government. Calhoun insisted that the unanimity requirement would lead neither to anarchy, nor to domination of the majority by the minority. Instead it would make possible a true harmony of all parts of the body politic and for that reason was more truly "popular" and republican than majority rule.

Calhoun emphatically denied that requiring unanimity would make government ineffective. On the contrary, he argued that this form of government was "better suited to combine a higher degree of power and a wider scope of liberty"[2] than majority rule, because the energies of government would be harnessed only to legitimate ends supported by all portions of the community. Calhoun did not believe his model of government sacrificed power in order to safeguard liberty. He believed it maximized both liberty and the right kind of power; it delivered the best of both worlds.

This point is worth emphasizing. The key question is not whether it is *possible* to design a political system in which some or all "portions" or "interests" possess veto rights over collective decisions. Such arrangements are possible in theory and have existed in practice. (The United States under the Articles of Confederation, for example, operated under a consensus rule because one state could block any significant action.) Systems are clearly possible where each "portion or interest" employs its veto rights to obstruct whatever rival interests attempt.

Instead the key question is: under what conditions (if any) would a system of mutual vetoes accomplish what Calhoun intended? Mutual obstruction without positive action is not what Calhoun envisioned. On the contrary he argued it was precisely the high cost of inaction that would make a consensus model work: "When something *must* be done,—and when it can be done only by the united consent of all,—the necessity of the case will force to a compromise;—be the cause of that necessity what it may." He claimed this would "unite the most opposite and conflicting interests, and . . . blend the whole in one common attachment to the country."[3]

This chapter critically examines the assumptions and preconditions necessary for Calhoun's consensus model to function as he designed. Some scholars dismiss Calhoun's consensus model at the outset as pure fantasy. I will argue here that it is highly unlikely Calhoun's model could function as he envisioned, but the examination is worth making anyway. Several interesting theoretical problems emerge once one asks whether and under what conditions a consensus system could work. Political systems granting veto rights to one or more interests have existed, continue to exist today, and will be created or at least proposed in the future, whether or not Calhoun's own theory is consulted. By highlighting the (perhaps unrealistic) preconditions for such a system to work effectively and fairly, Calhoun's theory might serve, ironically, to caution against too quickly embracing a system of mutual vetoes to solve the governance problems of divided societies.

Three Critical Questions

This examination of Calhoun's consensus model (or what he called the concurrent majority) will be driven by three critical questions.

First, where every "portion or interest" possesses veto rights, what prevents anarchy or deadlock? Calhoun himself anticipated the anarchy objection and addressed it at some length. He clearly intended the exercise of veto rights as the first stage of a two-stage process, to be followed by effective collective action. He believed political decision making could function according to the model of the jury, which likewise requires that decisions be unanimous.

Second, what prevents minority domination under Calhoun's system? This is actually a variant of the anarchy/deadlock objection, because where the negative consequences of inaction are unequally distributed, a minority might be able to extort an extremely high price for its cooperation.

Third, where do the vetoes stop? If a minority can veto actions of the majority, why shouldn't a minority-within-a-minority have the same rights? On one hand, denying veto rights to internal minorities risks reproducing *within* a "portion or interest" the same oppression that Calhoun sought to prevent in the larger political community. On the other hand, if every internal minority enjoys veto rights one risks an infinite regression of ever smaller minorities-within-minorities wielding vetoes-within-vetoes, culminating in anarchy. The problem is not merely finding some stopping point (for in practice the vetoes always stop somewhere) but a *justifiable* stopping point, one that does not merely shift the location of oppression. All of Calhoun's responses to this question presuppose there exists some point at which interests are homogeneous enough—or can be *made* homogeneous enough—that internal vetoes are no longer required.

The Anarchy/Deadlock Objection

Calhoun himself anticipated the anarchy/deadlock objection. Someone might object, he observed, that under his proposed system "it would be impracticable to obtain the concurrence of conflicting interests, where they were numerous and diversified; or, if not, that the process for this purpose, would be too tardy to meet, with sufficient promptness, the many and dangerous emergencies, to which all communities are exposed." Calhoun admitted that "when there is no urgent necessity" for action, each interest may be unwilling to yield. But "when something *must* be done,—and when it can be done only by the united consent of all,—the necessity of the case will force to a compromise."[4]

Taken as an unqualified proposition, this is an unconvincing answer. It would be comforting to believe, for instance, that if civil war must be avoided, because the consequences for all sides are so dire, and if no party alone has the power to prevent it, civil war will be avoided because each side will recognize the need to compromise. Yet civil wars with all their terrible consequences nevertheless occur. Calhoun's answer cannot be taken seriously if it is simply the bland proposition that every crisis creates its own solution; we need some description of the *process* by which crises are averted.

Calhoun did attempt to describe such a process. First, he argued that political decision making under his system could be compared to a jury. To those who maintained that a unanimity rule was unworkable, Calhoun replied that juries, despite the unanimity requirement, rarely fail to reach a verdict. The requirement itself, he argues, creates a *"disposition to harmonize* . . . Nothing, indeed, can be more favorable to the success of truth and justice, than this predisposing influence caused by the necessity of being unanimous."[5]

Second, he admitted that patriotic statesmanship of the highest order was necessary to resolve a crisis, but claimed his system would draw into service exactly the type of patriotic statesman needed to make it work. Under governments based on ordinary majority rule, where it is easy to override the interests of others, "each faction, in the struggle to obtain the control of the government, elevates to power the designing, the artful, and unscrupulous." But where every portion or interest possesses a veto,

> each portion, in order to advance its own peculiar interests, would have to conciliate all others, by showing a disposition to advance theirs; and, for this purpose, each would select those to represent it, whose wisdom, patriotism, and weight of character, would command the confidence of the others. Under its influence,—and with representatives so well qualified to accomplish the object for which they were selected,—the prevailing desire would be, to promote the common interests of the whole; and, hence, the competition would be, not which should yield the least to promote the common good, but which should yield the most. It is thus, that concession would cease to be considered a sacrifice,—would become a free-will offering on the altar of the country, and lose the name of compromise.[6]

Elsewhere Calhoun made clear he considered himself exactly the type of statesman required to make a consensus system work.[7] He also believed the compromise tariff of 1833, which resolved the crisis occasioned by South Carolina's Ordinance of Nullification, exemplified a "spirit of mutual compromise" among key congressional leaders. His description of those deliberations, and his own role in them, closely parallels what he says about patriotic statesmanship in the *Disquisition*.[8]

The jury and statesmanship arguments reveal a great deal about how Calhoun believed a consensus model could function and deserve to be examined at length.

Social Sympathy and Distance

We should first ask whether either the jury or statesmanship arguments are consistent with Calhoun's own description of human nature in the *Disquisition*. Calhoun opens that work by asserting that "man is so constituted as to be a social being" and "has, accordingly, never been found . . . in any state other than the social" (here rejecting state-of-nature theories of the origin of government). But he next asserts that, though man is "created for the social state, and is accordingly so formed as to feel what affects others, as well as what affects himself, he is, at the same time, so constituted as to feel more intensely what affects him directly, than what affects him indirectly through others . . . His direct or individual affections are stronger than his sympathetic or social feelings."[9]

Calhoun's argument here might be criticized as an inconsistent mix of purely selfish (e.g., Hobbesian) and naturally social (Aristotelian) descriptions of humanity. Ralph Lerner argues that for Calhoun, "self-interest forms the warp and woof of every significant political act" and that Calhoun's system proceeds inconsistently "from irreducible self-interest to enlarged patriotism by way of a dread of stalemate and anarchy."[10] If indeed Calhoun's description of human nature is essentially Hobbesian (in milder dress) then Lerner is right to see a fundamental contradiction between Calhoun's diagnosis and remedy. One cannot imagine Hobbesian men effectively administering a consensus-based political order.

Conversely, if human nature is not pervasively selfish and we stress instead the "naturally social" side of Calhoun's description, then it is unclear why the whole machinery of mutual vetoes would be necessary. If human beings can deliberate and act in politics like impartial jurors, and if patriotic states-

CHAPTER SIX

men can put aside self-interest and the interest of party or section in pursuit of the common good, then why couldn't these same characteristics animate the ordinary workings of majority rule? Why then assume all power will be abused unless prevented by this elaborate system of mutual vetoes? If we stress the selfish side of Calhoun's description, his remedy would seem impossible; if we stress the social side, his remedy would seem unnecessary.

I do not believe Calhoun's argument here is fundamentally contradictory. To understand how his description of human nature might support his proposed remedy we should first set aside any stark dichotomy between "selfish" and "social." Calhoun himself insisted he was not describing human nature as "selfish" because that word implies "an unusual excess of the individual over the social feelings . . . something depraved and vicious."[11] He insisted instead that socially concerned motivations were real, even if less powerful than individual motivations; that distinguishes his from any purely self-interested account of human nature.

Calhoun described these "individual" and "social" feelings in terms of *distance*—a matter of degree rather than either/or. A human being feels what "affects him directly" more intensely than what "affects him indirectly through others." It would follow that, within the range of social feelings, human beings will feel more intensely what affects those close to them, and less intensely what affects those a greater distance away. Thus it should not be surprising that democratically elected officeholders will have a more vivid sense of what affects their own section—their neighbors, people like themselves—than what affects fellow citizens in a different part of the country, with different habits and engaged in different pursuits. It is not necessarily individual selfishness that leads one group of citizens to mistreat another. It is instead the disposition that prefers the interests of those near and alike to the interests of those distant and different. None of this is earth-shatteringly novel, but it clarifies the links between Calhoun's description of human nature as not *completely* selfish, and his diagnosis of how one group of citizens comes to oppress another. This description of human nature is also consistent with Calhoun's preference for state sovereignty over national sovereignty and his insistence that the first loyalties of citizens in a federal union must be to their state.

However, this distance-reduces-sympathy argument does not immediately explain why Calhoun believed group differences could be bridged and consensus reached among all the diverse and distant interests in the larger political community. If one feels more intensely what affects those closer to oneself, then a consensus rule would seem most appropriate to small, homogeneous groups and least appropriate for decisions on a national scale. How would an ordinary citizen of South Carolina come to sympathize enough with an ordinary citizen of New Hampshire to come to a consensus—and do the same for every other state and interest?

The answer is that for ordinary citizens in Calhoun's world, these differences cannot be bridged. But they can be bridged at the elite level. Both Calhoun's jury model and his statesmanship argument presuppose a small, face-to-face community of highly placed leaders far more "national" in orientation than the citizens they represent, interacting under institutional conditions that overcome the effects of distance and make it possible for "the individual and the social feelings" to "unite in one common devotion to country."[12] Clearly Calhoun's description of human nature—its individual and social feelings and the interaction between them—is essential to his description of how potential deadlock is transformed into action in the common good.

The Jury Analogy

The deliberations of juries would seem to be a peculiar model for the legislative process. Jurors are not supposed to have personal stakes in the outcome of a case, whereas legislators—even if personally disinterested—are supposed to represent the interests of their constituents. In criminal cases jurors do not themselves suffer the penalties they impose through conviction; in civil cases they neither receive nor pay settlement money. Legislators and those they represent are directly affected by the consequences of legislation. Jurors typically face a much simpler, dichotomous choice: in criminal cases, they find the defendant guilty or not guilty; in civil cases, they find for one party or the other. In legislating, the range of possibilities is much wider. Creating a unanimously acceptable piece of legislation—which was Calhoun's goal—and balancing large numbers of very diverse interests and perspectives is rather different than jurors choosing between two straightforward and prefabricated options. Jurors deliberate upon the truth of a past event, a question which in principle has a correct answer. Legislators make policy for the future and deal in probabilities, not certainties. One cannot speak of a correct or incorrect tax law the way one speaks of a correct or incorrect verdict.

Moreover, with juries one can reasonably suppose that human beings of average intelligence and sensitivity deliberating in good faith will suffice;

CHAPTER SIX

extraordinary qualities are not required (and indeed are often discouraged). One cannot assume that the average citizen will have the expertise or diplomatic skills to craft a unanimously acceptable solution to a critical legislative deadlock. Legislators would need to be not ordinary but extraordinary human beings for Calhoun's system to function effectively (as Calhoun himself acknowledged).

For these reasons and more it would seem much easier for a jury to reach a unanimous verdict than for all interests affected by legislation to reach consensus. A better analogy for Calhoun's political model might be an out-of-court settlement in a civil case, where the parties themselves reach agreement by deliberately balancing their respective interests. But out-of-court settlements work only because courts can and will act if agreement between the parties fails; under Calhoun's system no such fallback option exists.

Thus Calhoun's jury analogy does little to demonstrate the workability of a legislative process constrained by a consensus requirement. However, the jury analogy is in other respects richly revealing of Calhoun's thinking.

One effect of the jury analogy is to remind readers there are certain rights and liberties too sacred to trust to simple majority rule. American citizens do not allow themselves to be deprived of life or liberty by a seven-to-five jury vote. By employing the jury analogy Calhoun suggests a similarity between the individual rights and interests at stake in a trial, and the minority rights and interests threatened by majority rule in the legislative process. To be victim of an unjust tariff passed by a close vote would be like being sentenced to pay a steep fine by a deeply divided jury. The jury model underscores Calhoun's sensitivity to those on the losing end of majority rule even if it does little to demonstrate the workability of his remedy.

Calhoun's attachment to the jury as model for the legislative process appears rooted in two types of jury-related "dispositions": the "disposition to give a fair and impartial hearing to the arguments on both sides," which we could label the truth-ascertaining function of jury deliberations; and the "*disposition to harmonize*" resulting from "the inconvenience to which they might be subjected in the event of division," which we could label the social-pressure effect of sequestered juries.[13] Both these jury-related dispositions inform Calhoun's vision of the legislative process constrained by a unanimity rule.

The jury analogy is problematic for a legislative process where all participants have interests, or represent interests, affected by legislation. But Calhoun believed that vesting every "portion or interest" with veto rights, by making it impossible for any one interest to dominate and putting all interests on an equal level, would *neutralize* all interests for purposes of deliberation. This would both force and enable legislators to deliberate like impartial jurors seeking only the truth. The operation of the concurrent majority, he argues, will "suppress the expression of all partial and selfish interests" and "give a full and faithful utterance to the sense of the whole community."[14] Calhoun's language here definitely does not describe ordinary bargaining among interests. It is as though, once all interests are included in the process and given equal obstructive power, interestedness itself ceases and legislators enter the realm of detached, even generous pursuit of truth and the common good.

Calhoun directly linked this disinterested pursuit of truth with the two elements of human nature described in the opening pages of the *Disquisition,* the individual and social affections. Ordinary majority rule (what he calls the numerical majority) encourages the expression of individual feeling at the expense of social attachments. But under the concurrent majority, "the individual and the social feelings are made to unite in one common devotion to country . . . And hence, there will be diffused throughout the whole community kind feelings between its different portions."[15] Calhoun was convinced that the institutional constraint of a unanimity rule would suspend the operation of self-interested motives and thereby allow the social affections—a real element of our nature, though ordinarily weaker than self-interest—to guide the political process.

This extraordinary assumption perhaps explains why Calhoun did not address the chief objection to his jury analogy, the disinterestedness of jurors as opposed to the interestedness of legislators. For Calhoun's key assumption about the psychological effects of a consensus rule on the legislative process erases this contrast between jurors and legislators. He remarks that with jurors "the love of truth and justice" will induce them to agree as long as this motive is "not counteracted by some improper motive or bias." He then immediately argues, in directly parallel fashion, that in governments of the concurrent majority, "love of country" is the most powerful of motives "if not counteracted by the unequal and oppressive action of government."[16] Calhoun believed the operation of a consensus rule, by eliminating the possibility of "unequal and oppressive action," would convert legislators into something like impartial jurors, capable of acting according to pure "love of country" and "love of truth."

Calhoun regarded the critical legislative and constitutional contests that

CHAPTER SIX

occupied him as a statesman as clashes between true and false principles; compromise and balancing of interests came only after agreement was reached on true principles. His critique of the protective tariff and his faith in nullification as remedy presupposed that he and his state were right—morally, economically, and constitutionally—and the protectionists wrong. Interests could be compromised and balanced (by phasing out protection gradually) only after agreement on the principle that protective tariffs were wrong. In allowing three-fourths of the states to override a single state's nullification, Calhoun was in effect setting up the co-states as a "jury of one's peers" judging which national economic vision was true and which interpretation of the Constitution was correct. On slavery Calhoun was even more convinced that at stake was a clash of true and false principles: slavery was positively good, abolitionism deeply evil, and there could be no compromise between good and evil. Calhoun was no relativist when it came to political and moral truth.

Unanimity through Pressure

Another key element of Calhoun's jury analogy was the "disposition to harmonize" under which "one after another falls into the same opinion, until unanimity is obtained."[17] It turns out that "love of truth and justice" is not the only motive shaping the deliberation of jurors. Each individual juror is also motivated by the "inconvenience" of being locked in the same room and unable to escape until there is either a unanimous verdict, or a final admission of failure. Jurors deliberate on the truth, not in isolation, but as members of a temporary but intense face-to-face community composed of individuals who previously may have been complete strangers to one another. Jurors are motivated not only by love of truth but also by their obligation toward fellow jurors to finish the business successfully. This social pressure cuts both ways with respect to discerning the truth. Jurors passionately convinced they are right, and willing to suffer continued inconvenience for the sake of that conviction, readily sway fellow jurors. Jurors less passionately attached to truth and more affected by the inconveniences of the situation may "harmonize" their opinion for the sake of closure.

Calhoun believed a legislative body constrained by a consensus rule would display a similar disposition to harmonize. A legislative body where numbers remain small (like the U.S. Senate) is an intense face-to-face community. Members may initially be strangers to one another, and the people and interests they represent very distant and distinct from one another, but once in the same room and forced to address the same problems the leaders of each section form a community. This overcomes the normal effects of geographical and social distance. According to Calhoun people naturally feel more intensely what is nearer than what is distant, and this tempts one section of the country to support legislation that injures another. But for a legislator locked in a difficult negotiation, the representatives of other sections and interests may at that moment seem much closer than constituents back home.

This will be especially true under a consensus rule where leaders of one section can accomplish nothing unless leaders of all other sections are satisfied. For jurors the penalty of failure to reach consensus is merely personal inconvenience. With legislators the penalty for failure is much higher:

> Impelled by the imperious necessity of preventing the suspension of the action of government, with the fatal consequences to which it would lead, and by the strong additional impulse derived from an ardent love of country, each portion would regard the sacrifice it might have to make by yielding its peculiar interest to secure the common interest and safety of all, including its own, as nothing compared to the evils that would be inflicted on all, including its own, by pertinaciously adhering to a different line of action.[18]

Note that Calhoun speaks of the "peculiar interest" yielding to "the common interest" in order to avoid a shared disaster. He does not suggest that the reverse might also occur: "the common interest" yielding to the "peculiar interest" to prevent an even worse outcome. Yet this possibility cannot be excluded, just as jury room pressures sometimes lead jurors to support bad verdicts.

Enlightened Statesmen Always at the Helm?

In an 1830 letter (with nullification in the background) Calhoun distinguished the ordinary politician, characterized by "intrigue and cunning," from the kind of statesman he conceived himself to be, who places himself "on principle and services as the means of advancement." The difficult challenge, he says, is to steer a course between tyranny on one side and anarchy on the other: "to unite liberty & power."[19] Calhoun never intended the consensus requirement to preserve liberty at the expense of effective government.

He believed it secured the best of *both* power and liberty. And he regarded enlightened statesmanship as the key to achieving these twin goals.

In *Federalist* No. 10 James Madison cautioned that we cannot depend solely upon enlightened statesmen to prevent majorities from acting unjustly, for "enlightened statesmen will not always be at the helm." A Madisonian limited-majority-rule system can usually function—though not necessarily at its best—with mediocre leaders.

Calhoun's proposed system, on the other hand, absolutely depends upon enlightened statesmen. Mediocre and/or venal politicians can certainly wield the veto powers of the region or interest they represent, the first stage of the process, but they would be unable to accomplish the second stage, the transformation of potential anarchy and shared disaster into true common good. This seems an argument against Calhoun's proposed system, but he turns it around by claiming that the urgent need for enlightened statesmen will guarantee their emergence. Where the majority can rule directly, he says, it will select "designing," "artful," and "unscrupulous" leaders. But where each interest can accomplish nothing unless it conciliates all other interests, it "would select those to represent it, whose wisdom, patriotism, and weight of character, would command the confidence of the others."[20]

Calhoun goes even further. Government based upon the concurrent majority would not only guarantee that enlightened statesmen would be sent to national councils, but even purge the citizenry itself of corruption. The purifying effects of his proposed system, Calhoun claims, would not be limited to "those who take an active part in political affairs" but "would extend to the whole community"; for if "knowledge, wisdom, patriotism, and virtue" are recognized as the only path to acquiring power and influence in government, these qualities will then be "highly appreciated and assiduously cultivated" and become "prominent traits in the character of the people." Simple majority rule will have exactly the opposite effect, and corrupt the people as well as those who hold office. "So powerful, indeed, is the operation of the concurrent majority, in this respect, that, if it were possible for a corrupt and degenerate community to establish and maintain a well-organized government of the kind, it would of itself purify and regenerate them; while, on the other hand, a government based wholly on the numerical majority, would just as certainly corrupt and debase the most patriotic and virtuous people."[21] Here there seem to be no limits to Calhoun's faith in enlightened statesmanship, or to his confidence that his proposed system will create the very preconditions necessary for its effective operation.

Clearly for such a system to work, statesmen representing each section must have a free hand in their internal deliberations and then persuade their constituents actively to support whatever consensus they have reached. As noted earlier, Calhoun did not envision mere interest-brokering but instead believed the possession of mutual veto rights would *neutralize* all interests during deliberation, allowing leaders to discern the truth and common good in jury-like fashion. For if leaders were tightly bound to the views of whatever "portion or interest" sent them to the national councils, the exercise of mutual vetoes would produce mere stalemate. (How Calhoun understood the relationship between leaders and those they represent, and leaders' responsibility for creating and preserving *internal* unity among their flock, will be examined below.)

In his early years Calhoun referred to the United States as a "nation." From the time he formulated his doctrine of nullification till the end of his life, he denied that the United States constituted a nation or that there existed any single "people of the United States."[22] But in the *Disquisition* his description of deliberations among statesmen constrained by the unanimity rule sounds very much like an intense, intimate nation: "Instead of faction, strife, and struggle for party ascendancy, there would be patriotism, nationality, harmony, and a struggle only for supremacy in promoting the common good of the whole."[23] Including "nationality" in the list is very telling. The aggregate of people collectively represented by these leaders do not form a nation; the people back home would ride roughshod over the interests of another section without a second thought. But Calhoun's small, face-to-face community of statesmen does seem to have a sense of shared nationality, one essential to their success in promoting the common good of the whole (even if Calhoun denied the whole constituted a nation). Without this intimate, elite-level sense of nationality Calhoun's system could not possibly work.

Consensus or Minority Domination?

A second critical question is whether Calhoun's consensus model would in practice enable the minority to dominate the majority. Madison's fundamental objection to Calhoun's doctrine of nullification was that it allowed a small minority to impose the law and its own construction of the Constitution on the vast majority.

While he anticipated and answered at length the anarchy/deadlock objection, Calhoun dismissed the minority domination objection fairly quickly where he addressed it at all. In the *Exposition* he wrote, "It may be objected that [nullification's] effects would be to place the minority above the majority." He admitted that "if the objection were well-founded it would be fatal" because "if the majority cannot be trusted, neither can the minority"; minority rule would simply repeat the old error of monarchy or aristocracy. But he denied that the power to check entailed the power to rule: "It is not the consequence of proper checks to change places between the majority and minority." He compared nullification to judicial review: "The power of the Judiciary to declare an act of Congress, or of a State Legislature unconstitutional" is "a most efficient check" but does not vest any "supreme power in the Court over Congress, or the State Legislatures."[24] Thus Calhoun presented nullification as an extension of the ordinary constitutional checks; if the latter were not minority domination, neither was the former. His argument here, though directed to the specific question of nullification, would also apply to the more general consensus model set forth in the *Disquisition*. For a single "portion or interest" to exercise its veto rights over the decisions of the whole is to check, not to dominate.

Whether the judiciary declaring laws unconstitutional amounts in practice to minority rule may be debated. But there are essential differences between judicial review and Calhoun's system of mutual vetoes that make the analogy questionable. The federal judiciary is a national body, its members appointed with the participation of the other two national branches; it is not, or not supposed to be, the organ of a *particular* section or interest as is the case with Calhoun's minority veto. Moreover the judiciary is responsive to majority opinion over a long enough time frame because those who appoint and confirm judges are themselves elected. Calhoun himself recognized the long-term responsiveness of the federal judiciary to majority opinion: exactly what he feared was that over time the same majority would control all branches of government, including the judiciary. He sought instead to vest minority interests with *permanent* checks no majority could ever take away, and to make each branch or division of the government the organ of a particular organic "portion or interest."

The question then is whether the exercise by a minority of veto powers which (unlike judicial review) are forever beyond majority control could under some conditions allow the minority to dominate the majority. Calhoun never addressed this question, even though it inevitably arises and was raised by Calhoun's contemporaries (including Madison).

My examination of the minority domination problem begins with an interesting essay by Douglas W. Rae, "The Limits of Consensual Decision," which analyzes Calhoun along with several more recent consensus theorists.[25] Rae's thesis is that the consensus model not only cannot be duplicated in practice, but should not be approximated either, because "some outcome to any decision must portend a violation of consent." This will be especially true where the costs of government inaction are unequally distributed. Under such conditions, "defensive minorities may use their special leverage—the potential cost of their votes to those who want change—as a means to exploit others." To be truly equal and impartial, rather than privileging those with an interest in blocking change, a consensus requirement would have to be such that one could veto *both* decisions and nondecisions, both action and failure to act. The status-quo privilege disappears only if there exists "a right of veto over every policy, including old laws in politics and the non-exchange outcome in the market." But this leads to absurd outcomes: one interest vetoes a new law and another interest vetoes the continuation of the old law and as a result "we might neither retain nor rid ourselves of a law." The only way to avoid such absurdity under Calhoun's system (whom Rae explicitly names) is to provide "that *some* outcomes and not others are subject to the requirement of unanimity." Rae observes that the consensus requirement "has enormous ideological value to people well placed in society, for no redistribution can be justified without the consent of those who stand to lose, even if they are numerically overwhelmed by prospective beneficiaries."[26] (Calhoun, of course, might concede the truth of this observation but consider it a benefit, not a disadvantage.)

Rae emphasizes two key problems that complement my own discussion below of the minority domination problem: first, that the consequences of stalemate may be very unequally distributed among sections and interests—which was the case when South Carolina nullified the tariff; and second, that Calhoun's model ultimately presupposes a distinction between outcomes subject to the unanimity requirement and outcomes that are not—which we will see in applying Calhoun's model to the expansion of slavery to the territories.

Blocking or Imposing?

Clearly Calhoun did not grant the minority any formal right to rule the majority. (At least among white fellow citizens; for in South Carolina a free white minority ruled an enslaved black majority.) All "portions or interests," including those in the majority, would enjoy the same veto rights, so conditions are formally equal for all: a system of mutual veto rights, not exclusive minority privileges. This may explain why Calhoun took seriously the problem of anarchy or deadlock, but not that of minority domination. He insisted that consensus was fundamentally different from, and superior to, either majority rule or minority rule.

But Calhoun's answer to the anarchy objection requires the assumption that the costs and risks of failure to act collectively are *equally distributed among all interests*. "Impelled by the imperious necessity of preventing the suspension of the action of government, with the fatal consequences to which it would lead," he argues, each portion would yield "its peculiar interest to secure the common interest and safety of all." He adds that each portion would have "an additional impulse derived from an ardent love of country."[27] His vision of statesmen deliberating impartially in jury-like fashion to realize the common good likewise presupposes equal risk and danger for all sides.

But failure of government to act is not always equally fatal to all interests. If a particular minority can use its veto power to impose greater risks and costs of inaction on other interests than it suffers itself, the assumption of an equal playing field as precondition to deliberation and action in the common good fails. A minority so positioned could instead force the majority to choose between agreeing to the minority's excessive demands, or refusing and creating anarchy (or worse), which hurts the majority more than the minority.

Calhoun's theory also assumes a clear difference between the negative power of a minority to *block* action by the whole, and the positive power of a minority to *impose* a decision on the whole. This distinction between negative and positive power is key to his judicial review analogy, noted above, and to his consensus theory generally. In certain instances the difference between negative and positive power is clear enough. The negative power to block the majority from imposing its religious views on a minority, for example, does not mean that the minority thereby imposes its religious views on the majority. The same is true of the right of free speech and many other constitutional checks that likewise presuppose a clear difference between blocking and imposing.

But in other circumstances the difference between blocking and imposing may be less clear, or altogether lacking. The veto rights Calhoun recommended were not limited to any specific issues or domains, and whoever exercised the veto was judge of whether it was used appropriately. This means veto rights could be exercised in precisely those cases where there is no clear distinction between blocking and imposing.

Thus minority domination is possible where one or both of the following conditions hold: (1) the consequences of failure to act are unequally distributed, and (2) there is no clear distinction between blocking and imposing. Many hypothetical cases could illustrate the effect of these conditions. But I will instead take up two actual cases with which Calhoun himself was intensely concerned, tariff law and slavery.

A tariff must apply with equal force in all sections of the country, otherwise its purpose is defeated. It would be fiscally self-defeating, as well as unconstitutional, to collect a high tariff in New York and no tariff at all in Charleston, South Carolina. Even as he supported South Carolina's Ordinance of Nullification, Calhoun recognized South Carolina could not permanently collect a different tariff than the rest of the country while remaining in the Union. His purpose was to block implementation of an obnoxious law in a way that would force Congress to reconsider the issue and pass a new, lower tariff—as indeed happened in 1833. From Calhoun's perspective South Carolina was not imposing a law but merely blocking a law, creating a crisis equally affecting all sections and interests, thereby forcing them to deliberate in the common good—exactly as outlined in the *Disquisition*.

But did the impasse created by South Carolina's nullification carry equal costs and risks for all? In answering this question we must distinguish between the actual course of events in the 1832–1833 nullification crisis[28] and how matters would have stood if Calhoun's own political and constitutional theory had been followed. What actually happened was that President Andrew Jackson rejected the supposed constitutional right of nullification and made clear he would enforce the tariff with military means, if necessary. This produced a dangerous crisis in which the possibility of armed conflict between national government and a state, and between opposing factions within South Carolina, was very real. It was amidst this dangerous crisis that the 1833 compromise tariff was passed, South Carolina rescinded its ordinance of nullification, and disaster was avoided. Here it could be argued that the costs and risks of failure to resolve the crisis were approximately equal for all parties—or at least too unpredictable to give any participant an interest in prolonging the showdown.

But this course of events occurred only because Calhoun's prescription was not followed. According to Calhoun, the state of South Carolina had a clear constitutional right to nullify federal law. (And the same would hold for Calhoun's more general version of the consensus model in the *Disquisition:* each portion or interest possesses clear constitutional rights to exercise its veto whenever it judges appropriate.) Jackson's threat to enforce federal law upon a nonconsenting state was in Calhoun's view completely unconstitutional and despotic.[29] In assessing whether Calhoun's consensus model produces minority domination, we should ask what might have happened if, according to Calhoun's script, both president and Congress accepted South Carolina's self-proclaimed right peacefully to nullify a national tariff law.

This too would precipitate a crisis, especially at a time when the tariff produced most of the federal government's revenue. All sides would recognize that administration of two radically different tariffs in different sections of the country could not continue. But the risks and costs of continued deadlock would *not* be equally distributed. South Carolina, free from the danger of armed intervention and already in practice administering its preferred tariff policy, would have far less to lose by deadlock than those states with a direct interest either in tariff protection or in tariff revenues (e.g., to fund roads and canals on the frontier). Far from moderating its demands, South Carolina might have increased them to the point of insisting on complete and immediate abolition of protective tariffs, or all tariffs for that matter. It might be rational under such circumstances for the national majority to accept South Carolina's demands rather than allow the crisis to continue and risk dismembering the Union—especially since Calhoun also argued that a state may peacefully and constitutionally secede if it loses the vote. Someone who considered all protective tariffs illegitimate from the outset might favor exactly such a course of events. But this scenario clearly entails minority domination of a majority, and it is definitely possible under Calhoun's consensus model.

The issue that most concerned Calhoun in the last decades of his life was the status of slavery in federal territories. Calhoun and the slave states insisted that slave owners had a right to transport slave property to the territories, regardless of the views of Congress or the territorial legislature. According to the unanimity rule underlying his joint-state-partnership interpretation of the Constitution, any one of the partners (in this case a state) could block decisions over use of the jointly owned property that violated its key interests or compromised its status as an equal partner.[30]

Here too there is no clear distinction between a minority using its veto powers to block something and using those powers to impose something on the majority—in this case on the national majority opposed to the expansion of slavery. One slave owner moving into a previously free territory would in fact convert it into a slave territory and possibly a future slave state. A majority opposed to the nationalization of slavery would understandably see this outcome as the positive imposition of slave-state law on the nation. Yet according to Calhoun the antislavery majority here enjoyed no equivalent veto right. If the antislavery interest did possess an equivalent veto right, it could veto the slave states' veto of the prohibition on slavery in the territories; the slave states would then veto the free states' veto of their veto; and the result would be the kind of absurd outcome Rae diagnoses. Only by making some outcomes and not others subject to the consensus requirement—in this case, by positively favoring the proslavery position and rejecting as illegitimate the antislavery position—could Calhoun avoid this absurd conclusion. (In this case it is unclear whether either side could have reasonably expected any advantage from failure to resolve the crisis: secession and civil war are difficult to calculate.)

Perhaps the reason Calhoun failed seriously to ask whether his system could lead to minority domination is that he was convinced in both key controversies (tariff and slavery) that the minority was right and the majority wrong. He believed the free-trade political economy behind South Carolina's nullifying the tariff benefited the entire United States, not only South Carolina or southern planters. His vision of freer international trade was attractive and plausible in many respects. But according to the ordinary rules of the democratic game, his own claim (or the claim of his state or section) to know the national common good of the United States has no privilege over other individuals' or sections' claim to understand the common good. Each makes their case and the majority, according to some system of constitutional procedures, ultimately decides. Calhoun, however, was not willing to wait. He and his state, though a minority, would act first and set the country straight. Calhoun never asked what would happen if a state or interest persisted in employing its veto for sinister purposes.

At this point deciding whether Calhoun's minority veto leads to minority domination becomes a matter of perspective. If one is genuinely convinced one is blocking action not for selfish reasons but for the good of the country, success in getting one's way will not appear to be minority domination but instead the true common good of the whole. This is exactly what makes Calhoun's consensus model so seductive: the theory's unsolved problems become invisible just when one most needs to recognize them.

Where Do Veto Rights Stop?

A third critical challenge to Calhoun's minority veto/consensus model of government is the question: where do veto rights stop? What prevents an infinite regress of vetoes-within-vetoes by minorities-within-minorities?

This question was posed by William Henry Harrison in 1832 in a series of public letters addressed to Calhoun. Harrison argued that Calhoun's principle of nullification could not stop at the state line.

> Would not the claim to its advantages be asserted by the minorities in the subdivisions of the States also? . . . Called upon to pay his tax for cutting of the Canal, the resident of the banks of the Ohio, or of Lake Erie, might say that it was an "act of robbery" which they were committing upon him. A principle of justice is not altered by the number of persons to whom it is applicable, whether it operates on a million or on a single individual.[31]

One elementary answer to this challenge is possible. In his constitutional writings Calhoun argued that the American states were fully sovereign, while the federal government was a creation of the states and therefore not sovereign. The political subdivisions within a state are also creations of the state, not sovereign. Thus states, because they are sovereign, have the right to veto acts of the federal government. Counties or other internal subdivisions are not sovereign and therefore enjoy no veto rights over actions of their state.

But even if one accepts Calhoun's version of state sovereignty, this does not answer the problem at hand. Vesting a state with full sovereignty, externally and internally, does not prevent the interest controlling that state from acting unjustly toward an internal minority. It would instead give it a sovereign right to do so. The justice question here does not depend on the location of sovereignty.

We could restate Harrison's challenge in the following way. If every interest within a state enjoys the same right to veto state action that the state itself enjoys to veto federal action (under Calhoun's theory), then the result is anarchy. On the other hand, if internal minorities with equally valid claims are denied veto rights, then the result is injustice.

This general problem is not limited to Calhoun's theory. It is of wider applicability and especially relevant to acts of partition or secession. It is a depressingly familiar story that when national minorities secede, or secure extensive autonomy short of secession, they often proceed to oppress their own internal minorities, who in turn press for secession-within-secession. Calhoun's consensus model was intended as an alternative to secession, but the infinite regression problem applies in both cases. Unless it can resolve the infinite regression problem, Calhoun's theory of government is unworkable.

Calhoun's consensus model requires, first of all, some practical limitation to the number of "portions or interests" exercising veto rights. Consensus among two or three key interests might be attainable; consensus among ten or thirty very diverse interests, each armed with veto rights, is not. Calhoun did insist that every American state was sovereign and entitled to nullify federal law, but in practice he assumed the number of significant interests (e.g., slavery, manufacturing, commerce) was smaller than the number of states and that states with similar interests would act as a bloc.

Second, Calhoun's model assumes that at some point in the internal regression the heterogeneity of interest that characterizes the wider community is replaced by a relative homogeneity of interests. For if there exist deep differences of interest *within* a "portion," then the leaders of that portion (or state), in exercising veto rights, might simply advance the interests of one internal group at the expense of another internal group. (Indeed, they might use their veto precisely to prevent the larger community from intervening to protect the rights of an internal minority.) Calhoun argued that within a "portion or interest," "every individual of every interest might trust, with confidence, its majority or appropriate organ, against that of every other interest."[32] By trust in one's own "majority or appropriate organ," Calhoun meant there came a point at which internal vetoes were no longer necessary to prevent injustice. We must ask how Calhoun located and justified this stopping point.

Calhoun answered the infinite regression challenge in a number of different ways. He argued that within a "portion or interest," despite internal differences, everyone had the same interest with respect to political decisions of the larger community. Second, he limited the range of what counted as "portions or interests" entitled to veto rights. Third, he recommended an internal version of the consensus model, based on the South Carolina constitution, which recognized some internal differences but stopped far short of providing every internal minority with veto rights. Finally, in leading his state and section he demonstrated in practice that internal unity and homogeneity had to be deliberately created and maintained; it was not automatic.

CHAPTER SIX

The Relative Homogeneity and Defensive Shield Arguments

Calhoun admitted some internal differences of interest. In the *Fort Hill Address* he observed that the "dissimilarity of interests" that leads to majority oppression is "to be found in every community, in a greater, or less degree, however small, or homogeneous."[33] In the *Disquisition* he argued that the tendency of government "to pervert its powers into instruments to aggrandize and enrich one or more interests by oppressing and impoverishing the others" is present in all communities: "the small and the great,—the poor and the rich,—irrespective of pursuits, productions, or degrees of civilization." He then adds that "the more diversified the condition and pursuits of its population, and the richer, more luxurious, and dissimilar the people," the easier it will be for one portion of the community to plunder another.[34]

Calhoun here makes a distinction of degree: the oppression of one interest by another can occur in either small, homogeneous communities or large, diversified communities but is more difficult to prevent in the latter. Presumably he would categorize the United States as an extensive, diversified community and a state like South Carolina as a relatively more homogeneous community. But he did believe an oppressive majority could develop within South Carolina. To argue that majority oppression is more difficult to prevent in large communities does not mean it cannot occur in small communities.

In admitting internal differences of interest, Calhoun made one important assumption: that conflicts of interest *between* "portions or interests" were far greater than the conflicts of interest *within* each portion or interest. "For whatever diversity each interest might have within itself,—as all would have the same interest in reference to the action of the government, the individuals composing each would be fully and truly represented by its own majority or appropriate organ, regarded in reference to the other interests." For this reason, "every individual of every interest might trust, with confidence, its majority or appropriate organ, against that of every other interest."[35] Internal differences, in other words, pale in comparison to every internal group's shared interest with respect to the action of the more distant government of the larger community. We could call this the relative homogeneity argument.

Calhoun made another and closely connected argument in explaining why it is unnecessary to give every interest a veto. "Where the organism is perfect, every interest will be truly and fully represented," he says, but it is impossible to create a perfect system. "But, although this be true, yet even when, instead of the sense of each and of all, it takes that of a few great and prominent interests only, it would still, in a great measure, if not altogether, fulfill the end intended by a constitution."[36] If the problem is to restrain the actions of a powerful and distant government, a small number of "great" interests enjoying veto powers will provide a protective shield for those smaller interests not possessing veto powers.

Thus in Calhoun's view a white non-slave-owning yeoman farmer from the hill country of South Carolina, though his interests differed in some respects from the slave-owning planters who dominated South Carolina politics, would have the same interest with respect to any action taken (or contemplated) by the government of the United States. In nullifying federal law, Calhoun's argument would suggest, the slaveholding planters who governed South Carolina shielded all interests within the state, great or small, against a distant and potentially oppressive national government.

The relative homogeneity and shield arguments both presuppose as a universal proposition what is more likely contingent and empirical. Differences of interest *within* a "portion" (or state, or section) might, or might not, be less marked than differences of interest *between* portions (or states, or sections). The shield metaphor implies that all of the deadly arrows come from the outside and none from inside. If any deadly arrows come from the shield-wielder himself, the shield ceases to offer protection. Calhoun does not raise the question—central to Madison's analysis of faction in *Federalist* No. 10—whether one sometimes has more to fear from the powerful interest dominating one's state than from a distant federal government. The effect of Calhoun's relative homogeneity and shield arguments is to delegitimize from the outset any *national* action to protect an *internal* minority against a state-level majority.

It is worth asking whether the relative homogeneity assumption held for South Carolina in Calhoun's time. To address such a question in Calhoun's own terms we must exclude slaves, and free blacks, from consideration. Calhoun denied that slaves constituted an interest in their own right. If they were instead counted as an interest and permitted to express their interests, neither the relative homogeneity nor the shield assumptions would hold: their differences of interest vis-à-vis the people holding them in bondage might be far greater than their differences of interest with respect to citizens of free states.

Assuming application is limited to free white South Carolinians, the following can be said for Calhoun's relative homogeneity argument. Though there were sharp conflicts between the Nullifier majority and Unionist minority in South Carolina during the nullification crisis, none of the Unionists supported a high protective tariff, which they agreed was bad policy and damaging to the interests of the state.[37] South Carolina Unionists called upon President Jackson to remedy the "fatal errors" that threatened the Union— meaning an unjust tariff.[38] Unionists and Nullifiers in South Carolina were divided by different constitutional principles, different political loyalties, and differences of political strategy (how best to get the tariff revised). But no one in South Carolina had an interest in preserving the 1828 tariff. In this respect it was true that all white South Carolinians had "the same interest in reference to the action of the [federal] government."

On slavery the tendency of white South Carolinians to close ranks against an outside threat was even more marked than for the tariff. When abolitionists began submitting antislavery petitions to Congress in the mid-1830s, South Carolina's erstwhile Nullifiers and Unionists joined to denounce the abolitionist threat.[39] Calhoun himself emphasized how slavery united the interests of all white citizens (a theme taken up below). When slavery was threatened, South Carolina citizens certainly acted as though they had the same interest with respect to outside powers. (This was not the case in every slave state.)

But at the same time, the growth of a national capitalist market and the increased fiscal role of state governments called into question Calhoun's assumption that internal differences of interest were always greater than external differences of interest. In his 1833 speech on the Force Bill, Calhoun specifically addressed the question why the principle of nullification should not apply within states. He first asserted that "the objects of expenditure which fall within the sphere of a State Government are few and inconsiderable, so that, be their action ever so irregular, it can occasion but little derangement." But then he turned around and observed that the tendency toward oppressive majorities "is perceptible in some of the larger and more populous members of the Union, whose governments have a powerful central action, and which already show a strong tendency to that moneyed action which is the invariable forerunner of corruption and convulsions."[40] Thus Calhoun initially argued (as noted above) that differences of interest within states were much smaller than differences of interest between states or sections. But his admission that states with a "strong moneyed tendency" may display internal divisions called the intra-state homogeneity assumption into question.

The tendency of fully developed capitalism is to reproduce everywhere its characteristic class divisions. If the major conflict of interest is between owners of capital and wage laborers, and both classes populate one's state or section, then one cannot assume all in-state groups have the same interest with respect to action by the federal government. South Carolina in Calhoun's time still remained predominantly agricultural; it was connected with capitalist markets through sale of its products, but had not yet developed the class division characteristic of capitalism. But there was an incipient manufacturing sector in the state, and sharp political and economic divisions existed over the Bank of the State of South Carolina that mirrored national divisions over the Bank of the United States.[41]

Fully developed class divisions reproduced in every geographic section of the country would completely disrupt the correspondence between Calhoun's consensus model of government and his strong doctrine of state sovereignty. State sovereignty (including the right of single-state nullification) advances a consensus model of government only if just one interest predominates in every state, and internal differences of interest are always narrower than external differences of interest. A state's power to nullify national law would do nothing to produce consensus or advance economic justice if employed by a capital-dominated state government against the state's wage laborers. Under such conditions Calhoun's consensus model could only be salvaged by jettisoning the principle of state sovereignty, moving to some nongeographical definition of key "portions or interests" (as in Britain and the Roman Republic), and creating entirely different types of veto rights.

Calhoun clearly did not want to go that route. It was essential that South Carolina—and the South as a whole—be fully united in defense of its sectional interests.

Who Counts as an Interest?

The concept of a "portion or interest" is centrally important to Calhoun's theory because it is "portions or interests" who wield veto rights and who must come to consensus for government to act. He never defined the term "portion or interest," perhaps because it would be impossible to do so for all political orders in all times and places. Key political divisions in the Roman Republic would be different from key divisions in Britain or the United States. The dividing line may be mode of production in one political order, language in another, religion somewhere else, and so on. What defines a "portion" depends upon the particular whole of which it is a part.

But Calhoun clearly did not intend the number and type of "portions or interests" to expand indefinitely. His consensus model could not possibly work with an endless proliferation of veto rights. Not every group that might be regarded, or that might regard itself, as a "portion or interest" counted as such under Calhoun's theory (even when limited to white male citizens). In practice Calhoun's "portions or interests" were (1) limited in number; (2) hierarchically structured, with internal government of some kind; (3) relatively stable over time; and (4) powerful enough to cause problems for the whole if its perceived rights and interests were disregarded. Calhoun presented veto rights as an alternative to secession or violent resistance by disaffected minorities; this works only for minorities already enjoying significant strategic advantages. Only a small number of putative "interests" in any society can meet all these criteria.

For example, Calhoun made clear that the poor—meaning here poor whites—were not a legitimate "portion or interest" at all and thus were not entitled to veto rights. He made this point while discussing the conditions under which universal (white male) suffrage could be safely granted. In governments of the "numerical majority" the extension of suffrage is dangerous, he says, because it brings the community "under the control of the more ignorant and dependent portions of the community."

> As the poor and dependent become more numerous in proportion, there will be, in governments of the numerical majority, no want of leaders among the wealthy and ambitious, to excite and direct them in their efforts to obtain the control.
>
> The case is different in governments of the concurrent majority. There, mere numbers have not the absolute control; and the wealthy and intelligent being identified in interest with the poor and ignorant of their respective portions or interests of the community, become their leaders and protectors. And hence, as the latter would have neither hope nor inducement to rally the former in order to obtain the control, the right of suffrage, under such a government, may be safely enlarged to the extent stated, without incurring the hazard to which such enlargement would expose governments of the numerical majority.[42]

Calhoun is not saying here that rich and poor constitute *different* "interests." He claims instead that the poor do not constitute a legitimate interest at all. Each "portion" or "interest" is hierarchically structured, including both rich and poor, and it is the responsibility of the rich and well educated of each "portion" to be "leaders and protectors" of the poor of their respective "portion." Thus, for example, small, economically struggling southern farmers or tradesmen, owning few slaves or none, would not constitute a different interest from that of large plantations with numerous slaves, but instead be a subordinate component of the same interest; the needs and rights of the less-favored members would be represented and defended by the "rich and well-educated" of that interest. The same would presumably hold for manufacturing, an "interest" composed not merely of capitalists, but of capitalists and laborers both, the former representing the interests of the latter in national councils.

Where capital and labor exhibit separate and conflicting interests, as was already beginning to occur in the non-slaveholding states, Calhoun already saw incipient disease and corruption. "There is and always has been in an advanced stage of wealth and civilization, a conflict between labor and capital. The condition of society in the South exempts us from the disorders and dangers resulting from this conflict." This "explains why it is that the political condition of the slave-holding States has been so much more stable and quiet than those of the North."[43] Slavery, among its other benefits, preserved the internal harmony and hierarchical structure of each "portion or interest."

Why did Calhoun claim the class of "poor and ignorant" citizens cannot constitute a portion or interest? It would be unconvincing to argue that their interests (using "interest" more broadly here) are always the same as those of the wealthy in their state or geographical section. Indeed, Calhoun's own observations about when it is or is not safe to grant universal suffrage presuppose potentially great conflicts of interest between rich and poor citizens. It would also be unconvincing (using another of Calhoun's criteria) to claim that rich and poor citizens are never differentially affected by the actions of government.

But to count as a "portion or interest" for Calhoun a group must have an internal governing structure—must possess its own "majority or appropriate organ" capable of acting and speaking authoritatively for the group. A portion or interest cannot be composed of what Calhoun elsewhere calls "a mere mass of individuals without organization."[44] The poor as such do not possess an organized structure with decision-making institutions, at least not naturally and automatically (and the same applies to other unfortunate but unorganized groups). Calhoun apparently assumed that the poor and dependent would always be incapable of self-organization. Under bad governments it would be wealthy and ambitious demagogues who organized the poor and dependent by exciting resentment against the wealthy; under good governments the poor and dependent, he believed, would look up to the wealthy and educated as their natural "leaders and protectors." Political organization is hierarchical in both cases; the poor and dependent never organized themselves.

The need for organizational structure and a decision-making process does limit the number of potential "portions or interests" able to claim veto rights. To put the matter bluntly, this requirement limits veto rights to relatively powerful minorities and shuts out powerless ones. For one of the effects of oppression carried far enough is that the oppressed group is deprived of the power of self-organization. This limits the degree to which consensus among relatively powerful "portions or interests" can advance any vision of justice.

Consensus and Dissent in South Carolina

In closing his *Discourse on the Constitution and Government of the United States,* Calhoun held up the South Carolina constitution as a model of internal justice and harmony. His description echoed the consensus model he recommended for the United States as a whole and for all constitutional republics. Recall that William Henry Harrison publicly challenged Calhoun on nullification, arguing that one cannot deny internal minorities equivalent veto rights and that the result would be infinite regression culminating in anarchy. Calhoun never directly answered Harrison, but Calhoun's description of the South Carolina constitution could be considered his answer. (Calhoun's praise of the South Carolina constitution in the *Discourse* abbreviated an argument he made in-state in an 1846 public letter against making the state constitution more democratic, and I will draw from both.)[45]

In the *Disquisition* Calhoun argued that among different "portions or interests" veto rights are essential; but *within* a portion or interest every individual "might trust, with confidence, its majority or appropriate organ, against that of every other interest."[46] On one hand, Calhoun clearly signals here that veto rights come to an end somewhere, to be replaced by "trust" in the decision-making organ of one's "portion" (or state). On the other hand, he is not saying the internal decision-making procedure must always be majority rule. He speaks of trusting one's own majority, "or appropriate organ," opening the prospect of internal decisions based on something other than majority rule. Within a portion or interest, in Calhoun's view, majority rule seems to be permitted but not required—and as we shall see, not always recommended.

The South Carolina constitution centralized power in the legislature in a way unparalleled in any other state; by Calhoun's own account the legislature "appoints all the important officers of the State."[47] The governor, all state judges, and presidential electors were appointed by the legislature, which also possessed the power to amend the state constitution by two-thirds vote in two consecutive sessions. Therefore neither the judiciary, nor executive, nor local governments, nor the written constitution itself could significantly check the power of the legislature. This would seem an odd model for Calhoun, given his preoccupation, at the federal level, with external checks on the power of Congress, including of course state nullification of federal law. If the problem that drives Calhoun's theory is unchecked power, the South Carolina constitution would seem a peculiar remedy.

But Calhoun's consensus model does not necessarily rely upon *external* checks. In the *Disquisition* he argues that each "division or interest" must be given "either a concurrent voice in making and executing the laws, or a veto on their execution." Thus two rather different methods exist for institutionalizing the consensus requirement. One is through external veto; state nullification of federal law would be the clearest case here. The other is through a mechanism internal to the legislative process itself, a "concurrent voice in making and executing the laws."[48] In the South Carolina constitution as Calhoun described it, the two key "portions or interests" that composed the state were already incorporated organically into the operation of the legislature. One interest controlled the upper house, the other controlled the lower house, and the consent of both chambers was necessary to make laws, appoint officials, and amend the constitution. Because the internal operation of the legislature required consensus, external checks on the legislature were unnecessary.

What then were these two key interests? In geographic terms they were an upcountry interest and a lowcountry interest; economically they were defined by different products (in the lowcountry, rice and long-fiber cotton cultivation, plus Charleston commerce; in the upcountry, short-fiber cotton cultivation). But the most important differences, in Calhoun's view, were "the great excess of the slave population of the [lowcountry] compared with the [upcountry], and the difference in the origin of their inhabitants and manner of settlement"—the lowcountry having been settled principally by English Anglicans and French Huguenots, while the upcountry "consisted principally of emigrants who followed the course of the mountains" and who "had very little connection, or intercourse for a long time with the old settlement on the coast."[49] In the lowcountry slaves vastly outnumbered white citizens, while in the upcountry the numbers of slaves and white citizens were more evenly balanced; the lowcountry contained the larger share of taxable wealth (above all property in slaves) while the upcountry contained the majority of the free white population (but also a sizeable share of wealth, including slave property).[50]

The structure of the South Carolina constitution guaranteed that the lowcountry interest would predominate in the Senate and the upcountry interest in the House. The Senate was composed of one member from each election district, regardless of population (except for Charleston, which had two members), guaranteeing the lowcountry a majority; in the House representation was calculated according to a compound of (white) population and taxable property, which in practice gave the upcountry a majority. Thus the Senate represented taxable property, while the House represented a compound of property and population. Straightforward majority representation (of white male citizens) was not a principle expressed in either chamber or anywhere else in the South Carolina constitution. (This complete exclusion of what Calhoun called "the numerical majority" from state government distinguished South Carolina from all other states, including other slave states.)

This complicated formula resulted from an 1808 compromise resolving a potentially violent political crisis occasioned by the nearly complete exclusion of the upcountry from political power in the state. "The upper country," Calhoun reported, "although it had become the most populous section" was according to the rules of the 1790 constitution left "in a minority in every department of the government." The upcountry agitated for "a weight in the government, proportional to its population" but in the end settled for a compromise giving it predominance in the lower house alone while accepting continued underrepresentation in the Senate.[51] It was this compromise and the constitution resulting from it that Calhoun held up as a model. "The lower section was wise and patriotic enough to propose an adjustment" and the upcountry "waived its claims" to unqualified majority rule and accepted the compromise.

The effect of this settlement, in Calhoun's view, was to make each chamber of the legislature the organ of one of the two major social and economic divisions of the state, and to give each the power to check the other. He described in glowing terms the benefits resulting from this compromise between sections:

The government . . . was converted into that of the concurrent majority, and made, emphatically, the government of the entire population,—of the whole people of South Carolina;—and not of one portion of its people over another portion. The consequence was, the almost instantaneous restoration of harmony and concord between the two sections. Party division and party violence, with the distraction and disorder attendant upon them, soon disappeared . . . The State, as far as its internal affairs are concerned, may be literally said to have been, during the whole period, without a party. Party organization, party discipline, party proscription,—and their offspring, *the spoils principle,* have been unknown to the State. Nothing of the kind is necessary to produce concentration; as our happy constitution makes an united people,—with the exception of occasional, but short local dissentions, in reference to action of the federal government [meaning internal divisions over nullification in 1832];—and even the most violent of these ceased, almost instantly, with the occasion which produced it.[52]

Calhoun closes the *Discourse* by holding up this "offspring of a conflict, timely and well-compromised" as an example of "concord and harmony" for other states and the United States as a whole. The complete absence of "party division" in South Carolina (it was the only state at the time without party competition) is extremely important for Calhoun because it signifies the kind of internal harmony and homogeneity upon which his consensus model depended.

The underrepresentation of the upcountry majority did not go unchallenged in the state, however, and it was in response to this challenge that in 1846 Calhoun comprehensively defended the 1808 settlement. The occasion was a proposal by some upcountry leaders to have South Carolina's presidential electors selected by popular vote (as all other states did by that time) instead of appointed by the legislature.[53] This proposed change would not have changed the organization of the state legislature itself but would have introduced the principle of majority rule into at least one corner of South Carolina politics. It was on precisely these grounds that Calhoun rejected the proposal. His first argument was that popular selection of presidential electors would introduce party divisions into the state: "There would grow out of this state of things two parties, with all the usual party machinery, of caucus, convention, cliques, managers to control the election."[54]

But Calhoun's chief objection was that the principle of straight majority rule "would not be fair or just" to the lowcountry "regarding the State in its federal relations" and would "disturb and endanger the compromise" underlying the state constitution. By its "federal relations" Calhoun meant the federal formula for counting slaves in determining representation (i.e., the three-fifths clause). He emphasized that because of its large slave population, South Carolina depended more than any other state on the three-fifths clause for representation in Congress and its quota of presidential electors, "because she has the greatest number in proportion of that description of population." The lowcountry had a vastly greater slave population than the upcountry and for that reason added more "to the federal weight of the State" than the upcountry. Thus selecting presidential electors within state by majority rule would violate the very principle (the three-fifths clause) that guaranteed South Carolina's power in the Union as a whole. South Carolina, Calhoun argued, cannot uphold one set of principles in its federal relations—the representational bonus for slave property—and practice another set of principles internally (straight majority rule); this would introduce a "radical assumption . . . of the most dangerous character." Calhoun in effect reminded white South Carolinians that the principle of majority rule, internally or externally, endangered the institution of slavery.[55]

Calhoun opposed not only this specific proposal but any alternation of the 1808 settlement, which he argued had "satisfactorily and permanently adjusted" the conflicts between the two sections of the state. Any shift in the direction of majority rule, "be it ever so small . . . will slowly and imperceptibly commence the process of absorption" and will ultimately terminate in rule by "the mere numerical majority." "Our State is organized on the far broader and more solid and durable foundation, of the concurrent majority to the entire exclusion of the numerical."[56]

Calhoun's insisting that the 1808 settlement was *permanent* shows how his consensus model required essentially unchanging interest formations as the legitimate bearers of veto rights.[57] A system based upon majority rule and open party competition can respond relatively easily to the emergence of new interests and the eclipse of old ones. The system favored by Calhoun, and embodied in the South Carolina constitution, cannot easily adjust to emerging new interests or a changed balance between interests. Existing divisions must be not only maintained but where necessary reinforced. The system was borne of a compromise that averted a crisis, and altering the system now, he believed, could precipitate another crisis.

Thus Calhoun avoided the infinite regression problem (i.e., vetoes-within-vetoes for interests-within-interests) by halting the series at its first internal division: within the state there were only two essential interests. Each predominated in one branch of the legislature. If there were more than two essential interests within the state, Calhoun's principles would require creating additional branches and organs of government. For if any "portion or interest" was left unrepresented in this arrangement, that interest would be far more unprotected in South Carolina, given the concentration of all powers in the legislature, than in states with independent executive and judicial branches.

Ultimately what is most striking about Calhoun's account of upcountry and lowcountry interests in South Carolina is how alike they are. The ratio of slaves to white citizens in the two regions differed (the difference Calhoun emphasized most), but this becomes relatively unimportant given the enormous commitment of both regions to the institution of slavery. In this respect, Calhoun underscored the two regions' essential similarity in the very act of describing their differences. In South Carolina—and to a lesser degree in other slave states—slavery was the glue that reconciled all other differences among white citizens; Calhoun never tired of making this argument. Even those white citizens who owned no slaves and had to endure poverty and misfortune nevertheless savored the "position and pride of character" that came from being a member of the white race.[58]

Homogeneity Political, Not Natural

Thus Calhoun answered in several ways the challenge to his theory posed by the problem of internal diversity: where do veto rights end, and how could any particular stopping point be justified? All of his answers had one paradoxical element in common: in each case Calhoun admitted the fact of internal diversity yet depended upon discovering a point at which homogeneity outweighed diversity and internal vetoes were no longer necessary.

How is such a point discovered? This may be the wrong question. A better question is: how are such points *created and reinforced?* All of Calhoun's attempts to address the problem of internal diversity reveal a keen (if understated) recognition that the unity and homogeneity of his state and region was not natural and automatic but required continual maintenance and intervention. Political unity between the rich and (white) poor of a state or region is not automatic. The same goes for internal unity against a perceived outside threat (the shield argument). The politically contingent character of internal unity leads us once again to Calhoun's ideal of statesmanship and to his own historic role as leader of his state and the South.

In *Origins of Southern Radicalism* Lacy K. Ford writes that what most fascinated outside observers about antebellum South Carolina "was not so much the state's fiery radicalism as its penchant for concealing its internal divisions, such as they were, from the eyes of the world." An outsider to the state observed in 1860: "The people of South Carolina, however widely they may differ in fact, have a politic desire to present an undivided front to outsiders, and to appear before the world as all of one mind."[59] This characterization of South Carolina's political culture equally describes Calhoun's own brand of political leadership and the preconditions necessary for his consensus model to function as he intended.

Calhoun repeatedly emphasized there were no party divisions in South Carolina, and he achieved this party-free ideal to a significant degree in his own role as leader of his state. Ford reports that from 1833 until 1850 South Carolina stayed clear of national party attachments and pursued its own independent course under Calhoun's leadership. There was a direct connection between the independent course Calhoun followed on the national level and the degree of unanimity he demanded at home: "In order to be effective as a 'free-lance statesman' . . . Calhoun had to be sure of virtually unanimous support for his actions from within South Carolina." This "virtually unanimous support" did not come without some fierce political battles within the state. Calhoun had to crush an incipient Whig revolt in the early 1840s, after which "no concerted effort was mounted to establish a viable two-party system within South Carolina."[60]

Calhoun's leadership of South Carolina might seem of more historical than theoretical significance. What links it to his broader political theory, and the critical challenges to that theory, is the way Calhoun recommended the South Carolina example to the South as a whole. For the last two decades of his life he persistently sought to achieve "the union of the entire South" as he put it in 1837 and underscored in 1847: "Henceforward, let all party distinction among us cease, so long as this aggression on our rights and honor [meaning opposition to slavery] shall continue."[61] This union of the South illustrates most clearly the contingent rather than natural character of the unity and homogeneity that characterized "portions or interests" in Calhoun's political theory.

Unlike the state of South Carolina on one side, and the United States on the other—both of which were constitutionally defined political communities—"the South" as a section had no legal or constitutional status. The U.S. government and the government of South Carolina could advance their respective (if contradictory) claims to political obedience, but no southern state could pretend that other southern states were obliged to follow its lead. In a legal and constitutional sense "the South" as such did not exist.

In another sense, however, "the South" was essential to Calhoun's thinking in a way that the state of South Carolina, or any individual state, was not. What mattered most from the perspective of the theory set forth in the *Disquisition* was that each "portion or interest" possess veto rights. It was the South, with its special economic needs and enormous investment in slavery, which constituted a "portion" here, not any individual state. State sovereignty, states' rights, nullification—all of these were ultimately means to an end. States were important only as stand-ins for organic interests, and they could play that role only if states with shared interests were internally united and acted in concert. The complete unity of South Carolina (without party divisions) was essential to the unity of the South. The unity of the South (without party divisions) was essential to the proper functioning of Calhoun's consensus model of government on the national level.

Absence of party division does not mean absence of division. It means that alternative methods must be found of handling the kinds of internal conflicts that would normally be taken up by political parties under the standard majority-and-opposition model of politics.

In the end Calhoun relied upon two things to resolve the problem of internal diversity: slavery and statesmanship. Slavery created a common bond among interests that would otherwise compete in ways disruptive to the operation of Calhoun's consensus model. But a common interest in slavery (and a common front against threats to slavery) could not resolve every internal conflict. Where the glue of slavery ended, the task of political leadership began. It would also follow that if slavery were removed from the picture, as it must be in any modern-day attempt to realize a consensus model of politics, the burden of political leadership in reconciling (or suppressing) conflicts *within* portions as well as *among* portions becomes even greater.

An Ill-Advised Exchange

The question this chapter has addressed is not whether it is *possible* to create a system where one or more key interests enjoy guaranteed veto rights over decisions of the whole. Such systems can exist, do exist, and will continue to exist, sometimes as a result of deliberate constitutional design, sometimes simply because one or more key interests are powerful enough to make trouble unless they possess veto rights.

The question instead is: *Under what conditions* would a political system that guarantees each key "portion or interest" veto rights over decisions of the whole accomplish what Calhoun expected? What would be necessary for such a government to be *effective*—not feeble or anarchic? What would be necessary for such a government to be *fair* to all interests—not just favoring some at the expense of others?

Calhoun's political thought is of enduring value because he forthrightly addressed these questions of effectiveness and fairness. But the conditions necessary, by his own admission, for his system to work effectively turn out to be either improbable or oppressive or both. Calhoun's system depends upon leaders transforming potential catastrophe into genuine consensus, not just during a once-in-a-century crisis but all the time. His system avoids minority domination only under the unlikely assumption that inaction or deadlock is equally costly to all sides. Calhoun avoids the problem of potentially infinite regression of veto rights by denying that some interests are truly interests; by assuming that the interests that really count remain static over time (as in South Carolina); and by embracing a degree of inequality and hierarchy *within* an interest that he completely rejects in relations *between* interests. If his racial and class hierarchies are rejected, it becomes all the more difficult to justify any stopping point in the regression of veto rights under his system.

None of this is meant to dismiss the importance of Calhoun's thought. He understood, better than anyone else before or since, the necessary (if unlikely) preconditions for a minority veto/consensus model of government to work. As long as minority-veto based political systems and/or federal systems based on the full sovereignty of the constituent parts exist, Calhoun's political theory deserves close attention.

But that such systems *exist* is not necessarily a reason to *choose* them in preference to a functioning democracy based on majority rule—at least if the latter is available, as it was in Calhoun's own time and place. It was this functioning (if imperfect) system of majority rule that Calhoun sought to undo and replace with his seductive vision of true consensus. Given the improbable—or in some cases highly repressive—conditions necessary for a consensus model of government to work as Calhoun envisioned, such an exchange would be ill-advised.

■

SEVEN

Contemporary Divided Societies and the Minority Veto

This chapter examines one contemporary theorist with affinities to Calhoun (Arend Lijphart); explores three cases where something akin to Calhoun's consensus model has been either attempted (Yugoslavia and Northern Ireland), or seriously considered though rejected (South Africa); and closes with Lani Guinier's Calhoun-like diagnosis and remedy for the racial divide in American politics.

Slavery has been long dead in the United States. Apartheid is dead in South Africa. Yugoslavia no longer exists. What is not dead, however, is the idea that guaranteed veto rights for each significant group in deeply divided political orders will produce consensus rather than anarchy or secession.

Going to the Source

During the 1970s and 1980s the idea of a constitutionally guaranteed minority veto in a reformed South African political order was widely discussed. Nelson Mandela (still in prison at the time) and the African National Congress rejected any permanent minority veto, which in their view meant continued white minority domination in another form. The argument in favor of minority veto held that white South Africans would force a civil war rather than put their fates into the hands of a black majority. Because South Africa is divided not only by race but also by language and ethnicity, the minority veto was advocated as a means of protecting the fundamental interests of all minorities, not just the white minority, in a reconstituted political order.[1]

The ruling National Party's 1983 constitution with its separate parliaments for Asians and individuals of mixed race and complete exclusion of black Africans was a transparently rigged minority veto, designed to make white minority rule permanent. A different version of minority veto, however, was proposed by a small, white-led antiapartheid opposition party called the Progressive Federal Party under the leadership of Frederick van Zyl Slabbert. In a 1979 book, *South Africa's Options: Strategies for Sharing Power,* van Zyl Slabbert and co-author David Welsh advocated a constitution founded on universal suffrage that would grant formal veto rights over national legislation to any minority enjoying 10 to 15 percent electoral support. The obvious objection was that this would generate deadlock or anarchy. The authors, however, denied it would produce deadlock; instead, they argued, "it is often the threat of deadlocks or vetoes that induces a consensus."[2] They cited Dutch political scientist Arend Lijphart's 1977 work *Democracy in Plural Societies* for support on this claim.

If one consults the specific passage cited by van Zyl Slabbert and Welsh (page 37 of Lijphart's book), what one finds is Lijphart quoting and paraphrasing Calhoun's own argument in *A Disquisition on Government* about why giving each interest a veto will not lead to deadlock. Lijphart describes the minority veto as "synonymous with John C. Calhoun's concurrent majority, which also had the protection of minority interests as its principal goal." Lijphart then quotes at length from Calhoun's *Disquisition,* emphasizing Calhoun's claim that minority vetoes will not lead to deadlock or minority tyranny because (in Lijphart's summary of Calhoun) "each segment will recognize the danger of deadlock and immobilism that is likely to result from an unrestrained use of the veto."[3]

In advocating the minority veto/consensus model van Zyl Slabbert and Welsh (indirectly) and Lijphart (directly) depended on Calhoun to answer the anarchy objection. This suggests that no one has proposed a *better* answer to the anarchy objection than Calhoun's. Thus Calhoun's own strengths, weaknesses, and presuppositions should matter to theorists and constitution-framers elsewhere who might never have read Calhoun but who seek to remedy the problems of deeply divided societies through a consensus model of government. The strengths of Calhoun's theory may be their strengths; the traps Calhoun fell into may be lurking for them also.

My theme here is permanent, constitutionally guaranteed minority veto power over any sphere of policy, where the minority itself is final judge of when and how to employ that power. This was what Calhoun himself considered essential and what was institutionalized or proposed in the three cases examined below (Northern Ireland, Yugoslavia, South Africa). A permanent, constitutionally guaranteed minority veto should be distinguished from: (1) minority veto as an informal political arrangement that can be overturned if the danger of obstruction becomes too great; (2) minority veto over some carefully circumscribed policy area; and (3) minority veto in the constitutional settlement itself, but not under the constitution once enacted.

With respect to point (1): under any set of democratic institutions it is possible for particular minorities to secure a position of more-than-ordinary power. In the United States, for example, it can loosely be said that the National Rifle Association enjoys a minority veto over firearms legislation favored by a majority of Americans, but this is a contingent political result. In parliamentary systems, smaller parties in the governing coalition sometimes enjoy informal veto rights over matters especially important to their base; this is something short of a constitutional guarantee. Under the rules of the U.S. Senate, a single senator can filibuster, and a 60 percent cloture vote is required to end it. But the filibuster itself is a Senate rule, not a constitutional guarantee, and could in principle be overturned by majority vote of the body. Thus even though the filibuster is often called a minority veto, it falls short of the constitutional guarantee Calhoun considered essential.

With respect to point (2): an all-purpose minority veto over any sphere of policy should not be confused with veto rights over specifically defined, subsidiary policy areas (such as educational policy or language use) of special concern to religious or cultural minorities. Nor should it be confused with federal systems that reserve specific powers to states or provinces, but do not make individual states or provinces final judge of the extent of their own powers or the range of issues to which their veto rights apply.

With respect to point (3): in enacting a wholly new constitution, especially after a political revolution has fundamentally changed the form of government and/or redefined membership in the political community itself (as in South Africa in the early 1990s), the argument for nearly unanimous support for the constitutional settlement itself is very strong. This is very different from requiring near-unanimity *under the ordinary operations of a constitu-*

tion. I argued in chapter 4 that Calhoun's political remedy resembled in practice a permanent constitutional convention, where the degree of consensus ordinarily reserved for successful constitutional settlements was demanded as an ongoing decision rule. The Yugoslavian constitution of 1974 and the Good Friday Agreement of 1998 for Northern Ireland made consensus an ongoing decision rule; the same would have applied to several forms of minority veto proposed in South Africa.

The three cases examined here are all very difficult ones, the Yugoslavian case a full-scale disaster. Thus they may seem an unfair test of the consensus model. But Calhoun himself regarded the consensus model as appropriate precisely for the most difficult cases. Comparisons among these cases and with Calhoun's own historical context are tricky (no two cases are exactly parallel). But that they are *difficult* cases with entrenched conflict is exactly what makes comparison appropriate in the first place.

Calhoun, Lijphart, and Consociational Democracy

Among contemporary political scientists Arend Lijphart is probably closest to Calhoun in theoretical approach. Lijphart coined the term "consociational democracy" and has championed this idea both theoretically and practically for at least thirty-five years.[4] The degree of Lijphart's influence on contemporary political science is evidenced by the frequent use of the term "consociational" in the literature of comparative politics. Few other comparative political scientists demonstrate familiarity with Calhoun, but Lijphart himself has been enormously influential, among policy makers as well as academics, and he is explicit about similarities between Calhoun's thought and his own.

By consociational democracy Lijphart means a "consensus model of democracy" characterized by "the cooperative attitudes and behavior of the leaders of the different segments of the population." He contrasts consociational democracy with majority/opposition democracy ("the Westminster model") where a majority party or coalition governs, in competition with a minority that remains in loyal opposition and seeks to replace the majority.[5] Lijphart argues that the majority/opposition model may be appropriate to homogeneous societies like Britain where the common interests that hold society together can be taken for granted, but is not appropriate to "plural societies"—"societies that are sharply divided along religious, ideological, linguistic, cultural, ethnic, or racial lines into virtually separate subsocieties with their own political parties, interest groups, and media of communication." European nations that (at least in the 1970s) Lijphart described as "plural societies" include Belgium and the Netherlands (on which he published book-length studies), Austria, and Northern Ireland; and elsewhere in the world Nigeria, Lebanon, Malaysia, and South Africa—the last another book-length study. Other political scientists, following Lijphart's lead, have applied his consociational model to other parts of the world.

In a society deeply divided into segments, Lijphart argues, "the flexibility necessary for majoritarian democracy is absent" because voters' loyalties are rigid rather than fluid, and there is little chance that "the main parties will alternate in exercising governmental power." Under such conditions, Lijphart argues, "majority rule is not only undemocratic but also dangerous, because minorities that are continually denied access to power will feel excluded and discriminated against and will lose their allegiance to the regime . . . What these societies need is a democratic regime that emphasizes consensus instead of opposition." The primary characteristic of Lijphart's consociational (or consensus) democracy is that "political leaders of all significant segments of the plural society cooperate in a grand coalition to govern the country."[6] For Lijphart, as for Calhoun, the consensus requirement is intended among other things to stave off the threat of violent resistance or secession by minorities who regard the governing majority as equivalent to a foreign power.

Lijphart's consociational democracy has four essential characteristics: (1) "government by a grand coalition of the political leaders of all significant segments of the plural society"; (2) "the mutual veto or 'concurrent majority rule'"; (3) "proportionality as the principal standard of political representation"; and (4) "a high degree of autonomy for each segment to run its own internal affairs."[7]

The purpose of Lijphart's first characteristic, the grand coalition principle, is the same as Calhoun's central goal: "to unite the most opposite and conflicting interests, and to blend the whole in one common attachment to the country."[8] The general problem Lijphart and Calhoun seek to remedy is also the same: majority rule under conditions where entrenched majorities and minorities make it unlikely that the minority can ever replace the majority as a governing party.

Lijphart directly follows Calhoun in his second category, the "mutual veto or concurrent majority" (using Calhoun's own terminology). The minority veto requirement follows from the failure of grand coalitions to offer "absolute or foolproof protection" to minority partners; even if included in the cabinet they "may nevertheless be outvoted by the majority." (In other words, there is a difference between being consulted and getting what you want.) A minority that considers its vital interests at risk will not cooperate in a governing coalition. "A minority veto must therefore be added to the grand coalition principle; only such a veto can give each segment a complete guarantee of political protection." Lijphart then adds that "the minority veto is synonymous with John C. Calhoun's concurrent majority."[9]

Lijphart addresses the chief objection to the minority veto, i.e., "that it will lead to minority tyranny, which may strain the cooperation in a grand coalition as much as the outvoting of minorities." He lists three reasons "why this danger is not as serious as it appears," all drawn from Calhoun's own answer to the same objection and supported with quotations from Calhoun's *Disquisition*. First, because it is a *mutual* veto ("Calhoun uses the term 'mutual negative,'" Lijphart notes), its too frequent use can be turned against the minority's own interest. Second, "the very fact that the veto is available as a potential weapon gives a feeling of security which makes the actual use of it improbable."[10] Finally, "each segment will recognize the danger of deadlock and immobilism that is likely to result from an unrestrained use of the veto." This statement is supported by a quote from Calhoun's *Disquisition:* "Impelled by the imperious necessity of preventing the suspension of the action of government . . . each portion would regard the sacrifice it might have to make by yielding its peculiar interest to secure the common interest and safety of all, including its own, as nothing compared to the evils that would be inflicted on all, including its own, by pertinaciously adhering to a different line of action."[11] This was the very page cited by van Zyl Slabbert and Welsh to support their argument that a minority veto in postapartheid South Africa would not generate deadlock. Thus Lijphart's theory of consociational democracy resembles Calhoun's consensus model, not only in its institutional mechanisms (the "mutual veto") but also in Lijphart's response to the anarchy and minority rule objections.

In another respect, however, Lijphart's minority veto is broader than Calhoun's. Lijphart includes both formal veto powers "anchored in the constitution" and "an informal and unwritten understanding" that governs political cooperation among the different segments. Whether the minority veto should be a constitutional guarantee or an informal arrangement depends for Lijphart on the nature of the society and/or the specific policy at issue: in the Netherlands and Switzerland the veto is an informal arrangement; in Belgium it is informal on most issues but constitutionally recognized on "laws affecting the cultural and educational interests of the language groups."[12] But like van Zyl Slabbert and Welsh—and as we shall see, like Prime Minister F. W. de Klerk in the early 1990s—Lijphart recommended a permanent, constitutionally inscribed minority veto over national legislation for postapartheid South Africa.[13]

For Calhoun the minority veto had to be a clear constitutional guarantee. The informal political arrangement whereby slave states and free states were kept in balance, giving slave states equality in the U.S. Senate and consequently a veto on legislation, was in the process of breaking down toward the end of Calhoun's life and he insisted that only a constitutionally guaranteed veto would suffice.

Where the minority veto is an informal arrangement rather than a constitutional guarantee, there is some protection against the minority's using its veto in excessively obstructive or extortionate ways; what is created by the ordinary political process could be overridden the same way. On the other hand, this flexibility and "safety valve" character of the informal veto undermines Calhoun's argument—which Lijphart himself accepted and quoted—that the very danger of deadlock will force all segments to work together. Informal arrangements lack the "imperious necessity" essential to Calhoun's consensus model.

If in some respects Lijphart's "consociational democracy" is more broadly defined than Calhoun's "concurrent majority," in another respect Lijphart's theory is more narrowly targeted. Lijphart does not claim that consociational democracy is best for all political orders, but only for "plural societies," i.e., societies deeply divided into a number of segments, or subsocieties. Calhoun, on the other hand, rejected this distinction, arguing instead that every democracy will over time develop entrenched majorities and minorities unlikely to alternate in power.

Lijphart, like Calhoun, acknowledges that for a consensus system to work, ordinary voters within each "segment" must defer to the judgments and decisions of their top leaders. "Segmental leaders have the difficult task of, on the one hand, reaching political accommodations with and making concessions to the leaders of other segments and, on the other hand, maintaining the confidence of their own rank and file. It is therefore helpful if they possess considerable independent power and a secure position of leadership."[14] Elsewhere Lijphart makes the point more strongly: consociational democracy requires "an inherently strong tendency to be obedient and allegiant" on the part of the rank and file within each segment.[15] He admits that consociational arrangements come at some cost to democratic participation and partly for this reason does not recommend them for all times and all places. For Calhoun, in contrast, it is a good, not a drawback, that the "poor and ignorant" within each "portion or interest" defer to the "wealthy and intelligent" who "become their leaders and protectors."[16] In his own career as a political leader Calhoun insisted upon and largely received from his home state the kind of independence, flexibility, and deference that Lijphart describes.

One of Lijphart's essential characteristics for consociational democracy is proportionality, by which he means more than just proportionate representation in parliament (which of itself has no necessary relation to a consensus model of government) but proportionality in "the decision-making process itself" whereby "all groups influence a decision in proportion to their numerical strength."[17] He admits this is difficult with unavoidably dichotomous decisions, but believes it can be honored in spirit through reciprocity among groups over time.

Lijphart does not, however, discuss the potentially great tension between proportionality and the minority veto, both of which he considers essential, and this tension is significant for comparison with Calhoun. The U.S. electoral system (in Calhoun's time as well as the present) does not easily allow for proportionality except proportional representation of states by population in the U.S. House of Representatives. But it was precisely *this* proportionality that Calhoun considered most dangerous. Calhoun demanded for the South not simply the weaker protection of proportionality, but a guaranteed veto—in other words, whatever degree of power was required to guarantee what slaveholders themselves judged to be their vital interests. In practice this would have to be not proportional but more-than-proportional power; it follows in turn that the majority (or some less-favored minority) would enjoy less-than-proportional power.

The difference between proportionality and minority veto mattered very much to the slavery issue in Calhoun's own time. The slaveholding interest in the United States was already significantly *overrepresented* proportional to their numbers (both as a result of their equality in the Senate, and the three-fifths clause in the House). Yet Calhoun did not consider this overrepresentation sufficient to guarantee the interests of slaveholders. Slave owners were overrepresented, but *not overrepresented enough;* what mattered was a veto. Other minorities with vital interests at stake, far distant in place and time from Calhoun and the peculiar institution he sought to defend, may be equally unsatisfied with merely proportional power when the consensus model promises them a veto. Lijphart admits that proportional representation falls short of a minority veto, but does not explore the potentially enormous tensions between these two elements of consociational democracy.

Finally, neither for Calhoun nor Lijphart should *all* interests enjoy veto rights; for both theorists it is the "significant" interests, and those who regard one another as legitimate, that count. In Calhoun's case, the matter was settled by definition: slaves did not constitute an interest, internal dissidents within South Carolina did not count as an interest, abolitionists were beyond the pale. Lijphart is more willing to admit that some groups are excluded: the Communist Party, for example, was not included in the ruling consensus for any of the European nations he described as consociational. Lijphart also notes that consociational democracy works best where the number of groups participating in consensus is manageable, somewhere between three and five: "As the number of participants in negotiations increases, bargaining becomes more complicated and difficult."[18]

As a practical matter, Lijphart may be right that a consensus-based system—if it works at all—functions best where the number of veto-bearing participants is limited; or to put it another way, where consensus does not mean everyone. But this leaves unanswered the problem of justifying how and where that line is drawn, and of guarding the rights of those minorities that do not enjoy veto powers. In this respect Lijphart fails adequately to answer some of the same questions that Calhoun failed to answer.[19]

Concurrent Majority in Northern Ireland

John C. Calhoun was of Scotch-Irish descent, and his spirit seems to have presided over negotiations in his ancestral homeland. The Good Friday Agreement of 1998 attempts to resolve the longstanding bitter conflict between nationalists and unionists in Northern Ireland through constitutional arrangements that in many respects embody Calhoun's principle of the concurrent majority, including a dual executive and a concurrent majority rule for all significant legislation. There is no evidence that Calhoun's writings were directly consulted, but Arend Lijphart's theory of consociational democracy (which in turn draws from Calhoun) was an explicit influence on the architecture of the Good Friday Agreement; this is acknowledged by both supporters and critics of the agreement.[20] Thus in many respects the Good Friday Agreement may function as a test case for the theoretical prescriptions of both Calhoun and Lijphart.

The agreement requires that all "key decisions" receive majority support from both of the two key groups, the predominantly Protestant Unionists (who seek to remain part of Great Britain) and the predominantly Catholic Nationalists (who seek ultimately to join Northern Ireland to Ireland). All members of the assembly must designate themselves "nationalists," "unionists," or "others." Passage of important pieces of legislation requires "concurrent nationalist and unionist majorities as well as a majority of MLAs [members of the Legislative Assembly]." (Note that analysts Brendan O'Leary and John McGarry here employ Calhoun's own term, "concurrent majority.") The synonymous term "parallel consent" is also employed to describe these voting rules, which require, "among those present and voting, both an overall majority of Assembly members and a majority of both unionist and nationalist members to endorse a proposal." If a strict concurrent majority fails, there is a fallback procedure whereby legislation may be passed on the basis of "a weighted majority"—which requires 60 percent in the Assembly, including "the support of 40 per cent of nationalist members and 40 per cent of unionist members."[21] Thus key decisions require both a majority in the Assembly as a whole and majority support (or, in the fallback procedure, near-majority support) within both the nationalist and unionist groups, which gives each of these two groups a veto. The assembly members designated "other," such as the Northern Ireland Women's Coalition—which seeks to organize voters around issues that challenge the ideologies of both major groups—do not enjoy any such veto rights.

The concurrent majority/consensus model also has been built into the executive branch, which has been described as a "diarchy": the First Minister and the Deputy First Minister, each representing one of the two key divisions, are—at least in theory—of equal power. "If either the First Minister or the Deputy First Minister ceases to hold office, whether by resignation or otherwise, the other shall also cease to hold office." The purpose is not merely to allow each to veto decisions of the other, though this is one effect of the arrangement, but also, more positively, to force the two to work together: "This new diarchy will critically depend upon the personal cooperation of the two holders of these posts."[22]

The "diarchy" executive, whether by design or chance, closely resembles Calhoun's own proposal for a dual executive for the United States, each representing one of the two great sections of the country, and "requiring each to approve all the acts of Congress before they shall become laws."[23] It also exemplifies Arend Lijphart's broader consociational principle of "executive power-sharing" whereby "each of the main communities share in executive power." But the Northern Ireland "diarchy" has no exact counterpart in Lijphart's writings comparable to its exact counterpart in Calhoun. Not only the diarchy itself but also the assumptions and hopes about how it would function in practice directly parallel Calhoun's theory. For Calhoun (as noted in chapter 6) the purpose of the mutual veto was not merely to block action; stalemate was not the goal. The purpose was to force deliberation and cooperative action in the common good. The intention, at least, of the Northern Ireland diarchy—to force "personal cooperation" between top leaders of two antagonistic communities—is the same.

Several other features of the agreement should be noted. Elections are conducted according to the Single Transferable Vote rule, whereby voters can express both first and second party preferences. Supporters of the rule maintain it will encourage moderation by rewarding parties capable of achieving cross-community support (e.g., a nationalist voter might designate a moderate unionist party as his/her second preference). Whether it will actually have this effect is disputed.[24] The agreement also provides for proportional representation of parties in allocation of ministerial portfolios, employing a particular mathematical formula;[25] thus any party (including in theory those designated "other") that enjoys threshold-level support may be entitled to participate in a grand coalition cabinet.

The agreement leaves entirely open the key long-term question of whether Northern Ireland will remain part of Great Britain or join the Republic of Ireland—the central issue in dispute between the two competing communities. It attempts to establish instead a fair process for deciding that ultimate question; for resolving the immediate governance problems of Northern Ireland (above all ending the violence); and for guaranteeing the rights and respecting the nationalist loyalties of both groups regardless of whether Northern Ireland joins Ireland or remains part of Great Britain.[26] Thus whatever side ultimately "wins" on national affiliation, the rights and national identities of the "losers" would be protected.

The agreement was from the outset pushed by outside actors—the United Kingdom and the Republic of Ireland above all, with additional participation by the European Community and the United States. Built into the operations of the agreement itself is a network of federal and confederal arrangements between Northern Ireland and Ireland, Northern Ireland and the United Kingdom, and the United Kingdom and Ireland.[27] The agreement itself is in effect a treaty between the United Kingdom and the Republic of Ireland, and those sovereign nations remain its ultimate guarantors. The agreement provides as much self-government to the people of Northern Ireland as possible under the circumstances, but if self-government fails, the default policy is "London-Dublin cooperation in and over the region." McGarry and O'Leary call this "coercive consociationalism" and defend it as necessary where voluntary consociationalism fails.[28]

The agreement is not without its critics. I focus here on criticisms that are more broadly applicable to the minority veto/consensus model of government.

One criticism is that by according veto rights to nationalists and unionists, but not to "others," the agreement actually reinforces old divisions, privileges a particular group of elites, and systematically disadvantages any political movements attempting "to create new relationships of social interaction that transcend divisive political boundaries."[29] Though the groups designated as "others" may win seats in parliament and participate in coalition governments, they lack the veto rights accorded to nationalists and unionists and thus are excluded from the consensus. This exemplifies in the Northern Ireland context a fundamental dilemma explored elsewhere in this work: that in any consensus model of government the veto rights stop somewhere; consensus never means the agreement of every interest or perspective. To accord veto rights to *all* political groups in Northern Ireland would make the agreement unworkable from the outset; to accord veto rights to some groups and not others, as the agreement does, systematically privileges some political groups over others. That the agreement has this effect is undeniable; the question is whether this effect can be justified. A supporter of this feature would argue that, whatever other issues voters in Northern Ireland care about, the nationalist-unionist conflict is what must above all be managed because this is what disturbs the peace.[30]

Some critics fear the agreement's consensus requirement may prove *less* capable of resolving conflict than a carefully designed majority rule model. Donald Horowitz argues that the agreement rewards extremists on both sides by conferring veto rights and cabinet participation on political parties with no cross-community support whatsoever, making more difficult a government of the "moderate middle" at the very moment when a party appealing to the moderate middle might be capable of securing majority support. What ought to have been instituted, Horowitz argues, are rules that reward "parties moderate enough to secure marginal votes across group lines and able to compromise while in office." The assumption behind this argument is that political behavior is not fully determined by group affiliation, even in Northern Ireland; that instead, political deliberation and successful efforts at political persuasion can cross group lines *in the electorate itself*—not just among elites as in the consensus model. Horowitz thus challenges the fundamental assumption of the minority veto/consensus model—the inflexibility of political affiliations—and worries that the agreement will make political affiliations *more* inflexible than they are at present.[31]

It is too early to judge whether the Good Friday Agreement will bring about lasting peace and effective government in Northern Ireland. If the agreement succeeds, not only in restraining open violence, but also in creating a workable political community out of two embattled groups, it will be evidence in favor of Calhoun's principle of the concurrent majority—better evidence indeed than anything that occurred in Calhoun's original antebellum U.S. context.

At the same time there are features of the agreement and its context that limit its precedent for other deeply divided societies. If the agreement fails to produce effective and fair government, governance responsibilities revert to the safety net of Anglo-Irish cooperation. This removes the threat of dangerous anarchy, the "imperious necessity" that according to Calhoun (and to Lijphart, quoting Calhoun) would force all groups to work together in good faith. It would be a truer test of the theory to observe how the agreement would work in the absence of any safety net. (I am not recommending that this experiment be attempted.)

The role of the United Kingdom and the Republic of Ireland in the agreement is linked to another peculiarity of the Northern Ireland case. Almost no one, on either side of the communal divide, desires or intends Northern Ireland to become a permanent, independent sovereign state: "Nobody wants independence, even as their second-best option."[32] The decision instead is which sovereign state, Ireland or the United Kingdom, it will ultimately join. Whether the concurrent majority provisions of the agreement can function *permanently* as the governing rules of a viable sovereign state is a question that might not have to be answered (though we should remember the political maxim "nothing endures like the provisional").

The important short-range and medium-range questions are whether these arrangements will moderate or reinforce the stark oppositions that have scarred the region's history. The institutional arrangements might block effective action by either side instead of facilitating cross-community cooperation. Though in the short run political stalemate may be preferable to continued violence, if the agreement produces enduring deadlock it would have to be considered a failure. The concurrent majority/consensus model of government ultimately depends upon true deliberation and cooperation among leaders of conflicting groups in the effort to realize a common good. This is the standard by which to judge the success of the concurrent majority principle in Northern Ireland.

And even success will come at a cost, if the provisions systematically privileging two groupings over all others become permanent. In a healthy democracy new groups must be able readily to form around pressing new issues. This is difficult where one particular division, and the parties that owe their power to that division, are frozen permanently into place.

The strongest argument in favor of the mutual-veto solution for Northern Ireland is that all other attempts have failed. Majority rule as practiced in the past was a weapon used by one community against the other. Even if some version of majority rule that respected the rights of both communities would be preferable in theory (as Horowitz argues), nothing of the kind presently exists, and agreement by both groups on some set of political rules is probably better than no agreement at all. This distinguishes Northern Ireland from Calhoun's own antebellum U.S. context, where constitutional majority rule in a federal system had worked for two generations, and where Calhoun sought to replace it with a minority veto/consensus system. There was a *choice* possible between limited majority rule and a minority veto/consensus model in Calhoun's time and place. The people of Northern Ireland have not yet been offered a comparable set of political options from which to choose.[33]

Yugoslavia: The Failure of Consensus

The ill-fated former Federal Republic of Yugoslavia would seem an odd comparison with the political theory of John C. Calhoun. The Marxist political tradition from which the architects of Yugoslavia's 1974 constitution drew had almost nothing in common with the Anglo-American political tradition that produced Calhoun. The whole concept of a "workers' state" in which a single party enjoys an official monopoly on political power has no counterpart in American theory and practice. Calhoun's writings had no more impact on Yugoslavia than Yugoslavia (not yet existing) had on Calhoun.

And yet in many respects Yugoslavia was a good practical test of the consensus model of government championed by Calhoun. The particular causes of intergroup and interregional conflict in Yugoslavia were largely (not completely) different than in Calhoun's United States. But Calhoun believed that his minority veto/consensus model was universally applicable, whatever specific divisions and conflicts characterized a political community. That something close to Calhoun's proposal was institutionalized in a political order completely uninfected by his writings suggests the universal attractiveness of the *faith* that deeply divided political communities can bridge their differences through a consensus rule. The actual course of events in Yugoslavia calls this faith into question.

Yugoslavia consisted of six republics (Serbia, Croatia, Slovenia, Bosnia, Montenegro, and Macedonia) and two "autonomous provinces" within Serbia (Kosovo and Vojvodina). It was at the same time composed of a number of national groups with long histories (Croats, Serbs, Slovenians, and so on) whose demographic distribution corresponded only roughly to the republic that bore their name: thus in 1991 the population of the republic of Croatia was 78.1 percent Croat, 12.2 percent Serb, with a scattering of other groups; the republic of Serbia was 65.8 Serb, 17.2 percent Albanian (concentrated in Kosovo); and significant numbers of Serbs lived in Croatia and Bosnia. In Bosnia itself no single group composed a majority; 43.7 percent were Bosnian Muslims, 31.4 percent Serbs, 17.3 percent Croats. Slovenia was much more ethnically homogeneous than any other republic (87.6 percent Slovene) and thus largely free of the ethno-national divisions present in every other republic.[34] There were also religious divisions between Catholicism, Orthodox Christianity, and Islam that did not precisely coincide with either republican boundaries or national tradition.

Because of its problematic mix of nationality, ethnicity, and religion, Yugoslavia has sometimes been characterized as an "unnatural" state, doomed from the beginning by its divisions.[35] But the actual differences were no greater (and in the sphere of language significantly smaller) than in many other functional multinational states (e.g., Belgium, Spain, India). There was a high level of economic interdependency among the republics and a significant rate of intermarriage among groups; for a period of time Yugoslavia did function (if imperfectly) as a multinational, multiethnic, multilingual, and multireligious state.[36] Moreover, if it can be claimed that its divisions made a unified Yugoslavia "unnatural," any partition of the country was equally unnatural given the demographic distribution of groups. The principle of ethnic self-determination—i.e., that each national group is entitled to its own sovereign state—leads to insoluble contradictions when applied to a demographic patchwork like Yugoslavia, where one group can achieve national self-determination only by denying it to another group.[37]

The consensus-based federal system adopted by Yugoslavia in the 1970s was an attempt by the Communist leadership to resolve a number of governance challenges that had been building up over the late 1960s. Under Yugoslavia's 1974 constitution, key decisions were to be made by a process of "harmonization of views" among the several republics rather than majority rule; each republic possessed a de facto veto over federal decisions (which could be temporarily overridden in emergencies); and a rotating collective presidency was created to ensure the participation of each republic in the formation and implementation of federal measures.

One purpose of the 1974 constitution was to defuse nationalist conflicts through a timely decentralization of power. The Communist regime that took control of the country after World War II had made a "political commitment to multiethnic coexistence." All national groups were officially regarded as equal. The regime recognized "the separate existence of Yugoslav nations" and "freedom of cultural expression for nationalities," which included the right to use their own language in public forums and to be educated in their own language. But this ideal of national equality depended upon suppressing expressions of national*ism,* which meant "propagating or practicing national inequality and any incitement of national, racial, or religious hatred and intolerance."[38] The Communist Party under Tito, though by no means democratic, had successfully "forged a political movement with a multinational leadership and significant popular support among all the nations and nationalities and in all the regions of the Yugoslav lands."[39] This vision of national equality in a multinational state was incompatible with claims by any national group to superiority and sovereignty over the other groups within a particular republic or province. The consensus requirement under the 1974 constitution was supposed to reinforce this principle of national equality and prevent any one national group from dominating the others.

The other major challenge the 1974 constitution attempted to address was conflict between republics—not necessarily national groups—over the unequal distributive consequences of federal economic policy. Indeed, the Yugoslavian leadership, steeped in Marxist thought, tended to regard economic conflicts as primary and "nationalism and chauvinism" as reflexive responses that could be eliminated through successful economic development. Like every large, diversified modern state—including the United States, in Calhoun's day and our own—Yugoslavia had economically better-off and worse-off regions and sectors, and the immediate effect of any federal policy, whatever its long-term purposes, was to favor one republic at the expense of another. Much of Yugoslav economic development policy involved transfer of resources from wealthier republics like Slovenia to comparatively under-developed republics like Bosnia. This was resented by the wealthier republics, which began demanding more complete control over the economic resources at their disposal.[40] (In certain respects distributive conflicts among Yugoslavian republics in the 1960s and 1970s resembled conflicts over federal funding of "internal improvements" in the antebellum United States.)[41] Such distributive conflicts, far from indicating anything peculiar about Yugoslavia and its "ancient hatreds," are absolutely routine in modern states. What was not routine, however, was the consensus-based system Yugoslavia created to resolve these conflicts. (Recall here that it was precisely conflicts over the distributive consequences of government policy—the tariff—that spurred Calhoun to formulate his doctrine of nullification.)

The 1974 constitution (which codified several changes made between 1967 and 1971) replaced a highly centralized form of federal decision making with a highly decentralized form. According to historian Steven Burg, in 1970 the central party Presidium, at the initiation of the Croatian party leadership, decided that, "'as a rule, decisions in the federation should be taken on the basis of harmonization [of views] and agreement making among the republics' . . . Harmonization of views . . . calls for a negotiating process aimed at the formulation of policies that satisfy the interests of all the republican and provincial leaderships; it precludes the adoption of any policy without the complete agreement . . . of all republics and provinces." This meant "explicit recognition of a principle of unanimous decision making." Around the same time, at Tito's recommendation, a new collective state presidency was created "to be composed of highly authoritative individuals from each of the republics and provinces" and intended to provide "an arena for high-level resolution of interrepublican conflicts over governmental policy" and also "an answer to the question of [Tito's] own succession."[42]

The consensus requirement in the 1974 constitution was not airtight (in this respect diverging from Calhoun's prescription). It provided a temporary exception to the consensus requirement—"an alternative, non-consensual decision-making mechanism in cases of deadlock."[43] Though the constitution called for decision making based on consent, it did not *formally* accord each republic a veto over federal policy. In practice, however, "all federal policy depended on cooperation from republican leaders, who could veto any decision."[44] In theory, the Yugoslav constitution retained the principle of federal supremacy: "republican and provincial laws and other regulations . . . may not be contrary to federal laws." In practice, the constitution left entirely unclear who, if anyone, was empowered to enforce this theoretical supremacy of the federal constitution.[45]

Though the intention of the consensual decision requirement was to resolve interrepublic and internationality conflicts, its actual effect was the opposite. "Although these procedures aimed to protect smaller republics and to prevent majority tyranny, they tended to end in deadlock, which could be broken only by temporary measures that delayed real agreements . . .The consensual voting rules gave each party to the negotiation a veto. For those who believed their bargaining position was strong, there was little incentive to negotiate trade-offs and compromises and much potential gain from obstructionist tactics, stubbornness, or the threat of a walkout."[46] As a result the federal government was completely unable to make effective economic policy, which worsened the very ethnic and nationality conflicts the consensus system was intended to diffuse. Increasing numbers of individuals began turning to their ethnic or national group to provide the economic subsistence and physical protection the federal government was too weak to provide.[47]

When the Communist monopoly of political power was broken in the late 1980s and Yugoslavia attempted to establish itself as a true democracy, constitutional proposals were advanced by the republics of Slovenia and Croatia to reconstitute the federation on a more thoroughly consensual basis (proposals that bore even closer resemblance to Calhoun's understanding of federal union): each republic would be fully sovereign and have the constitutional right to nullify federal decisions. These proposals were advanced not with the declared aim of dissolving Yugoslavia, but at least ostensibly to preserve Yugoslavia in new and better form. The actual result was the breakup of Yugoslavia, which triggered a decade of civil war and ethnic cleansing in which more than a hundred thousand people were killed and millions forcibly relocated or turned into refugees.[48]

In 1988 Yugoslavia (still assumed then to have a future) began rewriting the federal constitution as an open democracy with constitutionally guaranteed freedom of religion, the right peaceably to assemble, and other internationally recognized human rights.[49] With respect to the federal system itself, two very different reform models were proposed. One proposal, designed to remedy "the inefficiency and ineffectiveness of the federal structure," sought "to improve the efficacy of the federation . . . by giving the federal government greater authority to enforce federal acts."[50] In every republic except Slovenia and Croatia there was strong support for keeping Yugoslavia as a "federation" as opposed to transforming it into a "confederation."[51] It did not help, however, that the standard bearer for this position was Serbia,[52] which was in the midst of a nationalist revival of its own that made it increasingly ill suited to advance proposals for the federation as a whole.[53]

The other reform proposal, advanced by Slovenia and joined by Croatia, was to remodel Yugoslavia as a pure confederation, with full sovereignty for the constituent republics, an explicit and unilateral right of secession, and an absolute consensus requirement for federal action whereby, even within areas explicitly within its jurisdiction, the federal government could act only with the consent of all republics. Slovenia proceeded to act on the assumption of full sovereignty in a manner directly parallel to South Carolina's action in 1832: Slovenia annulled twenty-seven federal laws and incorporated language into the Slovenian constitution giving Slovenian law precedence over the federal constitution and law.[54] When the federal Constitutional Court declared Slovenia's action to be unconstitutional, Slovenia declared the Constitutional Court's decision to be unconstitutional.[55] In October 1990 Slovenia and Croatia issued a joint declaration of "sovereignty based on a confederal arrangement" with a purely consultative parliament and a Council of Ministers in which "all decisions, with the exception of procedural decisions, would be made unanimously."[56] While asserting the unqualified right of secession, both Slovenia and Croatia claimed it was not their intention to secede (unless forced to do so by opposition to their proposals).[57] Their proposals were put forward ostensibly as efforts to preserve Yugoslavia in a new and more perfectly consensual form.

The procedure for unanimous decision under the 1974 constitution was clearly established in the genuine (if mistaken) faith that it would be an effective and fair way to govern a diverse and contentious multinational state. The same probably cannot be said for the Slovenian and Croatian confederal proposals of 1990, which may have been designed from the outset as pretexts for secession.[58] These proposals were made at a time when majorities even in Slovenia and Croatia opposed outright secession, and commitment to preserving the union was very strong in every other republic. Political scientist Robert Hayden calls the proposals a "political fraud" designed "to overcome this resistance to the breakup of Yugoslavia by creating a structure that destroyed the country under the guise of restructuring it."[59]

But at least on the surface these proposals seemed to continue and perfect the consensus rule of the 1974 constitution.[60] The argument could plausibly be made that, if unanimity was truly the decision rule, the provisions for temporary nonunanimous federal decisions under the old constitution violated that rule and that the explicit, unconditional veto proposed by Slovenia more perfectly embodied the principle. Certainly that was Calhoun's argument, which he advanced genuinely believing his doctrine would preserve rather than dissolve the union.

Furthermore, Slovenia and Croatia could refer to theoretical and practical precedents apparently supporting their claim to be saving rather than dissolving the federation. Hayden notes the similarity between the Slovenian proposals and the consensus model proposed by Arend Lijphart (whose affinities with Calhoun are discussed above).[61] Slovenian leaders made "praiseworthy references to the U.S. articles of confederation," to Ronald Reagan's "new federalism," and to the structure of the European Community as precedents for the proposal that Yugoslavia be transformed into a loose confederation.[62] (To most students of American history it would seem odd to treat the Articles of Confederation as a model. But in Calhoun's view the Articles were still in force and the federal Constitution merely an alteration of superstructure.)[63]

It would be wrong to claim that Yugoslavia's consensus-based federal order was the chief cause of its tragic collapse. There were a number of causes, both old and recent, that drove the breakup of the country and the warfare that followed. However, it is clear that the consensus process established by the 1974 constitution *failed to prevent* exactly those problems it was intended to resolve. The more radical confederal proposals put forward by Slovenia and Croatia, even if they had been accepted (the two republics declared independence before any decision was made on their proposals), would neither have saved the federation nor made possible any series of clean, peaceful secessions for the ethnically mixed republics of the former Yugoslavia.

Calhoun's consensus model of federalism, and even his insistence on a right of secession, were intended to make actual resort to secession unnecessary, because secession itself meant a bloody "knife of separation through a body politic . . . which has been so long bound together by so many ties, political, social and commercial."[64] The case of the former Yugoslavia does not support Calhoun's faith in the workability of a federal system operating under a consensus requirement. But it reconfirms a hundred times over his observation about the bloody knife of separation.

South Africa: Minority Veto or Majority Rule?

The century-long struggle that culminated in a democratic South Africa in 1994 began as a contest between racial equality and racial monopoly. But toward the end, when it was clear that racial monopoly would fall, it became a contest between majority rule and minority veto. At stake here was a real decision between two options.

The aim of then prime minister F. W. de Klerk and the ruling National Party, in initiating the reform process in the late 1980s, was to design a form of government that included all races but did *not* turn over full political power to a black majority. In the end it was majority rule that won out, above all because Nelson Mandela and the African National Congress (ANC) refused to compromise on this point. But under different bargaining conditions and different leadership on one or both sides, some version of permanent minority veto might have been enshrined in the new South African Constitution, as the National Party intended from the outset of the reform process. Instead of a constitution that resembles that of the United States (majority rule limited by separation of powers and constitutionally guaranteed individual rights), South Africa might have ended up with something like the 1974 Yugoslavian constitution or the Northern Ireland accord.

The form of government envisioned by de Klerk, when he commenced the reform process, was described by journalist Patti Waldmeier as one under which "minorities have special rights, and whites special powers, in a political system constructed—as in the days of apartheid—from separate racial groups. De Klerk believed the presidency should rotate between white and non-white leaders, with matters of importance decided collectively by all of them—an arrangement that would have given whites a veto over the majority. He wanted this form of power sharing enshrined in the Constitution, forever."[65] Much later in the process (late 1993), when it was clear his original vision of power sharing was unacceptable and the ANC had gained the upper hand, de Klerk continued to insist on high supermajority rules for important legislation and a requirement that in the cabinet (where the National Party expected to participate as a minority partner) "decisions be taken by consensus, a system that would give each party an effective veto over the others." Only at the very end did the National Party reluctantly agree to drop the minority veto "in favor of a commitment from the ANC that it would make decisions 'in a spirit of national unity'"—i.e., a moral obligation on the part of the majority to seek consensus rather than a constitutional right on the part of the minority to demand it.[66]

The National Party's insistence on a constitutionally guaranteed minority veto can easily be seen as a last-ditch attempt to preserve apartheid. Certainly that was the intention at the beginning, and Mandela and the ANC always regarded the minority veto in that light.[67] But several other considerations must be kept in mind to understand the tenacity of the minority veto model in South Africa.

In the 1980s it was not only apartheid supporters who were urging the minority veto, but principled opponents of apartheid like van Zyl Slabbert and outside observers like Lijphart—both of whom argued that ordinary majority rule could not function properly in a political order so divided along racial and ethnic lines. A majoritarian system can include constitutional protections for individuals and minorities, but these are meaningless over the long term if the majority itself chooses to ignore them. It was not unreasonable to fear such an outcome in South Africa.

It was also clear that something approaching unanimity on the constitutional settlement itself was necessary if civil war was to be avoided. The consent of Mandela and the ANC to the Convention for a Democratic South Africa (CODESA) negotiations was essential to any peaceful settlement. But the apartheid regime retained unchallenged military superiority and could have fought on for decades if it had chosen; the consent of white South Africans, too, was essential to any peaceful constitutional settlement. The ethnic Zulu-based Inkatha Freedom Party led by Mangosuthu Buthelezi was locked in a fierce and increasingly violent power struggle with supporters of the ANC; Buthelezi's consent, though less essential to the new constitution's legitimacy (he was *not* included in CODESA), was indispensable to reducing levels of violence in the country. Meanwhile the National Party faced a possible revolt from its own right wing, while the ANC faced potential revolt from those who saw its negotiations as a sellout.

The number and range of groups that might have prevented a peaceful constitutional settlement was potentially quite large. The constitutional settlement required, if not exactly unanimity, then what CODESA negotiators labeled "sufficient consensus," which "was defined—by a process of circular reasoning—to mean the agreement of all those who needed to agree, to avoid a breakdown." It was ultimately the risk of "mutually assured destruction" that induced all sides to cooperate.[68] That was, of course, exactly Calhoun's argument about why a unanimity rule would not lead to anarchy. Recall that van Zyl Slabbert and Welsh had made this same argument in support of a permanent minority veto in postapartheid South Africa, citing Lijphart for support, Lijphart in turn citing Calhoun.

Given that any peaceful constitutional settlement in South Africa required something approaching consensus, the National Party's insistence on a *permanent* minority veto need not be seen only as a desperate attempt to preserve the last vestiges of apartheid. It could also be seen, more sympathetically, as an attempt to inscribe in the constitution as a permanent decision rule the same principle of "sufficient consensus" that governed the CODESA deliberations and made peaceful abolition of apartheid possible.

Recall from chapter 4 that Calhoun believed government in the United States could and should follow the same consensus rule that guided deliberations at the Federal Convention in 1787; Calhoun's ideal was a kind of permanent constitutional convention. De Klerk and the National Party's negotiators in CODESA might have had in mind something similar.

Mandela, in contrast, made a sharp distinction between consensus *on* the constitution and a consensus rule *under* it; he conscientiously and effectively sought the former and just as effectively fought to prevent the latter. After his election as president in 1994 Mandela instituted a limited form of power sharing by including representatives of the National Party and the Inkatha Freedom Party in his Government of National Unity, but these were interim arrangements, not permanent constitutional requirements, and there was no minority veto at all.

This brings us to Mandela's own peculiar version of consensus-seeking politics, which played an indispensable role in South Africa's peaceful revolution. Despite predictions to the contrary, white South Africans did ultimately turn over political power to Mandela and the ANC—thus to the black majority—avoiding a bitter civil war. Whether South African whites would have peacefully turned over power to a black leader other than Mandela is an open question. Without compromising on the essential principle of majority rule, Mandela was somehow able to reassure a critical mass of white South Africans that their interests would not be overlooked and that they would be honored citizens in a new South Africa.

In his autobiography *Long Walk to Freedom* Mandela praises the consensus model in traditional African governance: "The meetings would continue until some kind of consensus was reached. They ended in unanimity or not at all . . . Majority rule was a foreign notion. A minority was not to be crushed by a majority."[69] His admiration for the traditional consensus rule did not, however, make Mandela into an advocate of formal minority veto when he and the ANC began negotiating with the government in the early 1990s. (Ironically, in this respect de Klerk's insistence on a formal consensus rule comes closer to the African tribal model celebrated by Mandela.) But Mandela considered it a high *moral* duty that the majority not crush the minority, and he knew white South Africans' own history and heroes well enough to be able to honor their traditions even as he challenged their regime. He did not just give verbal assurances to white South Africans; he made them believable.

Recall from chapter 6 that Calhoun's minority veto/consensus model of government absolutely depends upon enlightened statesmanship to function at all. Calhoun was not content with the merely negative step of blocking action. He believed instead that the threat of deadlock or anarchy resulting from veto rights would in turn inspire true statesmen to resolve the crisis.

Mandela's example suggests that the kind of leadership required for a minority veto system to function might in fact make the minority veto unnecessary by achieving something approaching consensus in another way, at least during critical periods where consensus is indispensable. If the objection is that one cannot always count upon enlightened statesmanship under majority rule, the same objection holds at least equally for any consensus model of government—which Calhoun himself admitted cannot function at all without exemplary leadership.

One should also raise the counterfactual: what would have been the effect of a constitutionally inscribed minority veto rule in a country as divided and potentially ungovernable as South Africa in the mid-1990s? A postapartheid South African state that was fair and neutral with regard to race, but unable effectively to govern because every group could veto its operations on a continuing basis, would have been a disaster.

The success of negotiated settlement in South Africa invites comparison with Northern Ireland, and the connection here is not merely speculative. In 1997, a year before the Good Friday Agreement, key leaders of Northern Ireland political parties attended an intense three-day conference in Arniston, South Africa, where they were directly schooled by Nelson Mandela and "people from all parties in South Africa who had negotiated the historic settlement."[70] The most directly applicable element of the South African experience was the degree of trust and consensus seeking necessary for a peaceful settlement process to succeed at all.

The *process* that resulted in the Good Friday Agreement for Northern Ireland may have taken inspiration from the South African case. The institutional *outcomes* were, however, fundamentally different. The Good Friday Agreement (as noted above) institutionalizes a minority veto/consensus model in both the legislature and the executive. This is exactly what the South African process did not create. One might ask: if majority rule can work in South Africa, why not in Northern Ireland? Or conversely: if the consensus model ultimately proves successful in Northern Ireland, could it have been equally effective in South Africa? But in one crucial respect the two cases are fundamentally different. Failure of the consensus model in Northern Ireland comes with a safety net: resumption of direct rule by the United Kingdom or by a United Kingdom–Ireland consortium. There was no equivalent safety net in South Africa.

South Africa has thus decided in favor of majority rule despite predictions it could never work there. And it was a decision: the minority veto model could have been implemented, with results about which we can only speculate.

Calhoun's critique of majority rule still applies to South Africa even though his solution was (probably wisely) rejected. For majority rule to work effectively and fairly in a nation as deeply divided by race, ethnicity, and language as South Africa, and where there remain enormous inequalities of wealth and opportunity, at least two things are necessary. First, there must be an opposition, loyal to the constitution, which can criticize the governing party in ways the latter must take seriously. This requires in turn that voters not be so tied to the governing party by race or ethnicity that the government never needs to fear losing voters' support. Second, it requires that the already existing tendency of political divisions to follow lines of race, language, and ethnicity be resisted rather than reinforced by political parties and political leaders. Political divisions over distribution of wealth, however fierce, are more amenable to resolution through constitutional majority rule than political divisions tracking ascriptive characteristics like race, language, ethnicity. As soon as political divisions harden into conflicts between distinct, mutually exclusive groups, the preconditions for healthy majority rule begin to break down.

So far, the ANC, which has continued to enjoy the electoral support of large majorities, has successfully appealed beyond racial lines; to its credit it has resisted rather than reinforced the temptation to organize along strictly racial or ethnic lines. On the other hand, it has at present no effective opposition. Whether this is a temporary or permanent state of affairs remains to be seen, but in the long run healthy majority rule will require an effective loyal opposition in South Africa just as it does in every other democracy.

If the Good Friday Agreement in Northern Ireland stands the best chance of proving that a consensus model can work, the survival and health of constitutional majority rule in South Africa stands in the long run the best chance of proving the consensus model unnecessary.

Lani Guinier's Calhounian Diagnosis

Racial divisions of course have not disappeared from the United States. Our Constitution—especially as transformed by the Thirteenth, Fourteenth, and Fifteenth amendments, all of them utterly irreconcilable with Calhoun's constitutional theory—establishes a very different framework for managing racial and ethnic divisions than anything available in Northern Ireland, the former Yugoslavia, or South Africa. Our institutions are very different from theirs, but the underlying problem is not.

In the *Disquisition* Calhoun sought to show how a self-interested majority, employing formally neutral procedures and laws, can systematically dominate a minority. His diagnosis should be taken seriously even if his remedy is rejected—and even if the marginalized minority is one Calhoun himself sought to keep in slavery.

In *The Tyranny of the Majority: Fundamental Fairness in Representative Democracy* (1994), legal scholar Lani Guinier analyzes racially polarized politics in the United States in a way that parallels Calhoun's own diagnosis of majority tyranny. Her proposed solutions, which include cumulative voting and supermajorities, are Calhounian in spirit: like Calhoun, Guinier holds up the consensus-seeking jury as a political model. But her proposals are procedurally less extreme than Calhoun's iron-clad minority veto.[71]

Guinier shows that, where voting almost completely follows racial lines, a sizeable racial minority (for instance 40 percent of an electoral district) may end up completely shut out of representative bodies (like county boards, city councils, and multimember state legislative districts). This is especially likely to occur where all members are elected at-large and/or where there are second-round runoff elections between the two top vote-getters. At-large elections, she writes, "allowed a unified white bloc to control all the elected positions. As little as 51 percent of the population could decide 100 percent of the elections, and the black minority was permanently excluded from meaningful participation." Guinier points out that in the South in the 1960s, at-large multimember districts and second-round runoffs were often instituted specifically to minimize the political power of newly enfranchised black voters.[72] Historical evidence of a discriminatory intent may indicate violation of the Voting Rights Act and thus a judicially enforced remedy. But the basic problem follows from the existence of racial bloc voting itself, even where voting systems were instituted without discriminatory intent (thus beyond the remedial power of federal courts).

"Sometimes, even when rules are perfectly fair in form," Guinier observes, "they serve in practice to exclude particular groups from meaningful participation." Nor is the problem limited to multimember districts. Single-member districts facilitate representation of residentially concentrated minorities, but where minority populations are residentially scattered, assuming voting still follows racial lines, single-member districts will likewise shut out the minority. Moreover, the diagnosis would apply to *any* issue or characteristic that divides voters into fixed and inflexible majorities and minorities: not just race, but potentially also religion, ethnicity, or ideology. "When majorities are fixed, the minority lacks any mechanism for holding the majority to account or even to listen. Nor does such majority rule promote deliberation or consensus. The permanent majority simply has its way, without reaching out to or convincing anyone else."[73]

Recall Calhoun's hypothetical community of five,[74] where according to perfectly "fair" rules the community votes 3–2 to tax all members, then votes again by the same 3–2 majority to distribute all benefits of the tax to the three, leaving the minority of two disenfranchised and impoverished. Guinier's critique of majority rule under conditions of racial bloc voting exactly parallels Calhoun's scenario.

In *Federalist* No. 10 Madison argued that in an extensive and diverse republic it is more difficult for an unjust majority to organize and "carry into effect schemes of oppression." Madison's solution to majority tyranny presupposed, first, that majorities were fluid rather than fixed (one could be in the majority on one issue and the minority on another); and second, that members of the (temporary) majority would recognize the danger of allowing the strongest faction to oppress the rest. Madison's solution was not to prevent the majority from ruling, but to design institutions that encouraged deliberate and enlightened majorities: a "coalition of a majority of the whole society" on the principles of "justice and the general good."[75] Calhoun argued, on the contrary, that over time the Madisonian solution would fail:

majorities and minorities will become fixed, not fluid; the majority need not fear exchanging places with the minority and thus has no interest in restraining itself.[76]

Guinier favors Madison's solution in an ideal world. She calls a majority "that rules but does not dominate" a "Madisonian Majority," meaning that "the losers at one time or on one issue join with others and become part of the governing coalition at another time or on another issue. The result will be a fair system of mutually beneficial cooperation." But Madison's solution depends upon "fluid, rotating interests." Where "the self-interested majority does not need to worry about defectors"—especially on matters of race— "the problems of unfairness are not cured by conventional assumptions about majority rule."[77]

There is thus a clear parallel between Calhoun and Guinier, both in their general critique of majority rule and in their specific critique of Madison's solution to majority tyranny. Guinier's rejection of Madison's solution is less absolute than Calhoun's, however, because her long-term hope is "to create Madisonian Majorities" in a political order where voting does not simply follow racial lines. Calhoun on the other hand argued that rigid majorities and minorities, once formed, could not be reversed.

Guinier's proposed remedies to majority tyranny fall short of Calhoun's permanent, iron-clad minority veto. But she echoes Calhoun in her assumptions about *the type of political deliberation* that will occur where institutional rules make majority domination difficult or impossible.

One proposal is to institute cumulative voting in multimember, at-large districts such that "each voter is given the same number of votes as open seats, and the voter may plump or cumulate her votes to reflect the intensity of her preferences." Instead of casting three votes for three different at-large candidates, for instance, a voter could award all three of his or her votes to one intensely desired candidate. In this way a racial minority—or for that matter any self-conscious political minority of significant size—could concentrate its votes strategically to ensure at least one of its candidates is elected. To the charge that this establishes a racial quota system, Guinier replies that the mechanism is not racially biased because "it allows voters to organize themselves on whatever basis they wish."[78] Any organized group of large enough size and sufficiently intense political preferences could use this system strategically.

A second reform proposal concerns the workings of deliberative bodies themselves. Even if minorities are represented there in rough proportions to their share of the voting population, they may be outvoted on policy decisions in a way that reproduces the racial divide in society as a whole. To remedy this Guinier proposes "legislative cumulative voting" whereby "over a period of time and a series of legislative proposals, votes on multiple bills would be aggregated or linked" and minority representatives' votes given extra weight on issues of critical importance to them.[79]

A final proposal (and the one closest to Calhoun) is to require a supermajority vote "or its equivalent, a minority veto on critical minority issues."[80] Guinier explains that "the minority veto is simply another way of referring to the effect of supermajority requirements."[81] She presents the minority veto as an "exceptional remedy" to be employed only where a "court finds proof of consistent and deeply engrained polarization."[82] It is unclear how broad or narrow is the class of exceptional cases for which Guinier considers minority veto the appropriate remedy. ("Consistent and deeply engrained polarization" could describe racial voting in the United States electorate as a whole.)

The general aim of Guinier's proposals is the same as Calhoun's: to prevent the majority from unilaterally determining outcomes and to force majority and minority to engage in good-faith deliberation in the common good.

Guinier's cumulative voting proposal arguably overcomes the arbitrariness that plagued Calhoun's minority veto. Calhoun's theory encountered difficulties answering the questions: Where do veto rights stop? How is it determined which minorities enjoy veto rights and which ones do not? Guinier's cumulative voting scheme, by allowing minorities (racial or otherwise) to define themselves politically through strategic voting behavior, avoids arbitrary definitions of who or what constitutes a minority entitled to veto rights. The other side of the coin is that Guinier's remedy would reward *any* intensely committed and organized minority, however just or unjust its aims.

To answer the objection that a consensus rule would produce anarchy, Calhoun invoked the model of the jury, which requires unanimity but nevertheless functions effectively.[83] Guinier likewise invokes the jury as a political model. "My proposal pursues the analogy to jury decisionmaking by fashioning local councils in the image of the ideal, consensus-driven jury."[84] Like Calhoun, Guinier's goal is not merely to block action or to reproduce within representative bodies the same divides that mark the electorate, but to bridge those divisions through genuine deliberation and compromise within representative bodies.

Guinier says her purpose is not to guarantee "equal legislative outcomes" but instead "equal opportunity to *influence* legislative outcomes regardless of race."[85] (Calhoun's iron-clad minority veto, in contrast, was indeed designed to guarantee favorable legislative outcomes for the minority.) Given a choice between voting rules that produce zero minority representation and rules producing least one minority representative, the latter would doubtless be an improvement.

This would be a pretty minimal accomplishment, however, and Guinier tries to promise something much better. She acknowledges that the mere presence of, for instance, two black or Hispanic city members in a city council of seven, while better than zero, does not by itself promote cross-racial coalitions. If the leaders of each group merely mirror the divisions of the society on every important vote, the policy result will be the same as if no minority members had been elected at all.

Guinier's proposed solution depends upon an additional and unstated assumption: that political elites will be more willing and able to bridge racial, social, and political divides than members of the voting population as a whole. Here she echoes Calhoun and Lijphart, both of whom made this assumption explicit.

Whether elected representatives in general are better able to bridge racial and social divides than the electorate as a whole is an open question. The more immediate question is what effect Guinier's proposed voting rules might have on the *type* of leaders elected; the effect might be counterproductive. Because her proposals reward intensely held preferences drawing limited wider support, they could just as easily elect white-supremacist candidates as black or Hispanic candidates—perhaps elect more black and Hispanic candidates *and* more white supremacists. This arguably increases "representativeness" but would probably not generate consensus-seeking deliberation.

Beyond the particulars of voting rules lies an enormous chicken-egg problem. Guinier assumes racially polarized voting behavior in the electorate as a whole and attempts to counterbalance this with new voting rules designed to modify the composition of representative bodies. Unless these new rules are judicially imposed (an unlikely prospect on any broad scale), the decision to implement them would belong to representatives elected according to current rules. But elected representatives are unlikely to institute new voting rules if the proposed rules are fiercely opposed by the majority of a racially polarized electorate. Passing new electoral rules would depend upon moderating racial polarization in the electorate as a whole—especially among white voters—not just among elites. No strategy of elite cooperation will be successful in the long run without changes in the attitudes and behavior of ordinary voters.

This is difficult but not impossible to achieve. But if one believes in the future possibility of "Madisonian majorities" and good-faith, cross-racial cooperation in the electorate as a whole, as Guinier does, then it should be possible to achieve this to some degree in the present, under existing rules, both among elites and in the electorate as a whole, by the ordinary methods of democratic persuasion.

Thus there is a positive side to the chicken-egg problem. The kind of democratic politics needed to persuade the majority to take race-related reform proposals seriously in the first place would itself begin to overcome the problem of racial polarization—whether or not voting rules themselves change at all. The possibility that fair rules might be used to produce unfair results is inherent in the democratic process itself, and it is there—among ordinary voters, through ordinary democratic persuasion—that the problem must be addressed.

EIGHT

■

Conclusion

Democracy promises more than it can consistently deliver. Rule by the majority (and its designated leaders) over the rest of the community is not necessarily the same as government "of the people, by the people, for the people," as Abraham Lincoln phrased it in his Gettysburg Address. Democracies around the world attempt through widely varying institutions to reconcile this basic tension between democracy's substantive goal—the good of the entire community, to the degree it can be approximated—and its principal mechanism, majority rule. No remedy works equally well everywhere; no remedy anywhere permanently resolves the tension. The U.S. Constitution as designed by its framers, and as defended by (among others) James Madison in the *Federalist Papers,* attempted to institutionalize deliberate, limited, and responsible majority rule. But even constitutionally limited majorities can act in unjust ways.

John C. Calhoun was unsatisfied with all of the available constitutional mechanisms for keeping majorities in check. He sought a form of government fundamentally different than majority rule, one that he believed better ensured rule by and for the entire community. Constitutional limits that merely slowed down majority rule might work temporarily, but over time, he believed, a deliberate majority would be as unjust as a hasty one. Freedom of speech and press did not guarantee the majority would actually listen and respond to the minority's arguments and interests. Formally neutral laws and procedures could be used to pursue systematically unfair laws and policies. Entrenched majorities and minorities, Calhoun believed, once formed would not alternate in power and thus the majority would have no incentive to treat the minority fairly. Federalism, if it lacked the minority veto, also failed in Calhoun's view to remedy the problem because local and regional interests could be deeply and adversely affected by national decisions on national matters.

Calhoun's solution was to replace majority rule with consensus: to give every key "portion or interest" in the community veto rights over collective decisions, thus ensuring only those laws and policies that genuinely benefited all parts of the community. He attempted deliberately to remodel the federal features of the U.S. Constitution into his consensus model of government: through full state sovereignty, state nullification of federal law, and a dual executive he sought to give regionally concentrated minority interests veto power over explicitly national decisions like the tariff and the spread of slavery to federally owned territories. Calhoun did not believe this form of government would lead to anarchy, deadlock, or minority domination. He believed on the contrary that it would be more energetic, effective, fair, and truly popular than government based on majority rule.

Calhoun was emphatic on this point. Over the centuries many federations have existed where joint action depended upon unanimous consent because any one of the parties could block action; the United States under the Articles of Confederation is the most obvious example. But these unanimous-consent federations have been on the whole ineffective and/or short-lived; reasonable men and women do not stake their life, liberty, and property on the effective performance of these loose federations.

Calhoun's version of unanimous consent was unique because he believed it was possible to combine the best of both: a federal government functioning on a unanimity requirement, yet capable of effective action under the most urgent of circumstances. The blocking of action that occurred when one or more "portions or interests" exercised their veto powers was in Calhoun's view only the first step; it could not end there. Instead the exercise of the negative was designed to force genuine, jury-like deliberation and the realization of a truly common good.

Calhoun's full-state-sovereignty theory of federalism under the U.S. Constitution absolutely depended upon the workability of his consensus model of government. He did not believe that state and federal spheres of authority could be cleanly separated or that state nullification of federal law should be restricted to legislation encroaching on matters reserved to the states by the Constitution. On the contrary, it was precisely on urgent national issues that

Calhoun insisted on each state's right to nullify federal law. He knew that a single state blocking national decisions on national questions imposed enormous consequences on the people of every other state. But in Calhoun's view this was good, not bad, because it would force deliberation and consensus.

I have argued in this book that Calhoun's consensus model of politics fails, or works only under very improbable and/or unjust conditions. Calhoun usefully set out the preconditions required for a consensus system of government to work effectively, and for this reason his theory deserves examination. Calhoun assumed the crisis caused by suspension of action on urgent matters would force all interests and regions to work together in the common good. This in turn assumed that the costs and risks of failure to act were equally distributed; for if inaction was a disaster for some but not others, the latter could use a crisis to extort peculiar advantages. Calhoun also assumed enlightened leadership on all sides and willingness on the part of the rank and file to defer to the agreements forged at the highest levels by their trusted leaders. Calhoun's theory further presupposed that groups wielding veto rights could be justifiably limited to a manageable number: that instead of an infinite regression of veto rights, group interests at some point became homogeneous enough—or could be *made* homogenous enough—that internal vetoes were no longer necessary.

Calhoun's assumptions about equal costs and risks of failure to act and universally enlightened leadership are unlikely to hold over any extended period of time. Meanwhile his understanding of where veto rights stop—the point at which opposed interest gives way to essentially shared interest—heavily depended in practice on the institution of slavery. For (as Calhoun made explicit) slavery gave all members of the white race the pride of being in the upper class and a shared interest in closing ranks against a common threat. Even apart from questions of justice, Calhoun's racial-solidarity answer to the question of where veto rights stop would be unacceptable in a world where all races and groups are presumed equal. A modern-day consensus-based political order would either have to find some functional equivalent of slavery—some other way of creating and preserving homogeneity *within* each "portion or interest"—or accept an indefinite expansion of diverse and mutually opposed interests demanding veto rights.

The historical track record of governments that distribute veto rights over collective policy in the way Calhoun prescribes is not good. Calhoun genuinely believed his own efforts as a sectional leader to demand veto rights for the South—by threat of secession if necessary—would tend to preserve the Union, but the reverse was true. He also had to torture the language of the Constitution and misrepresent the history of the framing period to adapt it to the needs of his political theory.

Even if Calhoun's system could function effectively in the sense of being capable of energetic collective action, his system is not one that protects *all* minority interests or liberty in general. What it does instead is guard the interests and liberties of *some* minorities, in particular those already relatively powerful and strategically positioned. A minority that was too powerless or marginalized to control a particular state or region would never enjoy veto rights under Calhoun's system; for veto powers cannot be exercised (as Calhoun phrases it) by an "unorganized mass of individuals." Disenfranchised and marginalized minorities—especially those victimized precisely by locally dominant minorities—are almost certainly better off under majority rule, where they can appeal to the justice of the national community, than under Calhoun's system where, unless they already enjoy superiority in some state or territory, they are shut out of decision making altogether. A newly emerging interest, small at present but potentially a player in the future, would also be better off under ordinary majority rule than under Calhoun's system, which locks a few dominant interests permanently into place.

Thus Calhoun's minority veto/consensus model of government falls even shorter of delivering what it promises—fair treatment of all interests in the community—than majority rule does. But his theory must be taken seriously all the same. To adapt an old saying: those who fail to understand the mistakes of political theorists are condemned to repeat them. Calhoun's consensus model, or something akin to it whether Calhoun is consulted or not, will continue to tempt constitutional architects in deeply divided societies where the preconditions for healthy majority rule are weak. At the very least constitutional architects tempted by the consensus model should consider what preconditions Calhoun himself considered essential for its effective operation, then somehow answer the questions Calhoun himself failed adequately to answer.

Calhoun's minority veto/consensus model must also be taken seriously because in many deeply divided political communities, one or more powerful, strategically placed minorities exist which, by threatening worse consequences if their demands are not met, attempt to secure for themselves veto rights over collective decisions. I don't mean here systems that accord veto rights to *all* interests, including the disadvantaged ones; that kind of system has never been seen. Instead I mean cases where purely by its factual might, an interest secures (or attempts to secure) for itself a power it denies to others. Such scenarios are depressingly common. Strategically placed minorities may very well view their veto power as a justifiable demand for consensus (as the white minority did in South Africa, and as Calhoun in his own time viewed the uncompromising stance of the slave states). It makes a difference whether we categorize attempts by privileged minorities to secure veto power as search for consensus or as strategies for minority domination, and Calhoun sheds some ironic light in this regard. The power of minority veto, simply of itself, does not ensure consensus, fairness, or justice and can very well guarantee the opposite.

Federalism and Majority Rule

This examination of Calhoun's attempt to replace majority rule with consensus leads me to the conclusion that there is no choice-worthy alternative to majority rule, even where conditions for healthy democracy are unfavorable. However, this statement requires several qualifications.

To call majority rule the only choice-worthy option assumes that a genuine choice is available; sometimes it is and sometimes it is not. For a majority to assert a right to rule a minority with which it is chronically at war, or even seeks to "ethnically cleanse" from the territory, is absurd; no shared political community exists under such conditions, and the minority has no obligation to respect majority rule. Even without open warfare, where a majority claims a right to rule a minority to whom it accords no rights in return (or whose rights it systematically violates), whom it does not permit to engage in fair political competition, or upon whom it imposes laws that it does not impose on itself, then all bets are off. No reasonable person would subject themselves to majority rule of this kind.

But in Calhoun's time and place a choice *was* possible. During debates over the protective tariff in 1828 and over the future of slavery in 1850 a functioning (if imperfect) system of constitutional majority rule existed, at least among white male citizens. The minority of slave-owning southern planters whose interests Calhoun sought above all to protect was fully included, indeed more than fully included, in the American political system. It was this functioning system of majority rule that Calhoun deliberately chose to reject in the hopes of achieving something he believed would be better. In South Africa in the early 1990s and Yugoslavia in the mid-1970s a genuine choice was made (in opposite directions in the two cases) between majority rule and minority veto. In the long run a similar choice will have to be made in Northern Ireland between entrenching the mutual-veto model and transitioning to majority rule.

A second qualification is that we should distinguish between majority rule as an enduring decision method and decision on *the constitutional settlement itself*—the fundamental agreement on the part of a number of groups or interests to be part of the same political community under a shared set of institutions and rules.

In a constitutional settlement itself (as in the United States in 1787 and in South Africa in 1994), the argument for consensus or near-consensus is a strong one. This simply restates the point that majority rule is meaningless among groups at war or who recognize no shared law. But consensus *on* a constitution (a discreet and exceptional decision) is different from a permanent consensus decision rule *under* a constitution, which was what Calhoun considered both possible and necessary. Calhoun rejected the distinction between consensus on and consensus under a constitution (as described in chapter 4), idealizing instead a kind of permanent constitutional convention.

A third qualification concerns federalism. To argue that there is no good alternative to majority rule does not entail the rejection of federalism, if by federalism we mean that local or regional majorities, not the national majority, decide some constitutionally defined range of issues. On the contrary, federalism is an essential method of defusing conflict in deeply divided societies where key groups are regionally concentrated. In theory federalism allows for a separation between those matters that principally concern the whole political community, to be decided by institutional processes of the whole, and those matters that should be decided by the local or regional majority best acquainted with the circumstances and most directly affected by the decision.

Unfortunately the terms "federalism" and "federal" are used so broadly that they frequently obscure the most important questions. (The word "federalism" seems to have a special attraction for purveyors of political snake oil, because it magically makes all democratic dilemmas disappear.) Many scholars of American political thought are trained to see a clear distinction between "federal" (as exemplified in the U.S. Constitution) and "confederal" (as exemplified by the Articles of Confederation). But usage here is not as clear or stable as we often assume, especially when conflating the two concepts serves some political purpose. For Calhoun, "federal" meant, by definition, a political community composed of fully sovereign parts with veto rights over collective decisions; the difference between "federal" and "confederal" was superstructural, not foundational. For Madison, in contrast, it was exactly the relinquishing of full sovereignty for the parts that defined a truly federal union (as opposed to full state sovereignty under the Articles of Confederation).

Because the terms "federal" and "federalism" sweep so broadly it is useless to prescribe federalism, simply as such, as the solution to anything. Instead one must be as specific as possible about *what kind* of federalism and its specific relation to the practice of majority rule.

Federalism at its best moderates the conflicts produced by majority rule in deeply divided societies. It does not make those conflicts disappear, for at least two reasons. The first is that it is impossible perfectly to separate what principally concerns the whole community and what principally concerns a specific group, region, or state. Someone or something must decide where and how the line is drawn. There is nowhere this power can reasonably be placed except in some national institution or process accountable to a national majority. To hedge on this, to give equal or superior line-drawing authority to the individual members or regions (as Calhoun intended), is to once again make effective federalism depend upon an implausible faith in consensus.

The second reason is that, even assuming the clearest possible boundaries between the two levels of decision, some decisions must inevitably be made nationally because of the common interests at stake. It may be possible to defuse some otherwise divisive matters by devolving them to state or local decision. But it is impossible by definition to assign *all* the important and potentially divisive decisions to the local and regional sphere. For if there were *no* significant common interests at stake, there would be no point in maintaining a federal system at all. To deeply antagonistic, regionally concentrated groups who share nothing but their own mutual animosity, secession or partition, however painful, may be preferable to the alternative; it is impossible to make fixed rules about this. But that is not the type of federal system Calhoun was talking about.

Where a federal system consists of people, member states, and interests who genuinely want to remain together, then on matters genuinely national, a national majority or some body ultimately accountable to a national majority must ultimately make decisions. These decisions will inevitably have a significant impact on the outvoted minority. There can be no guarantee that national decisions will never be biased against the minority in the way Calhoun diagnosed and sought unsuccessfully to remedy.

To argue for choosing majority rule when a genuine choice is possible is not a trivial claim, and it is not intended in a spirit of democratic self-celebration.

It is not a trivial claim because there are alternatives to majority rule, some of them hypothetical (Calhoun's consensus model), some of them very real (dictatorship, oligarchy, rule by a strategically placed elite). Minority rule in one form or another has been predominant throughout most of human history and probably still predominates in the world today despite the universal rhetorical commitment to democracy. Thus to call majority rule the only choice-worthy option should not be confused with an embrace of the global status quo.

The commitment to majority rule is also not trivial if in making it one is fully aware that even at its best—given equality under the law, genuine respect for constitutional rights, full freedom of the press, and so on—majority rule can be deployed in systematically unfair ways. From the failure of Calhoun's remedy one should not leap to the conclusion that some better institutional remedy to the same problem is waiting to be discovered. The more probable conclusion is that there is no remedy—at least no permanent and fundamental remedy.

It will always be possible in a democracy for decision makers to *aim* for consensus on crucially important matters. That consensus is unworkable as a decision rule does not make it any less worthy a moral and political goal. Consensus on some matters may be impossible. But it is always possible—and not even difficult—for decision makers to take into consideration the interests of more than fifty-percent-plus-one of the population.

For example, if there is any justification for the peculiar U.S. Senate practice of filibuster—often mislabeled a "minority veto" though Calhoun would not have classified it that way—it is that it exemplifies a majority's standing moral commitment to accommodate a greater range of interests than is constitutionally required for the vote at hand. The filibuster rule could be undone by simple majority vote in the Senate. Whether it should be undone is a question I leave open; but that it *could* be undone by majority vote is as it should be. The alternative—to make filibuster a constitutionally guaranteed power enjoyed by a legislative minority—would be a disaster, empowering the minority far beyond what is reasonable or fair. (The accidental, ad hoc minority that sometimes elects presidents under our Electoral College system no better realizes the ideal of consensus than does any other variant of minority rule.)

Instead of guaranteeing permanent veto rights to a minority (as Calhoun insisted was necessary) our constitutional provisions constrain the majority of the moment to act in accordance with certain structural rules. These rules make it more difficult, though in the long run not impossible, for a single majority party or coalition to control all branches of government. Our system also obligates the majority of the moment to respect an array of rights guaranteed to *individuals*—not to groups (like Calhoun's veto-wielding "portions or interests"), except insofar as groups make use of the individual protections. These rights, which include freedom of speech and press, the right to form opposition parties, and the right to challenge incumbents for election, in theory raise the level of democratic discourse by confronting the majority with alternative arguments and inconvenient facts.

A majority coalition (and its leadership) that genuinely seeks the good of the whole community will thus have available to it abundant sources of information and argument about the actual or potential effects of its decisions on the community as a whole and on the rights and interests of the outvoted minority. If the majority chooses, it can establish institutional channels through which alternative arguments and inconvenient facts can be communicated. (We should keep in mind, of course, that the minority itself may be biased, misinformed, or enamored of weak arguments—another reason not to arm minorities with veto rights.) None of this comes close to the kind of strong medicine Calhoun demanded. But it is probably the best a democracy can do, and if practiced in good faith it is sufficient to prevent the majoritarian pathologies Calhoun feared.

On the other hand, nothing in our system guarantees that the opposite will not occur. The fact that the minority may speak does not guarantee that the majority and its leadership will listen. In extreme cases it is possible for the majority and its leadership to shut out alternative arguments and sources of information altogether, at least in its internal deliberations (which are what ultimately matter the most). This pathology has afflicted the internal processes of Congress on more than one occasion and will doubtless occur again in future. Under such circumstances the diseases Calhoun diagnosed are on full display.

Readers familiar with the *Federalist* will recall the authors' caution against too great a dependence on enlightened leadership. "Enlightened statesmen will not always be at the helm," Madison famously warned in *Federalist* No. 10. One purpose of a well-constructed constitution is to limit the damage that can be done by short-sighted majorities and foolish leaders. But to reduce this risk is not the same as eliminating it. Constitutional provisions can take a popular government only so far. At some point political leadership really does have significant effects upon the health or sickness of a democracy, and selecting, cultivating, and politically rewarding enlightened leaders becomes a high priority. And this in turn depends upon a *moral* commitment, on the part of whatever majority happens to be in power at the moment, to honor the indispensable but difficult-to-enforce principle that majority rule is intended to serve the interests of more than the majority.

To look to enlightened leadership and collective moral commitments may seem like weak medicine. Calhoun's iron-clad minority veto seems at first a more concrete and realistic way of checking unjust majorities and bad leadership: power must be met with power, not moral suasion, he argued, and it would seem difficult to disagree. Yet Calhoun's proposed remedy simply shifted the location of the leadership problem and the moral commitment. Under his system of mutual vetoes it was not enough merely to block collective action—that certainly can and does occur with mediocre (or worse) leadership. His theory absolutely depended upon enlightened leadership from all sections to come to a meeting of minds on the common good. (Calhoun rigged the argument by insisting that under his system the very indispensability of such leaders would guarantee their emergence.) Thus in the end his remedy is far *more* dependent on enlightened leadership and moral suasion than the kind of majority rule he rejected. Calhoun's remedy is unworkable, or workable only in ways that are less fair or just than majority rule; but he performs a service by focusing attention on the unavoidable impact of good or bad leadership in a democracy.

The United States has recently taken on the self-appointed role of evangelist for democracy across the globe. The intensity of our democratic rhetoric is equaled only by the superficiality of our comprehension of what democracy entails, both among strangers and at home. We tend to be oblivious to the difficulties of establishing democracies in deeply divided nations (especially via military invasion) and to the significant and potentially widening divisions in our own society.

In my view neither Calhoun nor contemporary advocates of the minority veto offer workable models for building democracy in deeply divided nations. But studying Calhoun's critique of democracy can sensitize us to the many ways democracy can go wrong, and thus discourage policy founded in simplistic democratic evangelism. Critically examining his proposed remedy can guard us against embracing, and perhaps imposing on other peoples, seductive prescriptions that turn out worse than the disease. Our resolve should be to celebrate democracy less and understand it more. And that in turn requires a willingness to listen carefully to democracy's critics, including those like Calhoun toward whom one may be deeply ambivalent. Calhoun himself embodied some of our best American aspirations and several of our worst ones, and we can learn from both his better and worse sides without making him another American idol.

Constitutional checks and institutional design can only do so much to limit the diseases to which democracy is subject. Beyond that point, the health of democracy depends upon the leaders we elect and the politics we ourselves practice. The same set of democratic procedures can be used either to build walls or to build bridges. If nothing in democracy prevents it from falling sick, nothing also prevents us from deciding democratically to restore democracy itself to health.

Notes

Chapter One. Introduction

1. See, for example, Aristotle's *Politics,* Book III, chapters 7–8, and Book IV, chapters 2–10; Thomas Hobbes's *Leviathan,* chapter 19.

2. For the politics behind the 1828 tariff, see Merrill D. Peterson, *The Great Triumvirate: Webster, Clay, and Calhoun* (New York: Oxford University Press, 1987), 159–161; Harry L. Watson, *Liberty and Power: The Politics of Jacksonian America* (New York: Hill and Wang, 1990), 88–89; William W. Freehling, *Prelude to Civil War: The Nullification Controversy in South Carolina, 1816–1836* (Oxford: Oxford University Press, 1965), 136–140. For more detailed description of the tariff provisions and their effects, see F. W. Taussig, *The Tariff History of the United States* (New York and London: G. P. Putnam's Sons, 1923).

3. John C. Calhoun, *A Disquisition on Government.* In *The Papers of John C. Calhoun,* 28 vols. (Columbia: University of South Carolina Press, 1959–2003) 28: 20.

4. *South Carolina Exposition. Papers* 10: 512.

5. *Disquisition. Papers* 28: 34.

6. The most comprehensive biography is Charles M. Wiltse's three-volume work: *John C. Calhoun: Nationalist, 1782–1828; Nullifier, 1829–1839; Sectionalist, 1840–1850* (Indianapolis: Bobbs-Merrill, 1944–1951). Two newer biographies are more critical of Calhoun: John Niven, *John C. Calhoun and the Price of Union: A Biography* (Baton Rouge: Louisiana State University Press, 1988), and Irving H. Bartlett, *John C. Calhoun: A Biography* (New York: W. W. Norton, 1993).

7. See Calhoun's 12 December 1820 report to Congress. *Papers* 5: 480–490.

8. On internal improvements, see Calhoun's speech to Congress, 4 February 1817, *Papers* 1: 398–407; on the 1816 tariff bill, see his speech to Congress, 4 April 1816, *Papers* 1: 347–356; on Calhoun's early broad construction of the Constitution, see his 26 February 1816 and 4 February 1817 speeches, *Papers* 1: 331–339, 398–407; and Calhoun to

Robert S. Garnett, 3 July 1824. *Papers* 9: 198–202. Calhoun's early nationalism is discussed in chapter 3.

9. For Calhoun's disposition toward American Indians, see chapter 5.

10. The "corrupt bargain" (whereby Clay supposedly threw his support to Adams in the 1824 election in exchange for Adams's appointing Clay secretary of state) Calhoun called "the most dangerous stab, which the liberty of this country has ever received." Calhoun to Joseph Swift, 10 March 1825, *Papers* 10: 10. For the controversy over Calhoun's handling of debate in the Senate, see Calhoun's pseudonymous "Onslow" letters of 1826 in ibid., 99–104, 135–155.

11. In 1818 Andrew Jackson, ordered to put down a Seminole Indian uprising, crossed into Spanish territory and summarily executed two British citizens who were living among the Indians. Calhoun, then secretary of war, argued in cabinet meetings that Jackson had violated orders. Jackson during his presidency found out about Calhoun's criticism of his conduct during the Seminole War and demanded an explanation. See Calhoun to Andrew Jackson, 29 May 1830, *Papers* 11: 173–191. For the Peggy Eaton episode and its consequences for Jackson's cabinet, see Peterson, *Great Triumvirate*, 183–185.

12. According to Merrill Peterson, Calhoun "frequently passed notes to Hayne during the speech. Everyone understood that he spoke for the vice president as well as himself and this heightened the significance of the debate." *Great Triumvirate*, 175.

13. See the *Fort Hill Address* of 26 July 1831. *Papers* 11: 413–439. For Calhoun's statement urging nullification, see his 28 August 1832 letter to James Hamilton, Jr., governor of South Carolina. *Papers* 11: 613–649. For his actions during this period, see Bartlett, *John C. Calhoun*, 177–189; and Richard E. Ellis, *The Union at Risk: Jacksonian Democracy, States' Rights, and the Nullification Crisis* (Oxford: Oxford University Press, 1987), 64–68.

14. The Ordinance of Nullification and the test oath are included in William W. Freehling, ed., *The Nullification Era: A Documentary Record* (New York: Harper & Row, 1967), 150–152.

15. Calhoun defended the test oath in his 1833 "Speech on the Force Bill" (15–16 February 1833), *Papers* 12: 63–64.

16. "Hugh S. Legare on the Outrage of the Test Oath," in Freehling, *Nullification Era*, 167–169.

17. For Jackson's response to nullification, see Ellis, *Union at Risk*, 91–95. Calhoun responded at length in his "Speech on the Force Bill." *Papers* 12: 45–94.

18. For Calhoun's endorsement of the compromise, see his 12 February 1833 "Remarks on Compromise Tariff Bill," *Papers* 12: 41–42. For the compromise tariff itself, see Peterson, *Great Triumvirate*, 212–233.

19. For Calhoun's claim that without South Carolina's nullification there would have been no revision of the tariff, see his 1833 "Speech on the Force Bill," *Papers* 12: 78–79. In contrast Henry Clay, the chief sponsor of the compromise tariff, "sought to show that the goal could be reached through the give and take of the political process, without the awkward and ruinous contrivance of nullification." Peterson, *Great Triumvirate*, 230. Calhoun subsequently claimed that South Carolina's nullification had "dealt the fatal blow" to the entire system of political corruption. Calhoun to Christopher Vandeventer, 24 March 1833, *Papers* 12: 144–145.

20. "Remarks on Receiving Abolition Petitions," 6 February, 1837. *Papers* 13: 392–393.

21. Ibid., 395.

22. Niven, *John C. Calhoun and the Price of Union,* 264–314; Bartlett, *John C. Calhoun,* 306–349.

23. Quoted in Peterson, *Great Triumvirate,* 423.

24. For Calhoun's demand that northern states suppress abolitionist societies, see chapter 4.

25. "Speech on the Slavery Question," 4 March 1850. *Papers* 27: 201, 210; *A Discourse on the Constitution and Government of the United States. Papers* 28: 231–233.

26. John Niven observes that Calhoun "still hoped that somehow the Union would remain intact" but that in private correspondence he predicted "disunion is the only alternative." *John C. Calhoun and the Price of Union,* 343. In contrast Ross M. Lence describes Calhoun's speech as a "last desperate effort to avoid the necessity of choosing between the abolition of slavery and secession." Editorial note, *Union and Liberty: The Political Philosophy of John C. Calhoun* (Indianapolis: Liberty Fund, 1992), 571.

27. *Disquisition. Papers* 28: 22.

28. Abraham Lincoln, First Inaugural Address, 4 March 1861. Don E. Fehrenbacher, ed., *Lincoln: Speeches and Writings, 1859–1865* (New York: Library of America, 1989), 220.

29. James Madison makes this argument in *Federalist* No. 39.

30. See the discussion of Arend Lijphart in chapter 7.

31. "Speech on the Force Bill." *Papers* 12: 81–82.

32. *Disquisition. Papers* 28: 15.

33. Ibid., 29–30.

34. Ibid., 20.

35. *Discourse. Papers* 28: 200–201, 221–222.

36. *Disquisition. Papers* 28: 14–15, 50.

37. Ibid., 25–26.

38. Ibid., 19.

39. *Exposition. Papers* 10: 444.

40. Calhoun to Littleton Tazewell, 25 August 1827. *Papers* 10: 300–301.

41. Ibid., 301.

42. *Fort Hill Address. Papers* 11: 422.

43. Ibid., 421–424.

44. *Discourse. Papers* 28: 189–196.

45. In 1830 slaves made up 53.9 percent of total South Carolina population; in 1850, the year of Calhoun's death, it was 57.6 percent. Jean M. West, "Rice and Slavery: A Fatal Gold Seede." Posted on Slavery in America, www.slaveryinamerica.org/history/hs_es_rice .htm (accessed January 16, 2008). See also Manisha Sinha, *The Counterrevolution of Slavery: Politics and Ideology in Antebellum South Carolina* (Chapel Hill: University of North Carolina Press, 2000), 10–12.

46. For example, Arend Lijphart's sympathetic appropriation of Calhoun in *Democracy in Plural Societies* (see chapter 7) is silent on Calhoun's commitment to slavery. George Kateb's "The Majority Principle: Calhoun and His Antecedents," *Political Science Quarterly*

84: 4 (December 1969), acknowledges the depth of Calhoun's commitment to slavery, but argues that slavery is ultimately incompatible with Calhoun's argument in the *Disquisition*.

47. See, for example, William W. Freehling on Calhoun in *The Road to Disunion: Secessionists at Bay 1776–1854* (Oxford: Oxford University Press, 1990) and the portrayal of Calhoun in Sinha, *Counterrevolution of Slavery*.

48. Charles Wiltse downplays Calhoun's commitment to slavery in his three-volume biography, as does Clyde Wilson in his editorial introductions and notes for Calhoun's *Papers*. H. Lee Cheek's *Calhoun and Popular Rule: The Political Theory of the Disquisition and Discourse* (Columbia: University of Missouri Press, 2001), an admiring study of Calhoun's thought, says little about slavery.

49. "Speech on the Oregon Bill," 27 June 1848. *Papers* 25: 533. For discussion of this key passage, see chapter 5.

50. *Disquisition. Papers* 28: 39–40.

51. August O. Spain's *The Political Theory of John C. Calhoun* (New York: Octagon Books, 1968 [1951]) is comprehensive but workmanlike, more a summary than an examination of Calhoun's theory. Cheek's *Calhoun and Popular Rule* (2001) sheds light on Calhoun's understanding of human nature and his conception of local community but does not pose critical questions. Guy Story Brown, *Calhoun's Philosophy of Politics* (Macon, Ga.: Mercer University Press, 2000), likewise lacks a critical dimension.

52. This group would include Ralph Lerner, "Calhoun's New Science of Politics," *American Political Science Review* 57: 4 (December 1963), 918–932; Kateb, "Majority Principle" (1969); and Lacy K. Ford, "Inventing the Concurrent Majority: Madison, Calhoun, and the Problem of Majoritarianism in American Political Thought," *Journal of Southern History* 60: 1 (February 1994), 19–58, which gains critical purchase through the comparison with Madison. Roberta Herzberg's "An Analytic Choice Approach to Concurrent Majorities: The Relevance of John C. Calhoun for Institutional Design," *Journal of Politics* 54: 1 (February 1992), 54–81, is useful in elucidating the game-theoretic implications of Calhoun's concurrent majority but does not examine his ideas in historical context. Douglas Rae's "The Limits of Consensual Decision," *American Political Science Review* 69: 4 (December 1975), 1270–1294, is among the best critical treatments of Calhoun and is discussed in chapter 6.

53. Niven's *John C. Calhoun and the Price of Union*, though not a study of Calhoun's political theory, does illuminate important aspects of his thought. Bartlett, *John C. Calhoun* (1993), usefully keeps the slavery issue always in view. Wiltse's three-volume biography is good despite its minimizing slavery.

54. Studies of the period that feature Calhoun include Peterson, *Great Triumvirate;* Ellis, *Union at Risk;* Watson, *Liberty and Power;* Freehling, *Prelude to Civil War* and *Road to Disunion*. Calhoun's role in South Carolina politics is described in Lacy K. Ford, *Origins of Southern Radicalism: The South Carolina Upcountry, 1800–1860* (Oxford: Oxford University Press, 1988), and (in less complementary light) in Sinha, *Counterrevolution of Slavery*. Calhoun's commitment to nationalizing slavery is documented in Don E. Fehrenbacher, *The Slaveholding Republic: An Account of the United States Government's Relations to Slavery* (Oxford: Oxford University Press, 2001).

55. For instance, Lerner, "Calhoun's New Science of Politics."

Chapter Two. Calhoun and the Legacies of Jefferson and Madison

1. Here I differ with Harry Jaffa's presentation of Calhoun as a thinker coming from outside the American tradition, "influenced decisively by Rousseau and Hegel," for which I find little evidence. *A New Birth of Freedom: Abraham Lincoln and the Coming of the Civil War* (Lanham, MD: Rowman & Littlefield, 2000), 86. Jaffa rightly emphasizes the significance of Calhoun's rejecting the principle that all men are created equal. But Calhoun was as much an American product as Lincoln was.

2. John C. Calhoun, "Remarks on Receiving Abolition Petitions," 6 February 1837. *The Papers of John C. Calhoun,* 28 vols. (Columbia: University of South Carolina Press, 1959–2003) 13: 395.

3. See, for example, Douglas's remarks on race and the Declaration at the 15 September 1858 Jonesboro debate. Robert W. Johannsen, ed., *The Lincoln-Douglas Debates of 1858* (Oxford: Oxford University Press, 1965), 128.

4. Taney quotes the section of the Preamble that begins, "We hold these truths to be self-evident, that all men are created equal" and then proceeds to comment: "The general words above quoted would seem to embrace the whole human family . . . But it is too clear for dispute, that the enslaved African race were not intended to be included, and formed no part of the people who framed and adopted this declaration." Chief Justice Taney, Opinion of the Court, *Scott v. Sanford,* 60 U.S. 393 (1857).

5. Calhoun sent a copy of Smith's *Wealth of Nations* to James Monroe in 1819. *Papers* 4: 287. He read Locke intensively in his early years (John Niven, *John C. Calhoun and the Price of Union: A Biography* [Baton Rouge: Louisiana State University Press, 1988], 14–15) and during a Senate debate in 1837 implicitly identified himself as a Lockean by denying that his "positive good" defense of slavery made him a follower of Sir Robert Filmer. *Papers* 13: 391. In an 1840 letter to a young correspondent Calhoun recommended reading "the best elementary treatises on Government, including Aristotle's, which I regard, as among the best." *Papers* 15: 389. Calhoun did not indicate what aspects of Aristotle's thought he considered significant; Aristotle is simply included in a list of recommended readings headed by the *Federalist* and the Virginia and Kentucky Resolutions. Calhoun at one point called Edmund Burke "the greatest of modern statesmen" and elsewhere quoted Burke on American colonists sniffing "the approach of tyranny in the tainted breeze" and on the importance of revenue to modern states. *Papers* 13: 416; 14: 71,147. But there is no direct evidence that Burke's organic model of society in *Reflections on the Revolution in France* shaped Calhoun's own political thought. Most index entries on "Edmund Burke" in Calhoun's *Papers* refer to an American by that name.

6. August O. Spain's *The Political Theory of John C. Calhoun* (New York: Octagon Books, 1968 [1951]) makes the unsubstantiated claim that "Aristotle and Burke were without doubt [Calhoun's] favorite authors" (35). Equally unsupported are Spain's assertions that Calhoun "owed his inspiration directly to Greek sources" (105) and that Calhoun's defense of slavery was "probably derived" from Aristotle's discussion of the natural slave (227).

7. Calhoun to William C. Preston, 6 November 1828. *Papers* 10: 432.

8. Calhoun to Bolling Hall, 3 April 1832. *Papers* 11: 565.

9. "As Nullification became a monomania [in South Carolina], so did the idolatry of

Jefferson." Merrill D. Peterson, *The Jefferson Image in the American Mind* (New York: Oxford University Press, 1960), 54.

10. *South Carolina Exposition. Papers* 10: 506, 510.

11. *Fort Hill Address. Papers* 11: 416.

12. Ibid., 414–415.

13. Ibid., 415.

14. *A Discourse on the Constitution and Government of the United States. Papers* 28: 210–213.

15. Ibid., 213–214.

16. Ibid., 189–190.

17. Adrienne Koch and Harry Ammon, "The Virginia and Kentucky Resolutions: An Episode in Jefferson's and Madison's Defense of Civil Liberties," *William and Mary Quarterly* 3rd ser. 5: 2 (April 1948), 148–149, 157, 161–162. See also Peterson, *Jefferson Image,* 39, 56–58.

18. See, for instance, Jefferson to John Dickenson, 6 March 1801. Merrill D. Peterson, ed., *Thomas Jefferson: Writings* (New York: Library of America, 1984), 1084–1085.

19. For the uses of Jefferson's name across the political spectrum in the antebellum period, see Peterson, *Jefferson Image,* 17–111.

20. Calhoun to Robert S. Garnett, 3 July 1824. *Papers* 11: 198–201.

21. Calhoun to Andrew Jackson, 4 June 1826. *Papers* 10: 110.

22. Calhoun, writing as "Onslow," 12 October 1826. *Papers* 10: 232.

23. For Calhoun's support of directly elected presidential electors, see his 28 March 1825 and 10 June 1825 letters to Samuel L. Gouverneur. *Papers* 10: 13, 27; for abolition of caucuses, see Calhoun to Virgil Maxcy, 9 September 1825. *Papers* 10: 43.

24. Calhoun to Littleton Tazewell, 25 August 1827. *Papers* 10: 300–301. Merrill Peterson considers this letter a key turning point: "Calhoun thus shifted the focus of his political theory from the conflict of rulers and ruled to the conflict of sectional economic interests." Merrill D. Peterson, *The Great Triumvirate: Webster, Clay, and Calhoun* (New York: Oxford University Press, 1987), 154.

25. Calhoun to John McLean, 3 September 1827. *Papers* 10: 307. For a similar blending of these two types of "corruption," see Calhoun to James E. Colhoun, 26 August 1827, *Papers* 10: 304.

26. On this theme, see William W. Freehling, "Spoilsmen and Interests in the Thought and Career of John C. Calhoun," *Journal of American History* 52: 1 (June 1965), 25–42.

27. *Fort Hill Address. Papers* 11: 418.

28. Peterson, *Thomas Jefferson: Writings,* 449.

29. Jefferson to John Taylor, 4 June 1798. Ibid., 1055–1062.

30. Ibid., 453, 455.

31. Ibid., 449.

32. *Discourse. Papers* 28: 88.

33. *A Disquisition on Government. Papers* 28: 7, 11–12.

34. Ibid. *Papers* 28: 37–40.

35. "Remarks on Receiving Abolition Petitions." *Papers* 13: 391.

36. "Speech on the Oregon Bill, 27 June 1848. *Papers* 25: 522–524. Emphasis added by Calhoun to Jefferson quotation.

37. Ibid., 524–525.

38. Ibid., 534–536.

39. "Virginia Resolutions against the Alien and Sedition Acts." 21 December 1798. Jack N. Rakove, ed., *James Madison: Writings* (New York: Library of America, 1999), 589.

40. *Fort Hill Address. Papers* 11: 415.

41. For a comprehensive portrait of the elderly Madison's self-conscious role as guardian of the Founders' legacy, see Drew McCoy, *The Last of the Fathers: James Madison and the Republican Legacy* (Cambridge: Cambridge University Press, 1989).

42. Charles J. McDonald to Calhoun, 30 May 1831. *Papers* 11: 396–397.

43. For another perspective on the Madison-Calhoun comparison, see Lacy K. Ford, "Inventing the Concurrent Majority: Madison, Calhoun, and the Problem of Majoritarianism in American Political Thought," *Journal of Southern History* 60: 1 (February 1994), 19–58. I agree with Ford that for Calhoun, the advent of national political parties meant "the centrifugal tendencies of multiple factions had been easily overwhelmed and reversed by the centralizing pull of party discipline and spoils" (45). However, I disagree with Ford's observation that "Calhoun sought to check those [oppressive] majorities not by rejecting the principle of majority rule but by using one kind of majority to check another" (47). In empowering a state-level majority to veto a national majority on national issues, Calhoun rejected the principle of majority rule in favor of something quite different: a consensus model.

44. Quoted in *Exposition. Papers* 10: 508.

45. Madison to Joseph Cabell, 18 September 1828. Rakove, *James Madison: Writings,* 813–823.

46. Madison to Edward Everett, 28 August 1830. Ibid., 848.

47. Ibid., 842–852. Emphasis in original.

48. Ibid., 844, 849.

49. Ibid., 845.

50. Ibid., 846–848.

51. Madison to Nicholas P. Trist, 23 December 1832. Ibid., 861–862. It is possible that, in saying "until of late, there is not a State that would have abhorred such a doctrine more than South Carolina" Madison had in mind South Carolina's dependence on federal power to suppress slave uprisings. James Monroe, in his retirement, did raise exactly this issue in his correspondence with Calhoun during the nullification crisis. See Monroe to Calhoun, 4 August 1828. *Papers* 10: 410.

52. Madison, *Report of 1800.* Rakove, *James Madison: Writings,* 660–661.

53. For discussion, see McCoy, *Last of the Fathers,* 145–146, and Koch and Ammon, "Virginia and Kentucky Resolutions," 161–162.

54. Madison to Nicholas P. Trist, May 1832, and Madison to Trist, 23 December 1832. Rakove, *James Madison: Writings,* 860, 862–863. Madison was correct that Jefferson supported the right of Congress under the Articles of Confederation to coerce delinquent states; see Jefferson's "Answers and Observations for Demeunier's Article" in Peterson, *Thomas Jefferson: Writings,* 578–579.

55. Madison to Edward Everett, 28 August 1830. Rakove, *James Madison: Writings,* 842–843.

56. Ibid., 849. Emphasis in original.

57. Madison to William Cabell Rives, 12 March 1833. Ibid., 864.

58. Madison, "Advice to My Country." Ibid., 866.

59. In 1837, during Senate debate over proposed government purchase of Madison's notes on the Federal Convention (which Calhoun opposed), Calhoun remarked that in Madison's *Report of 1800* [Calhoun says 1799] Madison "had given his views . . . in the prime of his life and vigor of his manhood," implying that his denunciation of nullification thirty years later was the result of failing mental powers. *Papers* 13: 447.

60. "Speech on the Force Bill," 15–16 February 1833. *Papers* 12: 75. Madison praised Rives's "very able and enlightening speech" in his debate with Calhoun over the meaning of the Virginia Resolutions. Madison to William Cabell Rives, 12 March 1833. Rakove, *James Madison: Writings,* 863–864. Calhoun was incorrect to claim that in 1798 "no one denied" the right to form an organized political opposition aimed at overturning the ruling party through an election.

61. *Discourse. Papers* 28: 94.

62. "Speech on the Force Bill." *Papers* 12: 71.

63. Rakove, *James Madison: Writings,* 77.

64. Ibid., 298.

65. *Exposition. Papers* 10: 488. The original passage may be found in Rakove, *James Madison: Writings,* 297.

66. *Discourse. Papers* 28: 140.

67. Ibid., 203–206.

68. Ibid., 218.

69. *Disquisition. Papers* 28: 16–17.

70. Ibid., 15.

71. Ibid., 20.

72. Madison to Joseph Cabell, 18 September 1828. Rakove, *James Madison: Writings,* 819.

Chapter Three. Calhoun's Political Economy and the Ideal of Sectional Reciprocity

1. John C. Calhoun, *A Disquisition on Government. The Papers of John C. Calhoun,* 28 vols. (Columbia: University of South Carolina Press, 1959–2003) 28: 20–21, 28.

2. *Fort Hill Address. Papers* 11: 418.

3. For an excellent discussion of the meaning of "nation" and its interconnection with "the people," government, and the economic system, see Nicholas Onuf and Peter Onuf, *Nations, Markets, and War: Modern History and the American Civil War* (Charlottesville: University of Virginia Press, 2006), 144–185.

4. *Papers* 1: 347–356.

5. Ibid., 398.

6. "Speech on the Force Bill," 15–16 February 1833. *Papers* 12: 68.

7. *Discourse on the Constitution and Government of the United States. Papers* 28: 77.

8. *Papers* 1: 403–405.

9. For the constitutional argument over federally funded internal improvements, see David P. Currie, *The Constitution in Congress: The Jeffersonians 1801–1829* (Chicago: University of Chicago Press, 2001), 258–283. For comprehensive treatment of the issues

at stake, see John Lauritz Larson, *Internal Improvement: National Public Works and the Promise of Popular Government in the Early United States* (Chapel Hill: University of North Carolina Press, 2001).

10. *Papers* 1: 398, 400, 407.

11. Ibid., 401.

12. *Disquisition. Papers* 28: 28.

13. *Papers* 1: 399.

14. *Disquisition. Papers* 28: 8.

15. Calhoun to Augustine Clayton and others, 5 August 1836. *Papers* 13: 262–265. On the shift from publicly funded and owned roads and canals to privately owned but publicly subsidized railroads, see Larson, *Internal Improvement*, 225–255.

16. On the southern states' support for economic nationalism after the War of 1812 and their later sense of betrayal, see Brian Schoen, "Calculating the Price of Union: Republican Economic Nationalism and the Origins of Southern Sectionalism, 1790–1828," *Journal of the Early Republic* 23: 2 (Summer 2003), 173–206.

17. F. W. Taussig, *The Tariff History of the United States* (New York and London: G. P. Putnam's Sons, 1923), 17–36. The complicated schedule of duties on iron in the 1816 tariff is described in Taussig, 50–56.

18. *Papers* 1: 347–348.

19. Ibid., 349–356.

20. "Speech on the Force Bill." *Papers* 12: 52.

21. *South Carolina Exposition. Papers* 10: 448.

22. *Papers* 12: 46, 57.

23. Taussig, *Tariff History*, 71. See also Charles S. Sydnor, *The Development of Southern Sectionalism, 1819–1848* (Baton Rouge: Louisiana State University Press, 1948), 140–142; Merrill D. Peterson, *The Great Triumvirate: Webster, Clay, and Calhoun* (Oxford: Oxford University Press, 1987), 72–74.

24. Taussig, *Tariff History*, 80–82.

25. For accounts of the political maneuvering that produced the 1828 tariff, see Peterson, *Great Triumvirate*, 159–161; Taussig, *Tariff History*, 84–103.

26. "Speech on the Force Bill." *Papers* 12: 61.

27. Taussig, *Tariff History*, 103–105.

28. "Speech on the Force Bill." *Papers* 12: 62. Emphasis in original.

29. Ibid., 61.

30. Ibid., 62.

31. *Exposition. Papers* 10: 448.

32. Because the 1828 tariff combined a high ad valorem percentage on some goods with rates per pound on other goods and minimum valuations on still others, its actual impact as a percentage of the market value of goods required complicated calculations and guesswork, but the actual rate was certainly higher than the 33 percent base rate.

33. *Exposition. Papers* 10: 450–454, 460.

34. Ibid., 454, 458.

35. Jacob N. Cardozo, *Notes on Political Economy, With an Introductory Essay by Joseph Dorfman and with Selections from Cardozo's Other Economic Writings* (Clifton, N.J.: A. M. Kelley, 1972), 200. I am indebted to Peter Onuf for this detail.

36. *Exposition. Papers* 10: 448, 466, 468.

37. For a sympathetic discussion of the protectionist argument, which likewise included a carefully worked-out vision of the national common good, see Onuf and Onuf, *Nations, Markets, and War,* 243–307.

38. On this point, see Schoen, "Calculating the Price of Union," 203–205.

39. *Exposition. Papers* 10: 466.

40. Ibid., 468–470.

41. Ibid., 482.

42. Ibid., 484.

43. *Fort Hill Address. Papers* 11: 436–437.

44. My highlighting both the traditional and modern aspects of Calhoun's concern with corruption contrasts with William W. Freehling's "Spoilsmen and Interests in the Thought and Career of John C. Calhoun," *Journal of American History* 52: 1 (June 1965), which emphasizes its traditional character.

45. *Papers* 12: 65.

46. Speech in Senate, 10 January 1838. *Papers* 14: 84–85. See chapter 5.

47. Calhoun to Virgil Maxcy, 11 September 1830. *Papers* 11: 229.

48. William W. Freehling, *Prelude to Civil War: The Nullification Controversy in South Carolina, 1816–1836* (Oxford: Oxford University Press, 1965), 122–124.

49. For the Virginia slavery debate of 1832, see William W. Freehling, *The Road to Disunion: Secessionists at Bay, 1776–1854* (Oxford: Oxford University Press, 1990), 178–196.

50. *Papers* 12: 66.

51. *Exposition. Papers* 10: 460.

52. *Fort Hill Address. Papers* 11: 429.

53. *Exposition. Papers* 10: 460.

54. Calhoun to James Edward Colhoun, 27 March 1838 and 21 April 1838. *Papers* 14: 249, 274.

55. Later, as southern states moved toward secession, several southern economists concluded that a new southern nation would have to develop an industrial base and, if necessary, renounce free trade in favor of northern-style protectionism. Onuf and Onuf, *Nations, Markets, and War,* 324–333.

56. "Speech at the Meeting of the Citizens of Charleston," 9 March 1847. *Papers* 24: 251–252.

57. *Disquisition. Papers* 28: 15–16.

58. "Speech on the Bill to Establish a National Bank," 26 February 1816. *Papers* 1: 333–334.

59. "Speech on the Removal of the Deposits," 13 January 1834. *Papers* 12: 200–225.

60. "Speech on the Bill Authorizing an Issue of Treasury Notes," 18 September 1837. *Papers* 13: 548, 554–555.

61. Ibid., 560–561.

62. Ibid., 564–566.

63. "Edgefield Letter," 3 November 1837. *Papers* 13: 638.

64. Calhoun to Nathaniel Beverly Tucker, 2 January 1838. *Papers* 14: 45.

65. Calhoun to Duff Green, 26 June 1837. *Papers* 13: 516.

66. Calhoun to Duff Green, 27 July 1837. *Papers* 13: 528.

67. "Edgefield Letter," 3 November 1837, 638–639.

68. "Remarks on Receiving Abolition Petitions," 6 February 1837. *Papers* 13: 394.

Chapter Four. Calhoun's Constitution, Federal Union, and Slavery

1. John C. Calhoun, *A Discourse on the Constitution and Government of the United States*. In *The Papers of John C. Calhoun*, 28 vols. (Columbia: University of South Carolina Press, 1959–2003) 28: 225, 203.

2. Ibid., 230–231.

3. *A Disquisition on Government. Papers* 28: 22.

4. William Sumner Jenkins, *Pro-Slavery Thought in the Old South* (Chapel Hill: University of North Carolina Press, 1935), 157–158.

5. Calhoun's demand for wide-ranging federal action promoting the interests of slaveholders is documented in Don E. Fehrenbacher, *The Slaveholding Republic: An Account of the United States Government's Relations to Slavery* (Oxford: Oxford University Press, 2001), 51, 75, 80, 121–124, 268, 281.

6. Jenkins, *Pro-Slavery Thought*, 160.

7. *Discourse. Papers* 28: 93–94, 74–76.

8. Ibid., 73–74, 92–93.

9. Ibid., 100, 166; on citizens' allegiance, see also 77.

10. Ibid., 72.

11. John H. Rhodehamel, ed., *George Washington: Writings* (New York: Library of America, 1997), 654.

12. *Discourse. Papers* 28: 72–73, 77–78.

13. See, for example, St. George Tucker's *View of the Constitution of the United States, with Selected Writings* (Indianapolis: Liberty Fund, 1999), 24, 121–126.

14. On this point, see James H. Read, *Power versus Liberty: Madison, Hamilton, Wilson, and Jefferson* (Charlottesville: University of Virginia Press, 2000), 43, 89–117.

15. *Discourse. Papers* 28: 91.

16. *Papers* 12: 71.

17. *Discourse. Papers* 28: 94.

18. Ibid., 151–153, 156.

19. Ibid., 160; "Speech on the Force Bill," 15–16 February 1833, *Papers* 12: 130–131.

20. "Remarks on the Vermont Abolition Memorial," 19 December 1837. *Papers* 14: 13–14.

21. "First Remarks on Receiving Abolition Petitions," 7 January 1836. *Papers* 13: 27.

22. For the antislavery argument on congressional power over slavery in the District of Columbia and the southern response to this argument, see Fehrenbacher, *Slaveholding Republic*, 79–81.

23. *Fort Hill Address. Papers* 11: 424.

24. "Remarks in Debate on His Resolutions," 3 January 1838. *Papers* 14: 46.

25. "Resolutions on Abolition and the Union," 27 December 1837. *Papers* 14: 31.

26. Ibid.

27. Ibid., 31–32.

28. Commenting on Calhoun's resolutions, Forrest McDonald observes that resolution

three "went far beyond the tradition of states' rights and, in seeking to protect slavery, actually distorted the doctrine [of states' rights]." *States' Rights and the Union: Imperium in Imperio, 1776–1876* (Lawrence: University Press of Kansas, 2000), 134. McDonald's observation is correct, but makes it sound like Calhoun accidentally overshot the mark after resolution two. The whole purpose of Calhoun's entire set of six resolutions was to go "far beyond the tradition of states' rights."

29. "Remarks on Amending His Third Resolution," 4 January 1838. *Papers* 14: 54.

30. "Resolutions on Abolition and the Union." *Papers* 14: 32.

31. Ibid.

32. Ibid.

33. "Remarks on His Resolutions," 28 December 1837. *Papers* 14: 36.

34. "Remarks in Debate on His Fifth Resolution," 9 January 1838. *Papers* 14: 74.

35. George E. Baker, ed., *The Works of William H. Seward* (New York: Redfield, 1853), 1: 74.

36. "Remarks on His Resolutions," *Papers* 14: 37; "Remarks on Thomas Morris's Substitute Resolutions," 29 December 1837, *Papers* 14: 42.

37. Calhoun to James Edward Colhoun, 8 January 1838. *Papers* 14: 70.

38. "Debate in Senate over Maine Resolutions," 8 April 1836. *Papers* 13: 144.

39. "Speech on the Slavery Question," 4 March 1850. *Papers* 27: 210.

40. "Report from the Select Committee on the Circulation of Incendiary Publications," 4 February 1836, *Papers* 13: 53–66; see also the bill Calhoun introduced on the subject that same day, *Papers* 13: 67–69.

41. For a broader description of the episode, see William Lee Miller, *Arguing about Slavery: John Quincy Adams and the Great Battle in the United States Congress* (New York: Vintage, 1995); for description of a principled libertarian response from a member of Congress, see Richard R. John, "Hiland Hall's 'Report on Incendiary Publications': A Forgotten Nineteenth Century Defense of the Constitutional Guarantee of the Freedom of the Press." *American Journal of Legal History* 41: 1 (January 1997), 94–125.

42. "Report on Incendiary Publications." *Papers* 13: 57–58.

43. Ibid., 59–60.

44. In contrast, Hiland Hall's was a genuine strict-constructionist, states' rights response to the issue. Hall admitted the constitutional power of states to suppress speech within their borders but sought to keep the federal government entirely out of the business of suppression. John, "Hiland Hall's 'Report on Incendiary Publications,'" 100.

45. "Speech on the Slavery Question." *Papers* 27: 210.

46. *Discourse. Papers* 28: 87.

47. Ibid., 76.

48. It might be argued that the Confederate Constitution's silence meant the right of secession was so obvious as to go without saying. But explicitly authorizing secession would have undermined the Confederate nation-building project from the beginning; the Confederacy could not have been indifferent to member states seceding and rejoining the Union.

49. *Discourse. Papers* 28: 76.

50. Ibid., 87, 172.

51. William Rawle, *A View of the Constitution of the United States of America* (Philadelphia, 1829). In chapter 32, "Of the Permanence of the Union," Rawle argues that

the citizens of a state (not the legislature alone) may solemnly decide to secede from the Union. But unless and until secession occurs, "the United States cannot consider their legislative powers over such states suspended, nor their executive or judicial powers any way impaired, and they can not be obliged to desist from the collection of revenue within such state." Thus Rawle specifically rejected nullification-without-secession. Rawle's *View of the Constitution* is posted in full at www.constitution.org/wr/rawle-00.htm.

52. "Noon Oration by William Drayton," 4 July 1831, in William W. Freehling, ed., *The Nullification Era: A Documentary Record* (New York: Harper & Row, 1967), 125.

53. See discussion of Madison in chapter 2.

54. In *A Constitutional View of the Late War between the States* (Philadelphia: National Publishing Co., 1868), Alexander Stephens (vice president of the Confederacy) cited St. George Tucker and William Rawle as authorities endorsing a constitutional right of secession (503–506). Madison, who rejected a constitutional right of secession, might seem entitled to at least as much constitutional authority as Tucker or Rawle.

55. See, for example, William W. Freehling and Craig M. Simpson, eds., *Secession Debated: Georgia's Showdown in 1860* (Oxford: Oxford University Press, 1992). Secessionists bolstered their constitutional arguments with invocations of a "divine right of self-defence, which governments neither give nor can take away" (46; see also 144). Of course a *natural* right of revolution could equally be invoked by southern slaves to rise up against slave owners.

56. "Speech on the Oregon Bill," 27 June 1848, *Papers* 25: 534; *Discourse, Papers* 28: 225. Calhoun's estimate of the probabilities was probably correct. A coordinated act of secession by nearly one-third of the territory, organized by state governments and having majority support among the citizen population, is very difficult to reverse; secessionists need only hold the territory while the central government must conquer and occupy a vast hostile territory. Union victory was the less likely outcome in the Civil War.

57. The South Carolina Ordinance of Secession and the *Declaration of the Immediate Causes Which Induce and Justify the Secession of South Carolina from the Federal Union* are included as source documents in David Stephen Heidler et al., eds., *Encyclopedia of the American Civil War* (New York: W. W. Norton, 2002), 2240–2243.

58. "Speech on the Oregon Bill." *Papers* 25: 532. See also the close of Calhoun's 9 March 1847 "Speech at Charleston." *Papers* 24: 258.

59. *Disquisition. Papers* 28: 43.

60. *Discourse. Papers* 28: 225.

61. The New Jersey Plan called for a plural executive consisting of an unspecified number of persons. There was no indication that any of these persons, or the body as a whole, would have enjoyed the veto powers proposed in Calhoun's dual-executive model. The New Jersey Plan instead envisioned a weak executive "removable by Cong[res]s on application by a majority of the Executives of the several States," which both in its weakness and in its majority-rule assumptions is far removed from Calhoun's purpose. Max Farrand, *The Records of the Federal Convention of 1787* (1937; rev. ed., New Haven, Conn.: Yale University Press, 1966), 1: 244.

62. *Discourse. Papers* 28: 119–120.

63. *Disquisition. Papers* 28: 43. This reasoning behind Calhoun's jury analogy is examined at length in chapter 6.

64. Farrand, *Records* 2: 221, 364.

65. Ibid., 221.

66. Ibid., 364.

67. "Speech on the Slavery Question." *Papers* 27: 210.

Chapter Five. Calhoun's Defense of Slavery

1. In 1837 Calhoun denounced the American Colonization Society together with "all other schemes . . . calculated to disturb the existing relation between the races" and categorized Henry Clay and Daniel Webster as leaders of an "abolition" party for supporting colonization. In John C. Calhoun, *The Papers of John C. Calhoun*, 28 vols. (Columbia: University of South Carolina Press, 1959–2003) 13: 371, 516.

2. Speeches in Senate, 27 January 1837 and 29 December 1837. *Papers* 13: 371; 14: 42.

3. Quoted in Manisha Sinha, *The Counterrevolution of Slavery: Politics and Ideology in Antebellum South Carolina* (Chapel Hill: University of North Carolina Press, 2000), 86.

4. James Henry Hammond, *An Oration on the Life, Character and Services of John Caldwell Calhoun, Delivered the 21st November in Charleston, S.C.* (Charleston, S.C.: Walker & James, 1850), 53–54.

5. "Further Remarks in Debate on His Fifth Resolution." Speech in Senate, 10 January 1838. *Papers* 14: 84.

6. "Remarks on Receiving Abolition Petitions," 6 February 1837 (revised report). *Papers* 13: 395.

7. Ibid., 391.

8. Clyde N. Wilson, "Introduction" to Calhoun's *Papers*, Vol. 14: xxxiii.

9. Sir Robert Filmer's *Patriarcha* (1680) was a principal target of John Locke's *Two Treatises of Government* (1690). Rives's comment about Filmer to which Calhoun responded is omitted from Calhoun's *Papers* but included in Ross M. Lence, ed., *Union and Liberty: The Political Philosophy of John C. Calhoun* (Indianapolis: Liberty Fund, 1992), 468.

10. "Remarks on Receiving Abolition Petitions." *Papers* 13: 390–391.

11. Ibid., 390.

12. "Further Remarks in Debate on His Fifth Resolution." *Papers* 14: 84–85. On Calhoun's plan to publish these remarks in pamphlet form, see Calhoun to Armistead Burt, 24 January 1838. *Papers* 14: 104–106.

13. *A Disquisition on Government. Papers* 28: 20.

14. See discussion of Lani Guinier in chapter 7.

15. Three full-length studies of Calhoun's political theory have been published in the last half-century. All three either marginalize or misrepresent Calhoun's argument in defense of slavery. August Spain's *The Political Theory of John C. Calhoun* (New York: Octagon Books, 1968 [1951]), 224–247, conflates Calhoun's own defense of slavery with other proslavery writers and does not explore interconnections between slavery and Calhoun's wider theory. H. Lee Cheek's *Calhoun and Popular Rule: The Political Theory of the Disquisition and Discourse* (Columbia: University of Missouri Press, 2001) says little about slavery and misleadingly implies that Calhoun regarded African American slavery as merely temporary (22, 91). Guy Story Brown's *Calhoun's Philosophy of Politics* (Macon, Ga.: Mercer University Press, 2000) puzzlingly claims that in calling slavery a "positive good" Calhoun

55. Ford, "Republican Ideology in a Slave Society," 422.

56. "Remarks on Receiving Abolition Petitions." *Papers* 13: 390.

57. *Disquisition. Papers* 28: 32–33.

58. "Speech on the Oregon Bill." *Papers* 25: 532–533.

59. In his chapter "Masters and Mudsills" from *The Arrogance of Race: Historical Perspectives on Slavery, Racism, and Social Inequality* (Middletown, Ct.: Wesleyan University Press, 1988, 15–27), George M. Fredrickson places Calhoun convincingly within a shared South Carolina ideology of race and slavery, but without distinguishing Calhoun's thought from that of Harper, Hammond, and others.

60. Selections from these writers are included in McKitrick, *Slavery Defended,* and Faust, *Ideology of Slavery.*

61. Thomas Roderick Dew, "Abolition of Negro Slavery," in Faust, *Ideology of Slavery,* 21–77. See especially 41, 50–51, 58, 61–63, 67–68.

62. William Harper, *Memoir on Slavery,* in Faust, *Ideology of Slavery,* 78–135. See especially 80–85, 89, 94–95, 109–113, 120.

63. Ibid., 104–108, 131.

64. James Henry Hammond, "Mud-Sill Speech," in McKitrick, *Slavery Defended,* 121–125.

65. James Henry Hammond, *Letters to an English Abolitionist,* in Faust, *Ideology of Slavery,* 168–205. Hammond himself is featured in Drew Gilpin Faust, *A Sacred Circle: The Dilemma of the Intellectual in the Old South, 1840–1860* (Baltimore: Johns Hopkins University Press, 1977), and in O'Brien, *Conjectures of Order,* 2: 952–959.

66. Hammond, *Letters to an English Abolitionist,* 177, 193–196.

67. Hammond, *Oration on the Life,* 59–60, 72.

68. On reopening the slave trade, see Hammond, *Letters to an English Abolitionist,* 171. Calhoun himself strongly condemned the international slave trade early in his career. In 1816 he described as a "disgrace" that the trade was tolerated until 1808 and was ashamed of his own state's role in it. *Papers* 1: 312. In 1820, as President Monroe's secretary of war, Calhoun was responsible for suppressing the illegal transportation of slaves into the United States. *Papers* 4: 687, 742. Calhoun's condemnation of the international slave trade later weakened after abolitionists began denying any distinction between international and domestic slave trades, calling both "piracy"; Calhoun "was not willing to admit the parallel" but also denied that the international slave trade qualified as "piracy." "Remarks on Reception of the Ohio Abolition Petition," 19 January 1836, *Papers* 13: 45. In 1842 when the Webster-Ashburton Treaty was presented to the Senate, Calhoun supported in principle the continued ban on international trade in slaves, but opposed allowing Great Britain to enforce the ban against U.S. ships. "Speech on the Treaty," 19 August 1842, *Papers* 16: 401–407.

69. Hammond, "Mud-Sill Speech," 123.

70. Fitzhugh's *Sociology for the South* (1854) is excerpted in McKitrick, *Slavery Defended,* 34–50. His essay "Southern Thought" (1857) is included in Faust, *Ideology of Slavery,* 272–299. Fitzhugh is featured in a number of studies including Eugene D. Genovese, *The World the Slaveholders Made: Two Essays in Interpretation* (New York: Pantheon Books, 1969), and O'Brien, *Conjectures of Order,* 2: 972–992.

71. Fitzhugh, *Sociology for the South,* 40–43; "Southern Thought," 285, 293.

72. "Further Remarks in Debate on His Fifth Resolution." *Papers* 14: 84–85.

73. Ibid., 84.

74. Calhoun to Francis W. Pickens, 17 July 1835, *Papers* 12: 544; "Report and Resolutions of a Public Meeting at Pendleton," 9 September 1835, *Papers* 12: 550; "Remarks on Receiving Abolition Petitions," *Papers* 13: 394.

75. "Remarks on Receiving Abolition Petitions." *Papers* 13: 397.

76. "Speech on the Loan Bill," 25 February 1814. *Papers* 1: 229.

77. For the abolition of slavery in the British West Indies and its aftermath, see Fogel, *Without Consent or Contract,* 226–229, 407.

78. "Remarks on Reception of Abolition Petitions," 15 February 1836. *Papers* 13: 77.

79. Calhoun to William R. King, 12 August 1844. *Papers* 19: 574.

80. "Remarks on Receiving Abolition Petitions," 6 February 1837. *Papers* 13: 397.

81. "Remarks on Receiving Abolition Petitions," 18 December 1837. *Papers* 14: 12.

82. "First Remarks on Receiving Abolition Petitions," 7 January 1836. *Papers* 13: 24. The "manly" actions Calhoun praises include the following: in the summer of 1835 William Lloyd Garrison was beaten by a Boston mob and dragged through the streets at the end of a rope. Theodore Weld was pelted with eggs and stoned in upstate New York and in Ohio. Fogel, *Without Consent or Contract,* 271–272.

83. "Speech on Abolition Petitions," 9 March 1836, *Papers* 13: 105; "Remarks on His Fifth Resolution," 9 January 1838, *Papers* 14: 73.

84. "Remarks on Receiving Abolition Petitions," 19 December 1837. *Papers* 14: 13.

85. David Robertson, *Denmark Vesey: The Buried History of America's Largest Slave Rebellion and the Man Who Led It* (New York: Alfred A. Knopf, 1999), 120–121. Scholars dispute how real the conspiracy was, but white South Carolinians certainly believed it was real.

86. "Report and Resolutions of a Public Meeting at Pendleton." *Papers* 12: 549.

87. "Speech on Abolition Petitions." *Papers* 13: 104–105.

88. James Oakes in *The Ruling Race: A History of American Slaveholders* (New York: Alfred A. Knopf, 1982, 96–122) argues that many slaveholders secretly suffered religious or moral doubts about the justice of slavery. There is no evidence that Calhoun himself suffered doubt, but his "positive good" defense of slavery implicitly recognized the danger of doubt among other Southern whites.

89. Edmund S. Morgan, *American Slavery, American Freedom: The Ordeal of Colonial Virginia* (New York: W. W. Norton, 1975), 6, 381.

90. "Remarks on Receiving Abolition Petitions," 6 February 1837. *Papers* 13: 390.

91. See, for example, J. Drew Harrington, "Classical Antiquity and the Proslavery Argument," *Slavery and Abolition* 10: 1 (1989), 60–72.

92. *Disquisition. Papers* 28: 34.

Chapter Six. Calhoun's Consensus Model of Government

1. John C. Calhoun, *A Disquisition on Government.* In *The Papers of John C. Calhoun,* 28 vols. (Columbia: University of South Carolina Press, 1959–2003) 28: 21.

2. Ibid., 40.

3. Ibid., 3, 34.

4. Ibid., 43.

5. Ibid., 44.

6. Ibid., 45–46.

7. For example, in his 27 June 1848 speech on the Oregon Bill, where he insisted on the right to bring slave property to any U.S. territory, he claimed: "I am influenced neither by sectional nor party considerations. If I know myself, I would repel as promptly and decidedly any aggression of the South on the North, as I would any on the part of the latter on the former." *Papers* 25: 515. There are many similar self-descriptions throughout Calhoun's *Papers*.

8. "Remarks on the Compromise Tariff Bill," 12 February 1833. *Papers* 12: 41–42.

9. *Disquisition. Papers* 28: 7–8.

10. Ralph Lerner, "Calhoun's New Science of Politics," *American Political Science Review* 57: 4 (December 1963), 931–932. See also August O. Spain, *The Political Theory of John C. Calhoun* (New York: Octagon Books, 1968 [1951]), which speaks of the "predominance of selfishness" in Calhoun's description of human nature (80). For a more social, less self-interested interpretation of Calhoun on human nature, see H. Lee Cheek, *Calhoun and Popular Rule: The Political Theory of the Disquisition and Discourse* (Columbia: University of Missouri Press, 2001).

11. *Disquisition. Papers* 28: 8.

12. Ibid., 34.

13. Ibid., 44–45.

14. Ibid., 28.

15. Ibid., 34.

16. Ibid., 45.

17. Ibid., 44.

18. Ibid., 45.

19. Calhoun to Alexander Hamilton, 28 March 1830. *Papers* 11: 142. The recipient was the son of Alexander Hamilton (1755–1804).

20. *Disquisition. Papers* 28: 45.

21. Ibid., 35.

22. See chapters 3 and 4.

23. *Disquisition. Papers* 28: 34.

24. *South Carolina Exposition. Papers* 10: 522–524.

25. Douglas W. Rae, "The Limits of Consensual Decision," *American Political Science Review* 69: 4 (December 1975), 1270–1294. Rae also discusses contemporary consent theorists James Buchanan, Gordon Tullock, Robert Paul Wolff, and Knut Wicksell.

26. Rae, "Limits of Consensual Decision," 1270–1278.

27. *Disquisition. Papers* 28: 45.

28. For narrative of the nullification crisis and its resolution, see William W. Freehling, *Prelude to Civil War: The Nullification Controversy in South Carolina, 1816–1836* (Oxford: Oxford University Press, 1965); and Richard E. Ellis, *The Union at Risk: Jacksonian Democracy, States' Rights, and the Nullification Crisis* (Oxford: Oxford University Press, 1987).

29. This is the central point of Calhoun's long speech on the Force Bill, 15–16 February 1833. *Papers* 12: 45–94.

30. See chapter 4.

31. William Henry Harrison to Calhoun, 30 April 1832. *Papers* 11: 569–578. The letter was published in several Ohio newspapers. That Harrison's description of in-state distributional conflict was on target is clear from John Lauritz Larson, *Internal Improvement: National Public Works and the Promise of Popular Government in the Early United States* (Chapel Hill: University of North Carolina Press, 2001), 71–107.

32. *Disquisition. Papers* 28: 22.

33. *Fort Hill Address. Papers* 11: 417.

34. *Disquisition. Papers* 28: 15.

35. Ibid., 22.

36. Ibid., 21.

37. See for instance the speeches by William Drayton, Hugh S. Legare, and Richard Manning in William W. Freehling, ed., *The Nullification Era: A Documentary Record* (New York: Harper & Row, 1967), 120–135.

38. Freehling, *Nullification Era,* 136.

39. Lacy K. Ford, *Origins of Southern Radicalism: The South Carolina Upcountry, 1800–1860* (Oxford: Oxford University Press, 1988), 155.

40. "Speech on the Force Bill," 15–16 February 1833. *Papers* 12: 92.

41. Ford, *Origins of Southern Radicalism,* 177–180.

42. *Disquisition. Papers* 28: 32–33.

43. "Speech on Reception of Abolition Petitions," 6 February 1837. *Papers* 13: 396.

44. *A Discourse on the Constitution and Government of the United States. Papers* 28: 117.

45. For the in-state version of the argument, see Calhoun to James L. Orr and others, 1 November 1846. *Papers* 23: 507–521. For the *Discourse* version of the same argument, see *Papers* 28: 236–239.

46. *Disquisition. Papers* 28: 22.

47. *Discourse. Papers* 28: 236. See also Ford, *Origins of Southern Radicalism*: "Real political leverage in the state lay with the legislature, which elected not only the United States senators, the governor, judges and chancellors, and all the state officers but also the board of directors of the Bank of the State of South Carolina, trustees of South Carolina College, election officials and poll managers, and members of some of the numerous district commissions which handled the affairs of local government" (304).

48. *Disquisition. Papers* 28: 20.

49. Calhoun to James L. Orr and others, 1 November 1846. *Papers* 23: 510–512.

50. For more detailed description of the contrast between upcountry and lowcountry, see Freehling, *Prelude to Civil War,* 7–24; Ford, *Origins of Southern Radicalism,* 44–95, 281–307.

51. Strictly speaking, the lowcountry and slave property were overrepresented in both Senate and House, but to a higher degree in the Senate than in the House. For specifics of the representational formula, see Ford, *Origins of Southern Radicalism,* 281.

52. *Discourse. Papers* 28: 239.

53. For the politics behind this proposal, see Ford, *Origins of Southern Radicalism,* 284–285.

54. Calhoun to James L. Orr and others, 1 November 1846. *Papers* 23: 509.

55. Ibid., 511–512, 518.

56. Ibid., 513–515, 518.

57. Douglas Rae observes that Calhoun's consensual model presupposes "a cleavage structure without cross-cutting" and that "this structure must remain essentially constant through time, else repeated constitutional crisis." "Limits of Consensual Decision," 1277.

58. "Speech on the Oregon Bill," *Papers* 25: 533.

59. Ford, *Origins of Southern Radicalism,* viii.

60. Ibid., 146, 154, 157, 183–184.

61. "Edgefield Letter," 3 November 1837, *Papers* 13: 639; Speech at Charleston, March 9, 1847, *Papers* 24: 257–258.

Chapter Seven. Contemporary Divided Societies and the Minority Veto

1. See, for example, Arend Lijphart, *Power-Sharing in South Africa* (Berkeley: Institute of International Studies, University of California, 1985), which explicitly recommended a minority veto: "It is wrong to interpret the basic problem in terms of a dichotomous black-white conflict. Far from being homogeneous communities, the black and white groups are each deeply divided into a number of ethnic groups . . . Afrikaner . . . English . . . Africans, Coloureds, Asians . . . Zulus . . . Xhosas" (19–20).

2. Frederick van Zyl Slabbert and David Welsh, *South Africa's Options: Strategies for Sharing Power* (New York: St. Martin's Press, 1979), 153–154.

3. Arend Lijphart, *Democracy in Plural Societies* (New Haven, Conn.: Yale University Press, 1977), 37.

4. Lijphart explains that "the term 'consociational' is derived from Johannes Althusius's concept of *consocio* in his *Politica Methodice Digesta* (1603)." *Democracy in Plural Societies,* 1n. Lijphart first presented his theory of consociational democracy in "Consociational Democracy," *World Politics* 21: 2 (January 1969), 207–225.

5. Lijphart, *Democracy in Plural Societies,* 1; Arend Lijphart, *Democracies: Patterns of Majoritarian and Consensus Government in Twenty-one Countries* (New Haven, Conn.: Yale University Press, 1984), 1–36.

6. Lijphart, *Democracies,* 22–23; *Democracy in Plural Societies,* 25.

7. Lijphart, *Democracy in Plural Societies,* 25.

8. John C. Calhoun, *A Disquisition on Government.* In *The Papers of John C. Calhoun,* 28 vols. (Columbia: University of South Carolina Press, 1959–2003) 28: 34.

9. Lijphart, *Democracy in Plural Societies,* 36–37.

10. Lijphart supports this by quoting the following language from Calhoun's *Disquisition*: "By giving to each interest, or portion, the power of self-protection, all strife and struggle between them for ascendancy is prevented, and thereby . . . every feeling calculated to weaken the attachment to the whole is suppressed." Lijphart, *Democracy in Plural Societies,* 37.

11. Ibid. For the original passage, see Calhoun's *Disquisition, Papers* 28: 45.

12. Lijphart, *Democracy in Plural Societies,* 38.

13. Lijphart, *Power-Sharing in South Africa,* 6–9, 72–73 .

14. Lijphart, *Democracy in Plural Societies,* 49–50.

15. Arend Lijphart, *The Politics of Accommodation: Pluralism and Democracy in the Netherlands* (Berkeley: University of California Press, 1985), 144.

16. *Disquisition. Papers* 28: 32–33. See chapter 6.

17. Lijphart, *Democracy in Plural Societies,* 39.

18. Lijphart, *Power-Sharing in South Africa,* 123.

19. For Calhoun's answer to the minorities-within-minorities problem, see chapter 6.

20. On the explicit role of consociational theory in the design of the agreement, see John McGarry and Brendan O'Leary, *The Northern Ireland Conflict: Consociational Engagements* (Oxford: Oxford University Press, 2004), 1–4; Donald L. Horowitz, "The Northern Ireland Agreement: Clear, Consociational, and Risky," in John McGarry, ed., *Northern Ireland and the Divided World: The Northern Ireland Conflict and the Good Friday Agreement in Comparative Perspective* (Oxford: Oxford University Press, 2001), 89–108. Horowitz is consistently critical of consociational theory but concedes its key role in shaping the agreement.

21. McGarry and O'Leary, *Northern Ireland Conflict,* 33, 290–291.

22. Ibid., 264.

23. *A Discourse on the Constitution and Government of the United States. Papers* 28: 231.

24. McGarry and O'Leary, *Northern Ireland Conflict,* 31, 34; for criticism of the rule, see Horowitz, "Northern Ireland Agreement," 98–100.

25. McGarry and O'Leary, *Northern Ireland Conflict,* 15–16, 292–293.

26. McGarry and O'Leary call this the "double protection model," which "promises to entrench the identical protection of rights, collective and individual, on both sides of the present border. In effect, it promises protection to Northern nationalists now on the same terms that will be given to Ulster Unionists should they ever become a minority in a unified Ireland." McGarry and O'Leary, *Northern Ireland Conflict,* 280.

27. Ibid., 272–279.

28. Ibid., 6, 111–115.

29. Rupert Taylor, "Northern Ireland: Consociation or Social Transformation?" in McGarry, *Northern Ireland and the Divided World,* 38.

30. McGarry and O'Leary, *Northern Ireland Conflict,* 19–24.

31. Horowitz, "Northern Ireland Agreement," 92–93, 100–101. McGarry and O'Leary dispute the claim that political attachments in Northern Ireland display any significant degree of cross-communal flexibility. *Northern Ireland Conflict,* 20.

32. McGarry and O'Leary, *Northern Ireland Conflict,* 129.

33. McGarry and O'Leary assert bluntly that "Northern Ireland's constitutional choice is between consociational democracy and no democracy." Ibid., 110.

34. Susan L. Woodward, *Balkan Tragedy: Chaos and Dissolution after the Cold War* (Washington, D.C.: Brookings Institution, 1995), 33–35.

35. For a summary of this line of argument and a response to it, see Woodward, *Balkan Tragedy,* 18, 21–22; Robert M. Hayden, *Blueprints for a House Divided: The Constitutional Logic of the Yugoslav Conflicts* (Ann Arbor: University of Michigan Press, 2000 [1991]), 2–4.

36. For rates of intermarriage and other indications of social and economic interdependence, see Hayden, *Blueprints for a House Divided,* 27.

37. The zero-sum character of the nationality conflicts in the region is described forcefully in Vladimir Gligorov, "Is What Is Left Right? (The Yugoslav Heritage)," in Janos

Matyas Kovacs, ed., *Transition to Capitalism: The Communist Legacy in Eastern Europe* (New Brunswick, N.J.: Transaction Publishers, 1994), 147–172.

38. Woodward, *Balkan Tragedy,* 36–37.

39. Steven L. Burg, *Conflict and Cohesion in Socialist Yugoslavia: Political Decision Making since 1966* (Princeton, N.J.: Princeton University Press, 1983), 24.

40. Burg, *Conflict and Cohesion,* 45, 55–56.

41. Burg, *Conflict and Cohesion,* 88–100, describes the Slovenian road-building crisis of 1969, where Slovenia asserted the right to withhold funding from a national road-building initiative that in Slovenia's view did not offer them a large enough share of the road-building pie. If the names and the construction materials were changed, this could be mistaken for one of the antebellum controversies described in John Lauritz Larson, *Internal Improvement: National Public Works and the Promise of Popular Government in the Early United States* (Chapel Hill: University of North Carolina Press, 2001).

42. Burg, *Conflict and Cohesion,* 110, 117.

43. Ibid., 215. See also Hayden, *Blueprints for a House Divided,* 30.

44. Woodward, *Balkan Tragedy,* 38.

45. Hayden, *Blueprints for a House Divided,* 33, 38.

46. Woodward, *Balkan Tragedy,* 60. For other negative assessments of the consensual decision process, see the essays by Steven L. Burg, Vojislav Kostunica, and Julie Mostov in Dennison Rusinow, ed., *Yugoslavia: A Fractured Federalism* (Washington, D.C.: Wilson Center Press, 1988), 9–22, 78–92, 105–119. For a defense of Yugoslavia's consensual decision process, see the essay by Zvonko Lerotic in the same volume, 93–104.

47. This argument is made in Woodward, *Balkan Tragedy,* 15–17.

48. In Bosnia alone, "more than 2 million people of a population of 4.3 million became refugees or were displaced to other parts of the republic." Woodward, *Balkan Tragedy,* 1.

49. Hayden, *Blueprints for a House Divided,* 36.

50. Ibid., 31–32. See also Woodward, *Balkan Tragedy,* 65–68.

51. Milan Andrejevich, "Crisis in Croatia and Slovenia: Proposal for a Confederal Yugoslavia," *Report on Eastern Europe* 1: 44 (2 November 1990), 28–33.

52. Hayden, *Blueprints for a House Divided,* 32. See also Woodward, *Balkan Tragedy:* "the transfer of power in Serbia from federalist liberals to a leader [Milosevic] oriented to Serbian sovereignty dislodged from the federalist camp its longest standing and most reliable support . . . Milosevic's nationalism removed what might have been an important obstacle to Slovenian independence" (94).

53. Because so many Serbs lived outside the borders of Serbia, Serbian nationalism could take the form either of support for keeping Yugoslavia united (which would keep all Serbs within the same larger political community) or demands for a "greater Serbia" (annexing regions of Croatia and Bosnia).

54. Andrejevich, "Crisis in Croatia and Slovenia," 28–29.

55. Hayden, *Blueprints for a House Divided,* 44.

56. Andrejevich, "Crisis in Croatia and Slovenia," 31.

57. Hayden, *Blueprints for a House Divided,* 47; Milan Andrejevich, "Kosovo and Slovenia Declare Their Sovereignty," *Report on Eastern Europe* 1: 30 (27 July 1990), 45–47.

58. For example, on the day after Slovenia declared its sovereignty its foreign minister

told an Italian newspaper that "Yugoslavia no longer exists." Hayden, *Blueprints for a House Divided,* 47.

59. Ibid., 63–64.

60. Hayden observes that "the flaws built into the [1974] constitution gave the Slovenes the means to destroy the constitutional order while claiming they were actually following the constitution's provisions." Ibid., 52.

61. Ibid., 29, 49–50. Hayden notes that the Slovenian proposals went further in the direction of decentralization than Lijphart himself recommends. The Slovenian proposals were, however, nearly perfect embodiments of Calhoun's vision of federal union.

62. Woodward, *Balkan Tragedy,* 99.

63. See chapter 4.

64. Calhoun to Anna Maria Calhoun Clemson, 25 January 1838. *Papers* 14: 107.

65. Patti Waldmeier, *Anatomy of a Miracle: The End of Apartheid and the Birth of the New South Africa* (New Brunswick, N.J.: Rutgers University Press, 2001 [1997]), 135. My principal sources for this section are Waldmeier and Nelson Mandela's autobiography *Long Walk to Freedom: The Autobiography of Nelson Mandela* (Boston: Little Brown, 1994).

66. Waldmeier, *Anatomy of a Miracle,* 178, 214.

67. Mandela described the minority veto proposal as "apartheid in disguise, a 'loser takes all' system." *Long Walk to Freedom,* 504.

68. Waldmeier, *Anatomy of a Miracle,* 3, 226.

69. Mandela, *Long Walk to Freedom,* 19.

70. Padraig O'Malley, "Northern Ireland and South Africa: 'Hope and History at a Crossroads,'" in McGarry, *Northern Ireland and the Divided World,* 276. For the conference itself, and the particular lessons the South African participants sought to impress upon those from Northern Ireland, see 284–299.

71. In the controversy surrounding Bill Clinton's subsequently withdrawn nomination of Guinier for Assistant Attorney General for Civil Rights in 1993, Guinier's proposals were often mischaracterized as a "racial quota system." Parallels between Calhoun and Guinier were occasionally noted; see, for example, John L. Safford, "John C. Calhoun, Lani Guinier, and Minority Rights" in *PS: Political Science and Politics* 28: 2 (June 1995), 211–216.

72. Ibid. Lani Guinier, *The Tyranny of the Majority: Fundamental Fairness in Representative Democracy* (New York: Free Press, 1994), 7.

73. Ibid., 1, 9.

74. See chapter 1.

75. James Madison, *Federalist* No. 10 and 51, in Jack N. Rakove, ed., *James Madison: Writings* (New York: Library of America, 1999), 164, 298.

76. See comparison of Madison and Calhoun in chapter 2.

77. Guinier, *Tyranny of the Majority,* 4–5.

78. Ibid., 15, 149.

79. Ibid., 108. Arend Lijphart recommends something similar for decision making within a grand coalition cabinet under a consociational system. *Democracy in Plural Societies,* 39.

80. Guinier, *Tyranny of the Majority,* 108.

81. Ibid., 260 n.119. In practice whether a supermajority voting rule translated into

minority veto would depend on the size of a given minority in the voting population compared to the magnitude of the minority required to block passage of legislation.

82. Ibid., 17.
83. See chapter 6.
84. Guinier, *Tyranny of the Majority,* 107.
85. Ibid., 14.

Selected Bibliography

Bartlett, Irving H. *John C. Calhoun: A Biography*. New York: W. W. Norton, 1993.

Burg, Steven L. *Conflict and Cohesion in Socialist Yugoslavia: Political Decision Making since 1966*. Princeton, N.J.: Princeton University Press, 1983.

Calhoun, John C. *The Papers of John C. Calhoun*. 28 vols. Vol. 1 ed. Robert L. Meriwether; Vols. 2–10 ed. William E. Hemphill; Vols. 10–22 ed. Clyde N. Wilson; Vols. 23–27 ed. Clyde N. Wilson and Shirley Bright Cook; Vol. 28 ed. Richard K. Cralle. Columbia: University of South Carolina Press, 1959–2003.

———. *A Discourse on the Constitution and Government of the United States*. Richard K. Cralle, ed. Originally published by the General Assembly of the State of South Carolina, 1851. Republished in *The Papers of John C. Calhoun*, vol. 28: 71–239.

———. *A Disquisition on Government*. Richard K. Cralle, ed. Originally published by the General Assembly of the State of South Carolina, 1851. Republished in *The Papers of John C. Calhoun*, vol. 28: 3–67.

———. *Fort Hill Address*. Originally published in the Pendleton, South Carolina, *Messenger*, 26 July 1831. Republished in *The Papers of John C. Calhoun*, vol. 11: 413–439.

———. *Rough Draft of What Is Called the South Carolina Exposition*. Originally as secretly authored committee draft, 11 November 1828. *The Papers of John C. Calhoun*, vol. 10: 444–532.

Cheek, H. Lee. *Calhoun and Popular Rule: The Political Theory of the Disquisition and Discourse*. Columbia: University of Missouri Press, 2001.

Davis, David Brion. *The Problem of Slavery in the Age of Revolution, 1770–1823*. Ithaca, N.Y.: Cornell University Press, 1975.

Ellis, Richard E. *The Union at Risk: Jacksonian Democracy, States' Rights, and the Nullification Crisis*. Oxford: Oxford University Press, 1987.

Farrand, Max. *The Records of the Federal Convention of 1787*. 4 vols. 1937. Rev. ed., New Haven, Conn.: Yale University Press, 1966.

Faust, Drew Gilpin. *A Sacred Circle: The Dilemma of the Intellectual in the Old South, 1840–1860*. Baltimore: Johns Hopkins University Press, 1977.

Faust, Drew Gilpin, ed. *The Ideology of Slavery: Proslavery Thought in the Antebellum South, 1830–1860*. Baton Rouge: Louisiana State University Press, 1981.

Fehrenbacher, Don E. *The Slaveholding Republic: An Account of the United States Government's Relations to Slavery*. Oxford: Oxford University Press, 2001.

Fogel, Robert William. *Without Consent or Contract: The Rise and Fall of American Slavery*. New York: W. W. Norton, 1989.

Ford, Lacy K. "Inventing the Concurrent Majority: Madison, Calhoun, and the Problem of Majoritarianism in American Political Thought." *Journal of Southern History* 60: 1 (February 1994), 19–58.

———. *Origins of Southern Radicalism: The South Carolina Upcountry, 1800–1860*. Oxford: Oxford University Press, 1988.

———. "Republican Ideology in a Slave Society: The Political Economy of John C. Calhoun." *Journal of Southern History* 54: 3 (1988), 405–424.

Frederickson, George M. *The Black Image in the White Mind: The Debate on Afro-American Character and Destiny, 1817–1914*. Middletown, Ct.: Wesleyan University Press, 1971.

Freehling, William W. *Prelude to Civil War: The Nullification Controversy in South Carolina 1816–1836*. Oxford: Oxford University Press, 1965.

———. *The Road to Disunion: Secessionists at Bay 1776–1854*. Oxford: Oxford University Press, 1990.

———. "Spoilsmen and Interests in the Thought and Career of John C. Calhoun." *Journal of American History* 52: 1 (June 1965), 25–42.

Freehling, William W., ed. *The Nullification Era: A Documentary Record*. New York: Harper & Row, 1967.

Garson, Robert A. "Proslavery as Political Theory: The Examples of John C. Calhoun and George Fitzhugh." *South Atlantic Quarterly* 84 (Spring 1985), 197–212.

Genovese, Eugene D. *The Slaveholders' Dilemma: Freedom and Progress in Southern Conservative Thought, 1820–1860*. Columbia: University of South Carolina Press, 1992.

———. *The World the Slaveholders Made: Two Essays in Interpretation*. New York: Pantheon Books, 1969.

Guinier, Lani. *The Tyranny of the Majority: Fundamental Fairness in Representative Democracy*. New York: Free Press, 1994.

Hammond, James Henry. *An Oration on the Life, Character and Services of John Caldwell Calhoun, Delivered the 21st November in Charleston, S.C.* Charleston, S.C.: Walker & James, 1850.

Harrington, J. Drew. "Classical Antiquity and the Proslavery Argument." *Slavery and Abolition* 10: 1 (1989), 60–72.

Hayden, Robert M. *Blueprints for a House Divided: The Constitutional Logic of the Yugoslav Conflicts*. Ann Arbor: University of Michigan Press, 2000 [1991].

Herzberg, Roberta. "An Analytic Choice Approach to Concurrent Majorities: The Relevance of John C. Calhoun for Institutional Design." *Journal of Politics* 54: 1 (February 1992), 54–81.

Hofstadter, Richard. "John C. Calhoun: The Marx of the Master Class." In Richard Hofstadter, *The American Political Tradition and the Men Who Made It,* 86–117. New York: Vintage, 1974.

Horowitz, Donald L. "The Northern Ireland Agreement: Clear, Consociational and Risky." In *Northern Ireland and the Divided World: The Northern Ireland Conflict and the Good Friday Agreement in Comparative Perspective,* ed. John McGarry, 89–136. Oxford: Oxford University Press, 2001.

Jefferson, Thomas. *Thomas Jefferson: Writings,* ed. Merrill D. Peterson. New York: Library of America, 1984.

Jenkins, William Sumner. *Pro-Slavery Thought in the Old South.* Chapel Hill: University of North Carolina Press, 1935.

John, Richard R. "Hiland Hall's 'Report on Incendiary Publications': A Forgotten Nineteenth Century Defense of the Constitutional Guarantee of the Freedom of the Press." *American Journal of Legal History* 41: 1 (January 1997), 94–125.

Jordan, Winthrop D. *White over Black: American Attitudes toward the Negro, 1550–1812.* Baltimore: Penguin Books, 1969.

Kateb, George. "The Majority Principle: Calhoun and His Antecedents." *Political Science Quarterly* 84: 4 (December 1969), 583–605.

Koch, Adrienne, and Harry Ammon. "The Virginia and Kentucky Resolutions: An Episode in Jefferson's and Madison's Defense of Civil Liberties." *William and Mary Quarterly* 3rd ser. 5: 2 (April 1948), 145–176.

Larson, John Lauritz. *Internal Improvement: National Public Works and the Promise of Popular Government in the Early United States.* Chapel Hill: University of North Carolina Press, 2001.

Lence, Ross M., ed. *Union and Liberty: The Political Philosophy of John C. Calhoun.* Indianapolis: Liberty Fund, 1992.

Lerner, Ralph. "Calhoun's New Science of Politics." *American Political Science Review* 57: 4 (December 1963), 918–932.

Lijphart, Arend. "Consociational Democracy," *World Politics* 21: 2 (January 1969), 207–225.

———. *Democracies: Patterns of Majoritarian and Consensus Government in Twenty-one Countries.* New Haven, Conn.: Yale University Press, 1984.

———. *Democracy in Plural Societies.* New Haven, Conn.: Yale University Press, 1977.

———. *Power-Sharing in South Africa.* Berkeley: Institute of International Studies, University of California, 1985.

Madison, James. *James Madison: Writings,* ed. Jack N. Rakove. New York: Library of America, 1999.

Maier, Pauline. "The Road Not Taken: Nullification, John C. Calhoun, and the Revolutionary Tradition in South Carolina." *South Carolina Historical Magazine* 28 (January 1981), 1–19.

Mandela, Nelson R. *Long Walk to Freedom: The Autobiography of Nelson Mandela.* Boston: Little Brown, 1994.

McCoy, Drew. *The Last of the Fathers: James Madison and the Republican Legacy.* Cambridge: Cambridge University Press, 1989.

McDonald, Forrest. *States' Rights and the Union: Imperium in Imperio, 1776–1876.* Lawrence: University Press of Kansas, 2000.

McGarry, John, ed. *Northern Ireland and the Divided World: The Northern Ireland Conflict and the Good Friday Agreement in Comparative Perspective.* Oxford: Oxford University Press, 2001.

McGarry, John, and Brendan O'Leary. *The Northern Ireland Conflict: Consociational Engagements.* Oxford: Oxford University Press, 2004.

McKitrick, Eric L., ed. *Slavery Defended: The Views of the Old South.* Englewood Cliffs, N.J.: Prentice-Hall, 1963.

Miller, William Lee. *Arguing about Slavery: John Quincy Adams and the Great Battle in the United States Congress.* New York: Vintage, 1995.

Morgan, Edmund S. *American Slavery, American Freedom: The Ordeal of Colonial Virginia.* New York: W. W. Norton, 1975.

Niven, John. *John C. Calhoun and the Price of Union: A Biography.* Baton Rouge: Louisiana State University Press, 1988.

Oakes, James. *The Ruling Race: A History of American Slaveholders.* New York: Alfred A. Knopf, 1982.

O'Brien, Michael. *Conjectures of Order: Intellectual Life and the American South, 1810–1860.* 2 vols. Chapel Hill: University of North Carolina Press, 2004.

Onuf, Nicholas, and Peter Onuf. *Nations, Markets, and War: Modern History and the American Civil War.* Charlottesville: University of Virginia Press, 2006.

Peterson, Merrill D. *The Great Triumvirate: Webster, Clay, and Calhoun.* New York: Oxford University Press, 1987.

———. *The Jefferson Image in the American Mind.* New York: Oxford University Press, 1960.

Rae, Douglas. "The Limits of Consensual Decision." *American Political Science Review* 69: 4 (December 1975), 1270–1294.

Rusinow, Dennison, ed. *Yugoslavia: A Fractured Federalism.* Washington, D.C.: Wilson Center Press, 1988.

Schoen, Brian. "Calculating the Price of Union: Republican Economic Nationalism and the Origins of Southern Sectionalism, 1790–1828." *Journal of the Early Republic* 23: 2 (Summer 2003), 173–206.

Sinha, Manisha. *The Counterrevolution of Slavery: Politics and Ideology in Antebellum South Carolina.* Chapel Hill: University of North Carolina Press, 2000.

Spain, August O. *The Political Theory of John C. Calhoun.* New York: Octagon Books, 1968 [1951].

Stanton, William. *The Leopard's Spots: Scientific Attitudes toward Race in America, 1815–1859.* Chicago: University of Chicago Press, 1960.

Steinberger, Peter J. "Calhoun's Concept of the Public Interest: A Clarification," *Polity* 13 (Spring 1981), 410–424.

Sydnor, Charles S. *The Development of Southern Sectionalism, 1819–1848.* Baton Rouge: Louisiana State University Press, 1948.

Taussig, F. W. *The Tariff History of the United States.* New York and London: G. P. Putnam's Sons, 1923.

Van Zyl Slabbert, Frederick, and David Welsh. *South Africa's Options: Strategies for Sharing Power.* New York: St. Martin's Press, 1979.

Waldmeier, Patti. *Anatomy of a Miracle: The End of Apartheid and the Birth of the New South Africa*. New Brunswick, N.J.: Rutgers University Press, 2001 [1997].

Watson, Harry L. *Liberty and Power: The Politics of Jacksonian America*. New York: Hill and Wang, 1990.

Wiltse, Charles M. *John C. Calhoun*. 3 vols. Vol. 1, *Nationalist, 1782–1828*. Vol. 2, *Nullifier, 1829–1839*. Vol. 3, *Sectionalist, 1840–1850*. Indianapolis: Bobbs-Merrill Company, 1944–1951.

Woodward, Susan L. *Balkan Tragedy: Chaos and Dissolution after the Cold War*. Washington, D.C.: Brookings Institution, 1995.

Index

Calhoun, John Caldwell (*continued*)
   rejects natural rights theory, 18–19, 24,
      35–39, 120, 126, 128, 130–131, 164
   and South Carolina politics, 7, 187–194
   on sovereignty, 16–17, 23–24, 27–29,
      38–39, 47, 55, 80, 89–95, 105–109,
      179
Cardozo, Jacob, 67
Civil War, American, 19–20, 52, 110,
   117, 156, 250n48, 251n56
Clay, Henry, 6–7, 23, 31, 69, 75, 81–82,
   132, 240nn10, 19, 252n1
concurrent majority, 2, 5, 14, 21, 51, 54,
   86, 113, 158, 160, 162, 168, 171,
   185, 188, 200–202, 204–205, 208,
   242n52, 245n43
   defined, 5
   Lijphart on, 200–202
   in Northern Ireland agreement, 204–
      205, 208
   See also consensus model of
      government; minority veto
consensus model of government, 1–8, 15–
   16, 22, 51, 53, 70, 86–87, 113–117,
   119, 125, 158, 160–195, 228–237,
   245n43
   anarchy/deadlock objection, 22, 162–
      172
   compared with majority rule, 1–5, 51,
      160, 195, 199–204, 220, 227–230,
      236
   and federalism, 15–17, 180, 184, 228–
      229
   homogeneity and heterogeneity of
      interests, 18, 180–184, 190, 192–
      194, 229
   "interest" defined, 53, 184–187
   jury analogy, 114, 163, 166–170
   leadership essential, 163–164, 170–
      172, 229, 236
   minorities-within-minorities problem,
      22, 162, 179–195
   minority domination objection, 162,
      172–179
   and nullification, 4–6, 17, 172–173,
      176–178

   and slavery, 17–19, 119, 125, 158,
      177–178, 194
   and U.S. Constitution, 5, 86–87, 113–
      117
   See also concurrent majority; minority
      veto
consociational democracy. *See* democracy:
   consociational; Lijphart, Arend
Constitution, U.S., 5, 15–17, 25–29, 33–
   35, 39–47, 85–117, 221
   Calhoun's method of interpretation,
      15–16, 89–95, 97, 99–102, 107–
      109, 115–117
   Calhoun's proposed reconstruction of,
      86–87, 107, 113, 115–117
   dual executive proposal, 86, 107, 115
   Jefferson on, 26–29, 33–35
   Madison on, 39–47, 110
   and nullification, 5, 15–17, 26–29, 33–
      35, 39–47, 94–95, 108–110
   and secession, 106–113
   and slavery, 85–89, 95–106, 114–117,
      191
   and sovereignty, 11, 16–17, 23–25, 27–
      29, 33–35, 46–47, 55, 80, 89–95,
      98–100, 105–109, 233
   strict versus broad construction, 6, 31,
      57, 80, 87–88, 98–105, 250n44
   tariff provisions, 16, 65
   as unanimous state compact, 97–102,
      105–106, 109, 112
   See also Articles of Confederation;
      Federal Convention of 1787;
      federalism

Declaration of Independence, 24–26, 30,
   33, 35–39, 156, 243nn3, 4
   Calhoun's critique of, 36–39
   See also Jefferson, Thomas
de Klerk, F. W., 202, 216, 218–219. *See
   also* South Africa
democracy, 1–4, 9–13, 20, 22, 144–145,
   195, 202, 227–237
   consociational, 199–204
   and majority rule, 2–3, 9–11, 227–237
Dew, Thomas Roderick, 146–147

Douglas, Stephen, 24, 243n3
Dred Scott v. Sanford (1857), 24–25, 243n4

Federal Convention of 1787, 21, 48, 89,
    91, 93–95, 107, 109, 113–117, 218,
    251n61
federalism, 2, 5, 11, 15–17, 21, 44, 46–
    47, 85, 89–95, 99–103, 180, 195,
    198, 228–229, 231–233
  Calhoun's understanding of, 89–95,
    99–103
  and consensus model, 15–17, 180, 184,
    228–229
  Madison's understanding of, 42–47,
    92–95, 233
  and majority rule, 11, 43–44, 231–233
  and sovereignty, 7, 9, 16–17, 21, 23–
    25, 27–29, 34, 38, 42–47, 89–95,
    98–100, 105–109, 179–180, 184,
    213–214, 228–229, 233
  in Yugoslavia, 209–215, 262n61
  See also Constitution, U.S.; sovereignty
Federalist Papers
  No. 10, 13, 41, 48, 171, 182, 222, 235
  No. 38, 49
  No. 39, 26, 46–47, 90, 92–93, 241n29
  No. 51, 48
  See also federalism; Madison, James
Filmer, Robert, 121–122, 149, 243n5,
    252n9
Fitzhugh, George, 142, 149–150
Ford, Lacy, 144, 193, 245n43
freedom of speech and press, 2, 10, 14–
    15, 89, 103–106, 116, 227, 234–
    235, 250nn41, 44
  Calhoun on, 14
  and "incendiary publications," 103–
    106, 250nn41, 44
  and majority rule, 2, 10, 227, 234–235

Garrison, William Lloyd, 75, 82, 95,
    256n82
Gliddon, George, 133–134
Guinier, Lani, 22, 196, 221–226, 262n71
  compared with Calhoun, 221–226
  on majority tyranny, 221–223

Hamilton, Alexander, 30, 41, 92–93,
    257n19
Hammond, James Henry, 119, 142, 148–
    149
Harper, William, 132, 146–148
Harrison, William Henry, 82, 179, 187,
    258n31
Hayden, Robert, 214–215, 262nn60, 61
Hayne, Robert, 7, 240n12
Hobbes, Thomas, 164, 239n1
Hofstadter, Richard, 142, 144, 254n51
Horowitz, Donald, 207–208, 260n20

Indians, American, 6, 138–140. *See also*
    race
internal improvements, 6, 31, 54–59, 61–
    62, 83–84, 212, 261n41. *See also*
    Calhoun, John Caldwell: political
    economy

Jackson, Andrew, 6, 32, 55, 64, 80–81,
    97, 104, 139, 176–177, 183,
    240nn11, 17
Jaffa, Harry, 243n1
Jefferson, Thomas, 21, 24–40, 45–46, 75,
    245n54
  Calhoun's appropriation of, 25–29
  compared with Calhoun, 33–39
  Declaration of Independence, 30, 36,
    38–39
  Jeffersonian political tradition, 29–31
  Kentucky Resolutions, 25–30, 33–35,
    40–42, 45–46, 104
  on slavery, 24, 26, 36–39
  See also Declaration of Independence;
    Madison, James
Jenkins, William Sumner, 87–88
judiciary, federal, 7, 17, 29, 44, 93–94,
    173

Lerner, Ralph, 164
Lijphart, Arend, 22, 196–206, 215, 217–
    218, 225, 241n46, 259nn1, 4, 10,
    262nn61, 79
  compared with Calhoun, 197, 199–204
  on consociational democracy, 199–200

and the Constitution, 5, 15–17, 26–29, 33–35, 39–47, 94–95, 108–110

and Jefferson's Kentucky Resolutions, 26–29, 33–35

Madison's rejection of, 39–47, 172

as minority veto, 5, 15–16, 31–32

and secession, 106–110

and slavery, 74–75, 97

and South Carolina, 7, 26, 64–65, 72, 87, 164, 174, 176, 177, 214

Yugoslavian experiment with, 214

See also consensus model of government; minority veto; sovereignty; tariff

O'Leary, Brendan, 205–207, 260nn26, 31, 33

political leadership

Calhoun on, 21, 54, 163–164, 166, 170–172, 185–187, 193–194, 203, 219, 257n7

and consensus model, 163–164, 170–172, 229, 236

and democracy, 235–237

Madison on, 171, 235

Mandela as example, 218–219

Lijphart on, 202–203

protectionism, 60–72, 76–79, 248nn37, 55. *See also* tariff

race

Calhoun on, 18, 121–123, 127–128, 131–140, 143–145, 149–153, 158, 192, 229, 253n28

in contemporary U.S., 221–225

in South Africa, 192–193, 216–217, 220, 259n1

See also slavery

Rae, Douglas, 174, 178, 242n52, 257n25, 259n57

Rawle, William, 109–110, 251nn51, 54

Rives, William Cabell, 46–47, 120–121, 246n60

secession, 5–6, 9, 17, 44–45, 78, 89, 96, 99, 102, 106–112, 117, 118, 149,

178–180, 196, 214–215, 241n26, 248n55, 250n48, 251nn51, 55, 56

Calhoun on, 5–6, 17, 106–112

Calhoun threatens, 98–99, 102, 111, 117, 118

and consensus model, 112

Madison on, 44–45, 110

and nullification, 5–6, 106–110

South Carolina (1860), 111–112

in Yugoslavia, 214–215

Seward, William, 102

slavery, 6–8, 17–19, 21–26, 35–39, 52, 59, 74–80, 82–89, 95–106, 111–112, 114–117, 118–159, 169, 177–178, 182–183, 186, 194, 203–204, 229, 231, 241nn45, 46, 242nn48, 53, 243nn4, 5, 6, 245n51, 249nn5, 22, 28, 251n55, 252n15, 255n68, 256n88

Calhoun's defense of, 118–159

and capitalism, 123–125, 140–145

and consensus model, 17–19, 125, 119, 158, 177–178, 186, 194

and *Disquisition* argument, 119, 125–132, 140–141, 145

in District of Columbia, 8, 87–88, 96, 98–99, 101, 116, 134, 153–154

and Federal Convention of 1787, 114–117

in federal territories, 8, 24, 26, 36–39, 87–88, 96–99, 102, 106, 116, 145, 154, 174, 177–178, 257n7

fugitive slave issue, 88, 96, 102–103, 106–107, 111, 114, 116

Jefferson and, 24, 26, 36–39

as "positive good," 119–125, 140–147, 150, 155, 256n88

and race, 18, 121–123, 127–128, 131–140, 143–145, 149–153, 158, 192, 229, 253n28

slave trade, 132, 149, 255n68

in South Carolina, 17, 134, 139, 174, 188–189, 191–192, 241n45, 245n51, 254n45, 255n59, 256n85, 258n51

See also abolitionism and antislavery; Calhoun, John Caldwell: defense of slavery

Smith, Adam, 25, 71, 243n5
South Africa, 3, 20, 22, 196–199, 202,
    216–221, 231, 232, 259n1, 262n70
  and majority rule, 216–221
  minority veto proposal, 196–197, 216–
    221, 262n67
  and Northern Ireland, 219–220
South Carolina
  Calhoun's leadership of, 7, 190–194
  constitution of, 180, 187–192
  Declaration of Secession (1860), 111–
    112
  dissent within, 7, 181–184, 187–192
  at Federal Convention of 1787, 114, 116
  nullifies tariff, 7, 26, 64–65, 72, 87,
    164, 174, 176, 177, 214
  slavery in, 17, 134, 139, 174, 188–189,
    191–192, 241n45, 245n51, 254n45,
    255n59, 256n85, 258n51
sovereignty, 7, 9–11, 16–17, 21, 23–25,
    27–29, 33–35, 38, 46–47, 89–95,
    98–100, 105–109, 179–180, 184,
    213–214, 228, 233
  Calhoun on, 16–17, 23–24, 27–29, 38,
    47, 89–95, 105–109, 179
  Lincoln on, 9–11
  Madison on, 46–47, 90, 92–95, 233
  See also Constitution, U.S.; federalism;
    nullification; secession

Taney, Roger, 24–25, 243n4
tariff
  of 1816, 6, 55, 60–63, 247n17
  of 1828 ("Tariff of Abominations"),
    3–4, 7, 12–14, 48–49, 60–70,
    73–74, 83, 183, 231,
    247n32
  of 1832, 7, 62, 64–65, 69, 73–74
  of 1833 (compromise tariff), 7, 164,
    176, 240n19
  constitutional provisions, 16, 65
  Madison on, 42
  and slavery, 74–80, 97
  See also Calhoun, John Caldwell:
    political economy; nullification;
    protectionism
Taussig, F. W., 64, 239n2, 247n17
Tyler, John, 8, 135

van Zyl Slabbert, Frederick, 197, 201–
    202, 217–218
Vesey, Denmark, 134, 154, 256n85

Waldmeier, Patti, 216, 262n65
War of 1812, 6, 30, 54, 60, 63, 69,
    77, 83
Washington, George, 91–92
Webster, Daniel, 7, 23, 81–82, 252n1
Welsh, David, 197, 201–202, 217–218
Wilson, Clyde, 121, 242n48

Yugoslavia, 3, 20, 22, 196, 199, 209–215,
    231, 260nn36, 37, 261nn46, 48, 52,
    53, 58, 262nn60, 61
  consensus model fails, 209–215
  secession in, 213–215